# Questioning
# Qualitative Inquiry

# Questioning Qualitative Inquiry

## Critical Essays

Martyn Hammersley

Los Angeles • London • New Delhi • Singapore

SAGE Publications Ltd
1 Oliver's Yard
55 City Road
London EC1Y 1SP

SAGE Publications Inc.
2455 Teller Road
Thousand Oaks, California 91320

SAGE Publications India Pvt Ltd
B 1/I 1 Mohan Cooperative Industrial Area
Mathura Road
New Delhi 110 044

SAGE Publications Asia-Pacific Pte Ltd
33 Pekin Street #02-01
Far East Square
Singapore 048763

**Library of Congress Control Number: 2007941790**

**British Library Cataloguing in Publication data**

A catalogue record for this book is available from the British Library

ISBN 978-1-4129-3514-2
ISBN 978-1-4129-3515-9 (pbk)

Typeset by C&M Digitals (P) Ltd., Chennai, India
Printed in Great Britain by TJ International Ltd, Padstow, Cornwall
Printed on paper from sustainable resources

# Contents

# Acknowledgements

An earlier version of Chapter 1, entitled 'The lamentable failings of qualitative research', was given at an ESRC-funded research seminar on 'What's wrong with qualitative research?', organised by Maggie MacLure and held at Manchester Metropolitan University in 2003. I am grateful to the participants for their comments.

Material from Chapters 2, 3, and 4 was presented to a meeting of the British Sociological Association Realist Study Group in 2005. My thanks go to the members of the group for a fruitful discussion.

Earlier versions of parts of Chapter 5 were published in the *British Journal of Sociology of Education*, 24, 1, 2003, pp. 119–26, and in M. Holborn and M. Haralambos (eds), *Developments in Sociology, Volume 20*, Ormskirk, Causeway Press/Edinburgh, Pearson Education, 2005. I am grateful to Roger Gomm for allowing me to include this chapter.

A version of Chapter 6 was published in *Discourse and Society*, 14, 6, pp. 751–81, 2003. This stimulated an exchange with Jonathan Potter, which appears in the same issue. A few corrections and additions have been made, and some technical notes have been removed. Earlier versions of this paper were given at an Open University Discourse Analysis Group seminar, at the Brunel University Social Theory Seminar, and at a conference on 'Knowing the Social World' held at the University of Salford in July 2000. In addition to the discussions on these occasions, I have benefited from the comments of Jonathan Potter, Stephanie Taylor, Max Travers, Rod Watson, and Margie Wetherell.

An early version of Chapter 7 was given as the Annual Ethnography Lecture, University of Bristol, Bristol Institute of Public Affairs, 31 May 2007.

A version of Chapter 9 was published in the *International Journal of Research and Method in Education*, 30, 3, 2007.

# Introduction: Dentists, Dadaists or Discourse Analysts?

My starting point in this book is that qualitative research is currently facing a crisis. In part this derives from the fact that, in some fields, after a period of dominance, or at least of benign tolerance, it has recently come under increasing external pressure to demonstrate its value, and in particular its practical value for policymakers and practitioners of various kinds. Like other forms of publicly-funded activity, it is now being required to show that it 'adds value', and there have been attempts to steer funds back towards quantitative research, partly on the grounds that this alone can provide evidence of 'what works' in terms of policy and practice.[1]

There are those who warn against exaggerating this threat. Thus, Atkinson and Delamont (2006) have pointed out that, despite these recent moves, qualitative work continues to be funded, and they also note the huge commercial success of ventures like the *Handbook of Qualitative Research*, now in its third edition (Denzin and Lincoln 2005). However, it seems to me that there is a danger of complacency here, in the face of powerful forces seeking to 'reform' social science in ways that will be detrimental to at least some kinds of qualitative work. But, in any case, the problems are deeper than this external threat. Indeed, in many ways they are symbolised by the very success of Denzin and Lincoln's *Handbook*. There are several aspects to this. One is the fact that qualitative inquiry now takes a wide variety of very different forms, supported by discrepant rationales. A second concerns the particular sorts of approach championed by Denzin and Lincoln.[2]

Many years ago, the American comedian Woody Allen wrote what he called a 'fantasy' entitled: 'If the impressionists had been dentists'. This is a series of

---

1 For discussions of these developments, see for example Hammersley (2002:ch 1) and Biesta (2007).

2 While the *Handbook of Qualitative Research* is extraordinarily influential in many contexts, it is perhaps worth noting that there have been limits to the reach of its influence. These are not just to do with language barriers but also disciplinary fences. For example, while there has been considerable methodological debate within the fields of politics and international relations, over the role of case study (see Brady and Collier 2004; George and Bennett 2005), the *Handbook* rarely seems to be cited there.

imaginary letters from Vincent van Gogh to his brother Theo, in which he recounts his troubles as a dentist.[3] The first letter begins:

> Will life never treat me decently? I am wracked by despair! My head is pounding! Mrs Sol Schwimmer is suing me because I made her bridge as I felt it and not to fit her ridiculous mouth! That's right! I can't work to order like a common tradesman! I decided her bridge should be enormous and billowing, with wild, explosive teeth flaring up in every direction like fire! Now she is upset because it won't fit in her mouth! She is so bourgeois and stupid, I want to smash her! I tried forcing the false plate in but it sticks out like a star burst chandelier. Still, I find it beautiful. She claims she can't chew! What do I care whether she can chew or not! (Allen 1983:199)

To amusing effect, Woody Allen transposes the attitude or temperament of the artist on to a patently functional activity, dentistry. Putting it a little differently, he contrasts how we expect dentists to behave with modern (or, rather, modernist) ideas about the nature of art and the artist.

The relevance of this fantasy here is that, from a currently influential point of view, qualitative researchers could be, and to some extent are being, accused of misunderstanding their own role in much the same manner as this fictional van Gogh. A strong trend within academic qualitative inquiry over the past couple of decades, at least at the level of influential rhetoric, has been towards viewing it as a form of literature or art, with not just Impressionism but also Dadaism and Surrealism as important influences (see Chapter 7). And this trend is exemplified in the agenda and content of successive editions of the *Handbook of Qualitative Research* as well as elsewhere (Denzin and Lincoln 1994, 2000, 2005; see also Denzin 1997 and 2003; Lather 2007). However, as already noted, in the last few years of the twentieth century some powerful stakeholders began forcefully to reassert a view of social science as a functional activity. They have insisted that it should be designed to serve policymaking and practice directly; in other words, that it should be devoted to eradicating decay and promoting (social) health.

Of course, this conflict between Dada and dentistry by no means exhausts what is going on in qualitative research today. Indeed, we are now faced with a bewildering range of approaches, a situation of methodological pluralism or disarray. I will not attempt to map out all the available approaches in this book. However, I do discuss one other currently influential trend: towards the use of discourse analysis, particularly that concerned with detailed analysis of texts, usually transcriptions of 'naturally occurring talk' or of interview data. Not only has there been a considerable expansion in work focusing on discourse and narrative, but the ideas associated with some forms of discourse analysis have influenced qualitative research more widely. One of the most significant results is the raising of challenging questions about the sorts of data, the forms

---

3 This material was used by Dey (1993) in his guide to qualitative data analysis.

of inference, and even the kinds of conclusion common in much mainstream qualitative research.

In the opening part of this Introduction I will examine the demands for a functional, scientific approach to social science, then look at advocacy of 'Dadaist' qualitative research, and follow this up with an assessment of the claims of discourse analysts. In the final part of the Introduction there will be an outline of the contents of each chapter.

## Qualitative inquiry as functional

Most qualitative researchers have probably always regarded their work as relevant to policymaking and practice. However, much of it has been academic in character, in the sense of being aimed first of all at contributing to disciplinary knowledge. The primary audience here has been fellow researchers, despite hopes that it would reach more remote audiences and thereby shape policy and practice. But there have recently been influential demands, in several countries, that social science be much more directly policy- or practice-relevant. Furthermore, this has sometimes been associated with criticisms of qualitative research, on the grounds that it does not use what are seen as essential means needed for this purpose: the study of large samples so as to facilitate generalisation, the use of experimental designs to control for confounding variables, and so on. The emphasis, often, has been on the need to employ randomised controlled trials and systematic reviews if we are to discover whether policies and practices have the effects claimed for them, and in order to check that they do not have serious negative consequences (see Oakley 2000, 2001; Mosteller and Boruch 2002; Slavin 2002).

The demand is that social science research should serve, *and demonstrate its contribution to*, evidence-based policymaking and practice. The other side of this is that policymaking and various forms of professional practice, especially in the public sector, should be based much more on, or become more strongly informed by, research evidence. And it is argued that, if this is to be achieved, social science must be transformed to produce the kind of evidence that can provide an effective basis for decision-making by policymakers and practitioners.

Pressure in this direction emerged in the UK in the last years of the twentieth century, with severe public criticism, by powerful commentators, of research in the field of education (see Hammersley 2002:ch. 1). And qualitative inquiry was at the eye of this storm. It was charged by some with being largely irrelevant, weak in validity, and a waste of public funds. Furthermore, the pressure for research to be reformed spread outside the field of education. This was clearly evident in a speech by David Blunkett, then Secretary of State for Education and Employment, to the Economic and Social Research Council (ESRC) (Blunkett 2000; see Hammersley 2000).

More recently, a similar crisis has arisen in the United States; though there, as elsewhere, the roots can be traced further back. Once again the field of education became the main target. In 1997 the National Institute of Child Health and Human Development published a report about teaching children to read, based on a meta-analysis of research involving highly restrictive criteria of inclusion modelled on those appropriate in medical research. Subsequently, the re-authorisation of the Elementary and Secondary Education Act ('No Child Left Behind') established randomised controlled field trials as the preferred methodology for federally-funded educational research. While the National Research Council's report on *Scientific Research in Education* adopted a more catholic approach, the framework was very much the logic of quantitative research (Shavelson and Towne 2002; see also Feuer et al. 2002). As a result of these developments, qualitative research has come under considerable threat in the USA, particularly as regards funding.

Denzin and Giardina argue that these developments are part of a broader trend:

> Qualitative research exists in a time of global uncertainty. Around the globe, governments are attempting to regulate scientific inquiry by defining what is good science. Conservative regimes are enforcing evidence-, or scientifically-based, biomedical models of research. (Denzin and Giardina 2006a:ix–x)

Indeed, the shift towards a more functional conception of social research can be seen as integral to the emergence of so-called 'knowledge societies'.[4] This involves a move away from what might be referred to as the patronage model for funding research towards the investment model. In these terms, research is no longer to be treated as a good thing in itself, with funds being provided by the State in the same way that they have long been for the arts, so that researchers are largely left to determine what is worth investigating and how this should be done. Instead, it is argued that funding research must be treated as an investment on which a satisfactory return is promised and delivered; and, along with this, that it should be highly responsive to external demand, whether that of the market or of democratically-elected governments.[5]

It is not hard to detect the influence of positivist assumptions about the nature of research behind these criticisms and proposals for reform. And they have stimulated vociferous protest from some qualitative researchers – who have dismissed them as 'regressive modernism', 'methodological conservatism' or 'methodological fundamentalism' (Lather 2004; Lincoln and Cannella 2004; Denzin and Giardini 2006b; Denzin et al. 2006).[6] However, in my view this

---

4 On which see, for example, Gibbons et al. (1994) and Stokes (1997).

5 In the UK, and no doubt elsewhere, changes have also been taking place in state funding of the arts, in the same direction.

6 For some of the many responses of qualitative researchers to these developments, see Erickson and Gutierrez (2002); St Pierre (2002); Atkinson (2004); Bloch (2004); Maxwell (2004); Popkewitz (2004); Eisenhart (2005); Erickson (2005); Gee 2005; Howe (2005); Moss (2005a; 2005b); Schwandt (2005); Eisenhart (2006); Lather (2006); St Pierre (2006).

sort of dismissal is less than helpful: it is a mistake in intellectual terms, and probably unwise politically as well (Maxwell 2004). Above all, it discourages both a sober assessment of what is being proposed and careful examination of the criticisms that have been made of qualitative inquiry.

It is important to recognise that what is being demanded by those who would reform social science is not *simply* a reversion to the positivist past, nor is it a resort to irrationally held 'fundamentals'. Most new movements appeal to past ideas in one way or another – nothing is completely new. Moreover, the position of some advocates of reform can be seen as politically progressive in key respects.[7] An example would be Ann Oakley's arguments (Oakley 2000). These challenge professional dominance – which, in recent times, sociologists have portrayed as the core of professionalism (see, for example, Larson 1977; Macdonald 1995) – in the name of democracy. She insists not simply that the evidential basis on which policymakers and practitioners make decisions should be scientifically sound but also that it be made publicly available, so that the decisions can be assessed by those on the receiving end. An important requirement for this, she argues, is that the research supplying the evidence must itself be methodologically transparent.

However, while the advocates of research-for-evidence-based-practice may be neither conservatives nor fundamentalists, they do suffer from either amnesia or ignorance. They neglect the cogent implications of much work in the philosophy of science, and in social research methodology, over the past fifty years. As a result, there are serious problems with this neo-positivist view of the function and nature of research. For all its virtues, the randomised controlled trial is unable to deliver what it is held to promise, as regards most research questions in the social field. Not only does it not control all confounding variables, but its use will not be effective unless what is being investigated is a clearly distinct and standard 'treatment'. And this is rarely the case once we move away from drug trials. Furthermore, it does not avoid the severe problems of measurement that have always been a weakness of most quantitative research in the social sciences (see Howe 2004 and Hammersley 2009). Similar problems arise with 'systematic' reviews (Hammersley 2001 and 2006b).

I am not denying that the research methods typically advocated in the name of 'evidence-based practice' can be worthwhile, but I *am* arguing that the claims made for them in the context of reforming social science are often excessive: they can neither provide absolutely certain knowledge about the effects of particular treatments nor tell us what is good policy or practice. All methods produce fallible knowledge; and while experimental methodology has distinctive strengths, like other methods it also involves some serious threats to validity. Similarly, proceduralisation of research does not and cannot produce

---

7 As indeed was early positivism, see Hammersley (1995:ch 1).

'transparency'. Finally, judgements about what is and is not desirable policy and practice necessarily depend upon evidence from more sources than research, and involve value assumptions whose justification research cannot provide, at least not on its own.

Some advocates of research for evidence-based policymaking and practice recognise this, at least some of the time. They acknowledge that the range of useful methods transcends the quantitative–qualitative divide. And there have been attempts to promote the value of qualitative work in the context of arguments for evidence-based policymaking and practice (see, for example, Davies 2000). Moreover, there has been quite a lot of qualitative work that is close to the functional model, in the sense that it is aimed at addressing quite specific, practically-relevant questions – for example in the fields of policy and programme evaluation and the gauging of political and social attitudes (see Walker 1986; Rist 2000; Ritchie 2003).

There is, though, a more fundamental question than whether qualitative work can be functional. This is whether social research can or should have this character. Often, discussion of this centres on a contrast between what have been referred to as the engineering and enlightenment models (see Bulmer 1982; Hammersley 1995:ch 7 and 2002:ch 6). And, in the current external climate, the pressure seems to be all in the direction of the engineering model. But, in my view, it is important to recognise a distinction between academic and practical research, to treat both as of value, to stress their interdependence, and to insist that neither can substitute for the other. In particular, it is important to emphasise that academic research develops, refines and assesses ideas and methods in ways that are not usually possible in the practical context; and that are of great importance if we are to gain sound understandings of social phenomena. Furthermore, the production of knowledge relevant to human concerns and interests is worthwhile in itself, irrespective of whether it is found useful at any particular time, serves national or 'emancipatory' interests, and so on (Hammersley 1995: ch 7 and 2002). Currently, there is a danger that funds will dry up for research that is not practice- or policy-focused, or that cannot at least convincingly pretend to be; and this is a particular problem for much qualitative work.

At the same time, it seems to me that the attitudes of some of the most vociferous defenders of qualitative research against recent criticism pose at least as serious a threat to genuine academic qualitative inquiry as that coming from those they dismiss as methodological fundamentalists or conservatives. This is because their defence relies, to a considerable extent, upon ideas that are fundamentally mistaken, often deriving from what is frequently labelled 'postmodernism'.[8]

---

8  This is a problematic term, one that has come to be used by many commentators in a dismissive way. I have tried to be as clear as possible about what I am taking it to refer to, while recognising that its meaning is quite vague.

## A Dadaist alternative?

As I explain in Chapter 7, an important and sometimes neglected influence on postmodernist ideas has been art movements like Dada and Surrealism. Dada was an attempt to subvert art, and thereby society, to shock it into being something different. Today, in much the same way, some forms of postmodernist-inspired qualitative inquiry are concerned with subverting the notion of social science, in the apparent (perhaps Foucaultian) belief that this challenges wider forms of power. Furthermore, art and literature are sometimes believed to embody a kind of alternative ethos that is celebrated as running counter to what are seen as scientistic forms of governance dominant in the West. In fact, the aim, often, is to challenge precisely those kinds of governance that lie behind calls for evidence-based practice.

As with Dadaism and Surrealism, in postmodernist writing there is a turn away from 'Western' notions of rationality, and an appeal to what these are taken to exclude: 'indigenous' or non-Western modes of thought and belief; non-representational forms of art; reliance on the intuitive, the unconscious or sheer chance; intense spiritual experience; and so on. The model of science, in particular the image of the scientific research report as clear and authoritative, is rejected in favour of modes of representation – for example, collage, poetry, and drama – that allow or encourage diverse interpretations on the part of audiences. Furthermore, the impersonal stance of science is replaced by a celebration of acknowledged subjectivity and ethico-political engagement.

The starkness of the conflict between a functional conception of social science and an 'artistic' interpretation of qualitative inquiry of this kind can be pointed up by Hughes' commentary on an exhibition concerned with 'Surrealist design'. He suggests that this phrase 'seems almost a contradiction in terms':

> 'Design' is for us strongly identified with industrial process, with modules, with the rationalisation of process into clear repeatability. To 'design' something implies that it can be made not just once, but again and again and again, without loss of quality and intensity [...] That an object is 'designed' implies, or seems to, that every aspect of it from the first pencil scribble to the finishing touch and on to its intended use by the proposed consumer has been thought about and brought into full consciousness. It would therefore seem so remote from the spirit, the *modus operandi*, of surrealism as to have nothing to do with it. (Hughes 2007:12)

Perhaps what is hoped, in the context of qualitative research methodology, is that an approach modelled on art can provide an alternative version of social design, one that escapes the mechanical and technical imagery that now governs policy discourse. Furthermore, it seems to be believed that the ethos which informs this alternative is intrinsically egalitarian and anti-imperialist in character.

What has come to be referred to as 'postmodernism' in many Anglo-American contexts, including in qualitative researchers' writings about methodology, draws its main ideas, of course, from influential French philosophy of the 1960s and 1970s. While by no means homogeneous or internally coherent, this 'post-structuralism' challenged those forms of thought that had previously been dominant in French intellectual life, notably phenomenology, existentialism, humanistic Marxism, and structuralism. At the same time, there was also a significant inheritance from these sources. In particular, a great deal was taken over from structuralism.

Structuralists had reacted against the subjectivism of phenomenology and existentialism; notably, against their grounding of knowledge and reality in the immediacy of experience or the will of an individual subject. Instead, structuralists argued that what people perceive, what they desire, and so on, are constituted by underlying structures, whether those belonging to a universal human mind (Lévi-Strauss), a particular kind of culture (Barthes), the unconscious (Lacan, Kristeva) or a particular type of society, such as capitalism (Althusser, Godelier). Post-structuralism inherited this displacement of the Subject, including rejection of any notion of a collective historical subject – for example, the idea that the working class can be seen as embodying the spirit of History under capitalism. This was a notion that had been characteristic of much twentieth-century Western Marxism, reflecting the influence of Hegel. The 'anti-humanism' of structuralism amounted to an abandonment of the idea that there is a teleology built into history: that the process of historical development reflects an unfolding of true human nature. For Lévi-Strauss, for example, the diverse social forms to be found across history and in different geographical areas simply represent realisations of the limited possibilities that can be generated by underlying cognitive structures. While he has a view of the long-term history of humanity, representing something of a golden age mythology, this is very far from any Hegelian teleology. Moreover, while some post-structuralists, notably Foucault, have been interested in the 'archaeology' and 'genealogy' of particular social forms, they treat shifts from one to another as largely contingent in character, rather than as part of any grand meta-narrative of self-realisation.[9]

What the post-structuralists rejected in structuralism was the assumption that there is a coherent set of underlying forces generating unified patterns of human consciousness and social life, *and the idea that these can be identified by scientific means*. They argued that what needs to be recognised is the fragmentation of, and tension within, human experience and cultures. Furthermore, they emphasised that philosophers, writers, and social scientists are themselves subjected to forces that generate fractures and fissures, rather than being Subjects

---

9 Though in interviews in the wake of May 1968 he did offer the prospect of escaping structural constraint, see Turkle (1992: 78).

who are in control of a single, coherent discourse. Thus, any idea that it is possible to produce a stable, genuine, complete representation of the social world can only be an illusion, and/or a rhetorical strategy designed to secure power through claiming expertise. For this reason, they rejected expert claims to knowledge about the world, and particularly those which offered a comprehensive theory, as not simply false but also oppressive. They saw this kind of scientific theory as the cause of what had happened in the Soviet Union – notably the Gulag. And they treated this as a product of Marxism, not just of communism, a link to which many on the French Left had long turned a blind eye (see Khilnani 1993; Christofferson 2005). In other words, it was not just that there could be no scientific politics, but also that the attempt to apply science to politics (or to life more generally) carried totalitarian implications. At the same time, they denied that intellectual work could ever be without ethical and political assumptions, implications and consequences.

The reception of these 'post-structuralist' ideas in Anglo-American social science has been highly selective. The treatment of literature and art as a model for thought, rather than science, has been widely adopted by qualitative researchers.[10] However, this valorisation of literature and art has been less discriminating than in the case of French post-structuralists; in the sense that it has adopted forms that are rather conventional in artistic terms. The emphasis on the politically reflexive character of all thought – that it is part of and affected by those situations of which it tries to make sense – has also been very influential, along with an associated radical epistemological scepticism or relativism. From this point of view, thought cannot but be political, and should be consciously directed towards political goals. However, the political orientation of postmodernist qualitative inquiry has been rather different from that of much French post-structuralism. It has not usually been concerned with challenging Marxism, but rather those kinds of liberalism that prevail in the USA and Britain. And the framework from within which this criticism comes is a form of Leftism that shares much in common with the humanist Western Marxism, especially Critical Theory, that post-structuralists were concerned to reject.

---

10 There is an interesting historical parallel to this. In seventeenth-century England a move by Philip Sidney and others towards making poetry a practical art that is concerned with the inculcation of virtue preceded Bacon's reorientation of natural philosophy into a form that was to be useful to the state (see Gaukroger 2001:ch 2). Of course, the words 'poetry', 'art', 'philosophy', and 'science' had rather different meanings then. Furthermore, the guiding ideas were also different. The great value of poetry, according to Sidney, was that whereas natural philosophers and historians could only describe the corrupt world that existed after the Fall, poetry as fiction could invent a nature which more closely mirrors eternal archetypes, conceived in Platonic as well as Protestant terms. Furthermore, for him, poetry does not simply tell people about virtue, it moves them to virtuous action.

In methodological terms, what postmodernist interpretations of qualitative inquiry have rejected, in particular, are science's emphasis on seeking to test ideas against empirical evidence; its ideal of clear, 'plain' argumentation; and the notion that the purpose of inquiry is a 'value-neutral' pursuit of knowledge. The notion of evidence has been questioned on the grounds that it implies the 'metaphysics of presence': that there is some form of data that is simply given directly to us by an independent reality, and whose validity we can therefore treat as absolutely certain. Similarly, drawing on post-structuralist notions of language as necessarily unstable, constitutive and perhaps also deceptive, it has been insisted that any attempt to privilege clear argument that states conclusions and grounds for them is ideological in character. It is held to be a falsification of how discourse operates, and one that has negative political or ethical implications and consequences. Finally, any idea that research can produce knowledge that is superior to the experience of ordinary people, particularly those who have been socially marginalised or oppressed, is challenged as elitist, this challenge drawing on the resources of epistemological scepticism and relativism mixed with standpoint theory. And it is claimed that all forms of research, including – in fact, perhaps especially – social science, are themselves implicated in processes of marginalisation and oppression; that, in fact, this is built into the modes of thinking and writing on which they depend.

Now, there are serious problems with all this. First, these arguments are founded on some very questionable epistemological assumptions: ones that have long been subjected to extended discussion in the philosophical literature, and which do not so much re-orient qualitative inquiry as turn it into a form of politically-inspired literature or art. Moreover, it is not clear what arguments the advocates of this sort of postmodernism could consistently put forward, in their own terms, to justify what they propose and practice, or how they could believe that these would be found persuasive by others. How can they avoid assuming precisely what they purport to abandon, for example the idea that their position is in some sense superior to what it opposes? Even if we put aside this performative contradiction, their specific arguments are rarely convincing. They frequently take for granted precisely what those who disagree with them need to be persuaded about. For example, they treat it as axiomatic that research is inevitably political and partisan and should be explicitly so; or that the corrigibility of evidence means that it cannot provide a means of testing our ideas about the world. Yet there are well-known arguments in the philosophical and methodological literature which throw doubt on both these assumptions (see Hammersley 1995 and 2000).

More sophisticated exponents of postmodernism argue that it does not offer a new alternative approach but is necessarily parasitic on mainstream forms of qualitative work. In other words, its role is as a corrective, or perhaps even as a laxative – serving to free up the thinking of qualitative researchers in the face of an inevitable drift towards closure, towards specifying 'methods', and producing overly definitive conclusions.[11] However, while there is undoubtedly the occasional

---

11  This, for example, seems to be the view adopted by MacLure (2003 and 2006).

need for such medicine, it is unclear why postmodernism is required for this purpose – there is plenty of scope within mainstream ideas about social science for generating scepticism and creativity. Furthermore, using postmodernism in this way amounts to a celebration of excess that kills rather than cures the patient.

The final point I want to make here, all too obvious I would have thought, is that this postmodernist image of qualitative inquiry is not only ill-conceived but its prominence at the present time, not least in arguments against what it dismisses as methodological conservatism, is potentially very damaging – not just to qualitative research but to social science more generally. This is because it is, quite literally, indefensible; and also because the polarisation it promotes encourages precisely the neo-positivism of which it complains. Unless this dynamic can be interrupted, the future of qualitative research is endangered (Hammersley 1999:584).

A central element of postmodernist-inspired qualitative research is what has come to be called constructionism, the idea that multiple realities can be, and are, constituted through discursive practices. Under the influence of postmodernism, this often stimulates a radical reflexivity in terms of which social scientists must continually attend to and display how their work is constructing the social world. However, within a different version of qualitative inquiry, also highly influential today, constructionism is taken to carry somewhat different implications: it demands analytic explication of the discursive practices that people employ in their everyday lives. Here, often, commitment to science is retained, albeit modelled on phenomenology or linguistics rather than natural science. The explicit aim is to describe rather than to explain.

## Discourse analysis

The term 'discourse analysis' covers a variety of approaches.[12] But the distinctive identity of some of these, the ones I will focus on here, arises from an insistence on detailed analysis of transcriptions of audio- or video-recordings, and perhaps also the presentation of these data in research reports so as to allow readers to evaluate the analyses presented. Furthermore, closely associated with this is a denial that we can rely on interview or documentary data to draw inferences about 'the world outside' these texts. While some discourse analysts employ interview data, in doing so they are solely concerned (purportedly at least) with examining the discursive resources and strategies displayed in these data – rather than with drawing inferences either about the people and places referred to or about the attitudes and perspectives of the interviewees.

---

12 For an outline and guide to the literature, see Hammersley (2003b). See also the appendix to MacLure (2003).

There seem to have been two, in some respects at least partly overlapping, pressures behind the turn to studying discourse within qualitative research in the second half of the twentieth century. First, there was the desire to capitalise on what was perceived to be an increased analytic rigour made possible by the availability of portable means of audio-, and later of video-, recording. These devices transformed the sort of data that qualitative researchers could rely upon – previously fieldnotes had been used to record both observations and interview responses. Transcripts of electronic recordings made clear the degree to which fieldnotes were a highly selective source of data that often contained descriptive errors. With extensive audio- and video-recordings, the data became more detailed and more accurate, for example in terms of capturing the actual words used. One effect was to bring home the complexity both of social interaction in the settings observed and of informants' answers in interviews, and this – along with the opportunities afforded by detailed transcription – encouraged much more micro-focused analysis than previously.[13] Indeed, there has probably been a tendency not only to use these new means of data recording wherever possible, but also to select those research foci and settings of inquiry that allow their use. Above all, what audio-recording enabled was analysis of the actual language used: whole stretches of what had been said by the people studied could now be 'preserved' in transcripts in a way that had not been possible in writing fieldnotes. This was the new opportunity that discourse analysis exploited.

The other driving force behind the turn to discourse, as already mentioned, was the influence of constructionism, interpreting this term broadly. In early usage, it referred to little more than an emphasis on the active role that human beings play in making sense of their surroundings, devising forms of action, and thereby producing as well as reproducing social institutions (see Berger and Luckmann 1969). However, constructionism of this kind later came to be transformed through contact with influential linguistic turns in twentieth-century philosophical thought. This led to the conclusion that social phenomena are brought into being as particular types of phenomenon (situations, actions, events, institutions, etc.) through discursive practices. Within social science, this sort of constructionism was influenced both by phenomenologically-inspired ethnomethodology and by structuralism and post-structuralism; though the balance of influence between these very different traditions of thought has varied considerably across forms of discourse analysis.

What is distinctive about constructionism here, then, is that it takes the view that social phenomena can only be understood by describing *the processes by*

---

13  I am not suggesting that this is the only possible consequence of relying on transcriptions of electronic recordings. For example, Clifford has suggested that it 'can produce a more polyphonic final ethnography' (Clifford 1990:57).

*which* they are culturally constituted as the things they are. What is involved, if this approach is followed through consistently, is a fundamental re-specification of the goal of inquiry from that which is characteristic of mainstream social science. The focus becomes, not the phenomena themselves, but rather the processes by which they are discursively produced. This shift can be illustrated by looking at changes in the sociological study of social problems influenced by constructionism. Where, previously, sociologists had studied social problems by investigating what factors generated them – the causes of crime, of financial corruption, of environmental damage, etc. – social constructionists turned their attention to *how such phenomena come to be defined as social problems.* Initially this involved a focus on the role of various pressure groups in promoting particular social problems and the strategies they employ, including rhetorical ones. But, later, for some writers, the topic shifted entirely to the discursive practices involved in formulating particular actions or practices as problematic, as needing remedy, as being the product of certain causes, and so on (Holstein and Miller 1993).

Constructionism also raises questions about the sorts of data that many qualitative researchers have routinely used in the past, and continue to use today; and, even more significantly, about the kinds of inference they employ in analysing those data. This has been most obvious in disputes over the use of interviews (see Chapter 5), but the implications extend more widely. Much qualitative inquiry has employed data to draw conclusions about what happens in particular types of situation, what the orientations of particular types of actor are, what strategies they use, what consequences these have, and so on. But constructionists question the validity of such inferences, arguing that the focus ought to be, and for reasons of methodological rigour *must* be, on the discursive practices that can be identified in transcriptions of talk or in documents. Inferences beyond these to phenomena 'behind' the talk or the writing, including motives and interests, are often ruled out on epistemological and/or ontological grounds.

The influence of ethnomethodological conversation analysis is particularly important here because of its explicit attempt radically to re-specify the focus of qualitative inquiry (Button 1991; Button and Sharrock 1993; Watson 1994). This amounts to a shift away from investigation of the features and causes of particular events, actions, and institutions towards a focus on the methods or practices that are held to generate whatever intelligible sense participants (and, for that matter, researchers) make of them. Furthermore, these methods or practices are assumed to be involved not just in the recognition of social phenomena but also in their production: in 'bringing off' events, actions, and institutions as of distinctive kinds.

Ethnomethodological conversation analysis has had considerable influence within the broader field of discourse analysis, albeit often in watered-down form and mixed with other sets of ideas. Sometimes it has been combined with epistemological scepticism, such that events, actions, and institutions are held to exist only in accounts of them; though, inevitably, this scepticism has usually been only selectively applied. At the same time, and sometimes by the same people, constructionist analysis has often been inserted into more or less taken-for-granted accounts of the nature of the wider society (see, for example, Wetherell and Potter 1992). Here, to some extent, its function becomes parallel to what previously would have been called ideology critique.

It is certainly true that discourse analysts have pointed to some serious problems with older forms of qualitative research. However, neither the criticisms nor the means adopted to avoid these problems are entirely convincing. For example, conversation analysis makes appeal to the concrete reality and representational capacity of transcripts or audio-recordings in ways that would be difficult to defend on its own terms (see Chapter 6). Moreover, if applied consistently, ethnomethodological arguments undermine even the work of most conversation analysts (see Lynch 1993). It is also important to recognise the cost of the sort of refocusing of social science that ethnomethodology recommends. This undermines the traditional ethnographic concern with documenting the character of events and actions in particular times and places, and the attempt to locate these within some picture of the wider society. Also threatened is the idea that qualitative research is able to capture differences in people's perspectives and orientations. Indeed, virtually the whole enterprise of traditional social science is put in question. Of course, if the arguments were sound, then these costs would have to be borne; but they are not.

As yet, at least, most qualitative researchers have not become discourse analysts – instead, they have combined an increased interest in discourse and its constitutive character with a continuing commitment to studying particular people and situations, sometimes giving more emphasis to the 'voices' of those whom they study than previously. However, in some important respects, this sort of eclecticism simply compounds the problems.

The conflicts between a functional and an aesthetic conception of social science, between dentistry and Dadaism as models, and between discourse analytic and older approaches to qualitative research, form the background to this book. Of course, these models do not represent ends of single-stranded, clearly-defined continua. Rather, they are positions in a complex, multi-dimensional, terrain; one that is by no means fixed in its geography. While there is no justification for the kind of bulldozing of it that seems to be proposed by some would-be reformers of social science, in my view there is certainly a need for some landscaping - albeit more on the model of a *jardin anglais* rather than that of a French formal garden!

Reactions to the current methodological pluralism vary sharply: from 'let a thousand flowers bloom' to the idea that we can draw everything together into a 'third way', characteristic of some advocates of mixed methods (see Tashakkori and Teddlie 2002). Above all it seems to me essential that we try to learn from the different approaches to qualitative research that have been developed, while at the same time engaging in robust assessment of them. This is the task to which this book is devoted. Without wishing to over-dramatise, in my view the survival of social science depends upon our capacity to make sound and realistic assessments of its current state and of how it should develop. The need for this applies as much to quantitative as to qualitative work; indeed, the distinction between the two approaches itself demands scrutiny. However, in this book I restrict my focus to qualitative research.

## The chapters

Chapter 1 looks back at the rise of qualitative inquiry over the second half of the twentieth century, focusing on some key respects in which it has failed to realise its potential. I argue, first of all, that it has not fully lived up to the claims made for it in early battles with quantitative researchers. Advocates argued the superiority of qualitative work on the grounds that it offered genuine under-standing of people's perspectives and actions, and took proper account of the processual character of human social life. Yet, in both these areas, the achieve-ment has been much less than promised. Secondly, I argue that qualitative research has failed to develop adequate responses to the criticisms made of it by quantitative researchers: as regards the need for measurement, for causal val-idation, and for generalisation. I examine the standard responses by qualitative researchers to these criticisms and argue that none of them is very effective. In the course of the discussion I suggest some reasons for the two sorts of failing I have identified, and explain why they are significant.

Chapter 2 takes up one part of this, looking at the argument, frequently used by qualitative researchers, that their approach is superior because it captures the complexity of the social world, as against the oversimplified pictures provided by general theories and the reified measurements generated by quantitative research. I argue that all analysis involves both theoretical abstraction and data reduction. Moreover, even if it were possible, simply displaying reality in all its complexity would not serve the goal of research, or any other purpose. This does not mean that qualitative researchers are wrong about the failings of quantitative work, or that the strategies they use to deal with complexity are entirely ineffective. But it does mean that more thought needs to be given to what is involved in the tasks of describing, explaining, and theorising social phenomena in the context of qualitative inquiry.

The next two chapters follow on from this, examining two influential approaches that were designed to enable qualitative inquiry both to respect complexity and to generate theories about the social world. The first of these, Clifford Geertz's notion of 'thick description', has come to be very widely cited in recent times. However, the label is often used in a ritualistic way – to

mean little more than a description in which details of the character of a
particular event, situation, or person are woven together with more abstract
theoretical ideas, usually derived from the relevant literature. In Chapter 3, I
examine what Geertz meant by 'thick description', and what he drew from the
term's original use by the philosopher Gilbert Ryle. I also assess how far it represents an adequate solution to the problem of dealing with complexity. I conclude that it largely fails to do this, for all its suggestive value in indicating what
sort of description may be required if we are to understand many aspects of
human social life. This is because, while Geertz acknowledges the fundamental
dilemmas that face social science, he does not tackle them directly.

In Chapter 4, the focus is on analytic induction. This too starts from the
complexity of actually occurring social phenomena, but in sharp contrast to
thick description it is aimed at the systematic production of theory that has the
character of specifying universal, albeit conditional, laws. Where much ethnography has been concerned with studying particular cases in their uniqueness,
albeit at the same time both using and contributing to more general ideas, analytic induction has quite the opposite concern: in most versions, idiosyncratic
aspects of particular cases are eliminated in order to discover the essential features that mark them out as belonging to causally homogeneous categories. Of
course, the term 'analytic induction' has been used in several different ways, but
I argue that even the most useful discussions of it (from Znaniecki to Becker)
involve some interpretative puzzles and unresolved problems. My aim here is
to spell out the logic of analytic induction and to assess its value as a model for
qualitative analysis directed at producing theories.

In the next couple of chapters, the focus switches to issues raised by discourse
analysis. As we saw earlier, the approaches coming under this heading have generated some fundamental criticisms of established qualitative research practice.
One area where the challenge has been sharpest concerns the use of interview
data. This is ruled out by some forms of discourse analysis; and, even where it is
not, the uses to which such data can be put are highly restricted. The arguments
here have come to be labelled 'the radical critique of interviews'. While, previously, qualitative researchers, like other social scientists, had used interviews to
draw on informants' knowledge about the people and situations being studied
and to document the perspectives that shape their behaviour, it is now commonly argued that these uses are illegitimate. Instead, at most, interview data
must be examined solely for what they can tell us about the discursive practices
or kinds of interactional performance that take place in interview (and perhaps
other) situations. In this chapter, co-authored with Roger Gomm, this radical
critique is outlined and assessed. It is argued that while it points to important
dangers associated with exclusive reliance on interview data, the grounds for
restricting the use of such data so narrowly are not convincing.

Chapter 7 examines some of the ideas that stimulated this 'radical critique'
and the forms of qualitative research they recommend. The focus is twofold:

conversation analysis, and the seminal form of discourse analysis initially proposed and practised by Potter and Wetherell. Both of these are usually treated as self-sufficient approaches to studying the social world, rather than as mere methods that can be combined with others. And there are two areas where their conflict with other approaches is clearest. First, they reject the attribution of substantive and distinctive psycho-social features to particular categories of actor as a means of explaining human behaviour. Secondly, they abandon the use of what people say about the world as a reliable source of information for analytic purposes. These two negative commitments mark conversation analysis and discourse analysis off from almost all other kinds of empirical research in the social sciences. In this chapter, I consider how sound the justifications are for these radical methodological commitments. I conclude that, while these forms of research have made important substantive contributions, they involve serious problems and that neither approach should be treated as a self-sufficient paradigm.

In most forms of discourse analysis, a constructionist interpretation is applied to the phenomena being investigated, *but not to the research process itself*. If this further step is taken, as in the case of some ethnographic postmodernism, any notion of research as producing knowledge about independently existing social phenomena is undercut: it becomes a form of imaginative literature or political rhetoric. I outlined this development, and indicated the problems with it, earlier in this Introduction. In Chapter 7, I develop further the argument that it draws much of its inspiration from Dadaism and Surrealism, via French post-structuralism and the work of anthropologists associated with *Writing Culture* (Clifford and Marcus 1986). I suggest that despite some dilution and mixing with other sources, this kind of qualitative research inherits some fundamental misconceptions from post-structuralism, and that it amounts to an aping of work in the arts and humanities in much the same manner that earlier social scientists sought to mimic the work of natural scientists. Moreover, it is, if anything, even more dangerous since what is being treated as a model is not a form of inquiry, but quite a different enterprise. The result is that, in effect, postmodernist work amounts to the abandonment of research.

In the past few decades, considerable attention has been given to the rhetorical dimension of the texts that social researchers produce, particularly qualitative work. This is the focus of the next chapter. Some of this literature mounts a critique of the realism that has previously been integral to research writing. A key argument here is that, contrary to what is often claimed for it, such writing employs rhetorical devices, rather than using language that is transparent. Moreover, many of these devices are the same as those that can be found in realist novels, where the realities produced are knowingly fictional. Under the influence of post-structuralist and constructionist ideas, the critics argue that social science similarly creates the realities it purports to describe and explain, rather than simply capturing or representing them. Given this, it is sometimes concluded that the use of a realist writing genre is a form of deception or inauthenticity, one that is geared to establishing and maintaining the authority of social science, while perhaps also serving to reproduce the socio-political status quo. Furthermore, on the basis of these ideas some commentators call for social research to be a *just* rhetoric, a rhetoric designed to promote social justice – for instance, by challenging expert claims to knowledge and thereby opening up the space for marginalised or subordinated discourses to be heard. In Chapter 8, I assess the significance of the rhetorical dimension of research, and challenge this anti-realism. In doing so, I focus on three issues: the differences between inquiry and other activities that produce written texts; the relationship between rhetoric and truth; and the question of the legitimacy or illegitimacy of particular forms of research rhetoric. In the course of the chapter, I compare this more recent work on research texts with the longstanding discipline of Rhetoric, which dates from the time of the Sophists in ancient Greece.

The final main chapter addresses the perennial issue of the criteria by which qualitative research should be evaluated. At the present time, there are powerful demands for 'transparent' criteria, for example in order to serve systematic reviewing and evidence-based practice. However, some qualitative researchers have argued that criteria are neither possible nor their pursuit desirable. At issue here, in part, is what the term 'criterion' means, and what role criteria could play in the context of qualitative inquiry. I suggest that they cannot amount to 'transparent' procedures which can be simply applied, and that a distinction must be drawn between the standards according to which research should be assessed and the considerations that need to be taken into account in assessing it. Furthermore, attention ought to be given to the different aims that assessing research can have: whether the focus is on the validity of the findings, the adequacy with which the research is presented, the value of the methods used, the competence of the researcher, and so on. Different standards will apply, and different considerations will be relevant, in each case. Equally important, though, is the question of whether a single set of criteria, guidelines, or principles is possible across qualitative research – given the methodological pluralism currently found within it and the fundamental areas of disagreement this reflects. Divergent approaches are framed, in part, by value assumptions about what is and is not worth investigation. In addition, there are differences in general methodological orientation: over what counts as rigorous inquiry; between realist and constructionist assumptions about the nature of social phenomena; and over whether the goal of research is to produce knowledge or to serve other purposes. The chapter concludes with a brief discussion of responses to this methodological pluralism, and their implications.

The book ends with a short epilogue addressing the conclusions that might be drawn from questioning qualitative research in the ways that have been done here. I suggest that there is a need for moderation in the claims made for qualitative inquiry, and for social science more generally, that tough decisions need to be made about what it can and cannot achieve, and that there must be sustained attempts to resolve the difficult methodological problems it faces. It seems to me that many qualitative researchers overestimate the success of their enterprise, and underestimate the seriousness of its problems. The main purpose of this book is to assess some of these problems and the attempts that have been made to deal with them.

# 1

## On the Failings of Qualitative Inquiry

My focus in this first chapter is on how qualitative research has developed over the past forty years. I examine what many of us claimed for it, and how far it has lived up to these claims. In effect, then, what is offered is an internal critique of qualitative research, one which assesses it according to the clarion calls sounded in the 'paradigm wars' of the 1960s, 1970s, and 1980s. It is important to remember that at that time there was a great deal more consensus about the nature of qualitative research, and why it was desirable, than there is today. While I write as someone who has worked in a particular country (the UK), a particular discipline (sociology), and for the most part in a particular substantive area (education) these were, to a considerable extent, in the vanguard of the shift towards qualitative method in the second half of the twentieth century (Atkinson et al. 1993). So I believe that the arguments I present here have wide relevance. Readers can, of course, judge this for themselves.

The emergence of qualitative research as a distinct approach to social science was often portrayed by its advocates as a 'paradigm change' or 'scientific revolution' of the kind that Thomas Kuhn had outlined in his historical and philosophical work on the development of natural science (Kuhn 1970). Kuhn described scientific revolutions as historical moments when it became widely recognised by researchers in the relevant field that a previously dominant paradigm had severe problems, and a new paradigm had appeared on the horizon that some believed to be superior. He argued that there was little likelihood that the disagreement between defenders of the old paradigm and advocates of the new one could be resolved through discussion. This was not just because there is never any *logical* or *empirical* means whereby the superiority of one paradigm over another can be demonstrated, but also because at the time of a scientific revolution insufficient intellectual resources are available even for effective reason–based persuasion. Instead, necessarily risky assessments have to be made; and, where a revolution succeeds, the outcome is partly determined by defenders of the old paradigm dying off and the emerging generation of researchers taking over. So, Kuhn argued that, during the throes of a scientific revolution, there can be reasonable disagreement among scientists in judgements about the potential of the new paradigm. Achieving a reason-based consensus is only possible once further work has been done within the framework of the new paradigm, so that its potential can be properly assessed. (Even then, agreement is not guaranteed – the superiority of one paradigm over another still cannot be *demonstrated* by either logic or empirical evidence.) What is involved in this process of assessment is discovering both whether the new paradigm resolves the anomalies that had emerged in the old one, and whether it opens up new fields of productive puzzles for normal science to pursue.

Kuhn's work had a huge influence on qualitative researchers in the third quarter of the twentieth century, despite the fact that he explicitly excluded the social sciences from his account, viewing them as pre-paradigmatic at best. Moreover, his work was often misinterpreted.[1] For example, it was treated as showing that even the truth of a natural scientific theory is relative to the paradigm in which it was developed, so that it may be false from the point of view of a different paradigm. And it was taken to follow from this that the decision to adopt a particular paradigm is necessarily arbitrary: a matter of non-rational commitment, since what is and is not rational is always defined *within* a paradigm. Furthermore, the meaning of the term 'paradigm' was frequently extended by qualitative researchers to include political and ethical assumptions, not just theoretical and methodological ones.

While Kuhn's perspective was not intended to apply to social science, and was often misrepresented, it is still worth looking back on forty years or so of qualitative research to consider how far it has succeeded in resolving the problems that it initially identified as intrinsic to 'the quantitative paradigm'. As I have already indicated, Kuhn did not deny that paradigms could be evaluated, only that this could not be done in a presuppositionless way – especially not at the height of a scientific revolution. Others too have argued that, while it may not be possible to carry out a point-by-point comparison and assessment of competing paradigms, it is nevertheless feasible to make rational judgements about their relative potential. An influential example is Alasdair MacIntyre's discussion of 'three rival versions of moral inquiry' (MacIntyre 1990). For MacIntyre, assessment can proceed by examining how well a paradigm succeeds in its own terms, and then by looking at how well it comprehends and resolves the problems that competing paradigms encounter.

The rise in influence of qualitative inquiry, whereby it came to be seen by many as a separate and superior approach, certainly resulted in part from increasing recognition of the failures of various kinds of quantitative work.

---

1 It must be said that Kuhn's message was not always clear, and he changed his views somewhat over time, partly in reaction against the reception of his work. For illuminating accounts of Kuhn's argument, see Bird (2000) and Sharrock and Read (2002).

Whereas these failures were generally regarded by quantitative researchers themselves as technical problems – in other words, as manageable, if not resolvable – many advocates of qualitative inquiry came to see them as more fundamental in character, as pointing to basic flaws in the ideas behind quantitative method, these often being dismissed as 'positivist'. In part what was being rejected here was the very image of science that Kuhn's work had undermined. Moreover, in classic Kuhnian terms, there was a sizeable revolt on the part of a new generation, who saw qualitative research as based on fundamentally different assumptions from quantitative work; plus the defection of some more established scholars from that dominant paradigm.[2] In the process, the attitude of most quantitative researchers towards qualitative work, at least in public, came to be one of toleration and even appreciation. It is only quite recently that there have been signs of a change back to more severe assessments.

While I still believe that the criticisms qualitative researchers made of the conventional methodological wisdom of the 1950s were largely correct, and that some of the problems with quantitative work are intractable, here I want to focus on assessing the track record of qualitative work.[3] I will suggest that there is much to criticise in the way that it has developed over the past few decades. In particular, there are respects in which it has not achieved what was promised. I am not denying the major contribution it has made to many substantive fields; though I think that this is rather less than is often claimed. My focus is solely on respects in which it has failed to live up to expectations or to meet the challenges it faced.

The failings of qualitative research can be divided into two categories. The first relates to criticisms that qualitative researchers made, and continue to make, of quantitative work, thereby claiming superiority. I will call these 'offensive failings'. The second sort of defect concerns responses to criticisms that quantitative researchers have made of qualitative research. I will call these 'defensive failings'.

## Offensive failings

In the late 1960s and early 1970s, there were a number of grounds on which qualitative research was widely advocated.[4] I will pick out just two main ones:

---

2 For discussion of an interesting example of this defection, that of Egon Guba, and the effect on those he taught, see Lather (2007:21–2).

3 I have discussed the problems facing quantitative work elsewhere (Hammersley 2007a).

4 Here, I am taking what Hargreaves (1978) called the symbolic interactionist/phenomenological tradition as providing the theoretical underpinning for the turn towards qualitative method in social research during the late 1960s and early 1970s. This was, of course, not the only strand. There were other influences, some of which were at odds with symbolic interactionism and phenomenology in key respects. For an account of the different varieties of British qualitative research, in one field, at that time, see Atkinson et al. (1993).

first, the need to *understand people's perspectives* if their actions are to be explained; and, secondly, recognition of the extent to which social life is a *contingent, and even emergent, process* – rather than involving the repetition of law-like patterns. It was argued that, because of its reliance upon pre-structured data, quantitative research was not able to provide adequate understanding of people's perspectives. Similarly, as a result of its focus on variable analysis, it ignored the processual character of human sociation. Qualitative research was put forward as better able to meet these requirements. Here I want to examine the extent to which it has done so.

### Understanding

The first argument was that in order to be able to explain – in fact, even to *describe* – people's behaviour it is necessary to understand how they view the world, and themselves. What the term 'understanding' meant here was for the researcher to learn to be able to see things in the same terms as participants, and thereby to recognise and document the internal rationality or logic of their perspectives. Quantitative research was criticised for either ignoring these perspectives completely, focusing on external behaviour, or eliciting attitudes by structured means, which were believed by qualitative critics to introduce serious distortions. These arose, they argued, from the preoccupation of quantitative researchers with measurement. This involved too many assumptions being built into the structure of the questionnaires or interview schedules employed, assumptions which were likely to reflect the cultural background of the researcher rather than the interpretative assumptions of the people being studied. In other words, much quantitative research was criticised for being framed in terms of conventional wisdom about the field being investigated, whereas (it was suggested) proper understanding requires that prior assumptions be suspended, in order to open them up to challenge.

The danger of misunderstanding had always been obvious in anthropological and other cross-cultural research, since there were many occasions when people's behaviour was not immediately intelligible. However, it came to be argued that the risks of distortion operated even when Western researchers studied their own societies: because of the high level of cultural differentiation within them, and also because of the creative and contextually sensitive ways in which people make sense of the world. It was pointed out that much survey research tends to assume that the dimensions of attitudinal variation are already known, and that the task is to document the number of people who see things in each of the various anticipated ways, and to explain the distribution of attitudes discovered. More fundamentally, there was a tendency to assume the existence of a cognitive consensus: that the world appeared the same way to everyone, or should do so (see Wilson 1971). Qualitative researchers insisted that, by reducing perspectives to positions on an attitude scale, a great deal could be lost that might be significant if we want to understand people's behaviour. They argued that what is required, instead, is the use of less-structured methods, such as informal and/or open-ended interviews, since these allow people to talk freely in ways that can reveal the distinctiveness and complexity of their perspectives. Only in this way, it was suggested, could genuine variation in orientation be understood.[5]

In the field of educational research, to take an area where qualitative work gained influence very quickly in the UK during the 1970s, this resulted in detailed, exploratory investigations of students' perspectives, particularly in secondary schools. It was argued that quantitative research either tended to assume that all students went to school simply in order to be educated, in the sense of wanting to learn the official curriculum, or it treated any deviance from this as abnormal, as a form of pathology that had to be causally explained. By contrast, qualitative researchers stressed the importance of exploring students' perspectives and actions without prejudging the parameters of these from the outset, or using evaluative categorisations. The aim was to seek to understand students in their own terms, treating what they said and did as rational in context, and as requiring explication. This was especially important, it was argued, in the case of those who were treated as recalcitrant or deviant by the school system. The task was to discover the rationality of these students' responses to schooling.[6] One general way of formulating this contrast – used at the time, and deriving from the sociology of deviance – was between a correctionalist and an appreciative stance (Matza 1969).

Of course, as it emerged within sociology in the 1960s and 1970s, qualitative research was not simply a reaction against quantitative method. It was also opposed to theoretical approaches that evaluated people's perspectives as rational or irrational against the standard of some scientific body of knowledge or purportedly rational mode of thought.[7] For this reason, use of the concept of ideology – whether by structural functionalists or by Marxists – was often rejected as simply explaining *away* whatever was difficult to understand from the researcher's chosen theoretical perspective, or on the basis of her or his background assumptions. Also, qualitative researchers criticised the common dismissal of some forms of behaviour as 'mindless', such as 'vandalism' or 'hooliganism', and challenged explanations of the lifestyles of some groups, notably the poor, as the product of 'cultural deprivation' or a 'culture of poverty' (Cohen 1971; Keddie 1975). Such theoretical approaches were rejected as an obstacle to genuine understanding of the lives of the people being studied.

---

5 In effect, this represented an attempt to reverse a major shift that had taken place from the 1930s onwards in the study of attitudes. Stouffer (1930) had claimed to show that life history interviews do not provide better data than attitude questionnaires; and this, among other things, led to a decline in the use of life histories and open-ended interviews within US sociology.

6 For examples of work in this genre, see Werthman 1963, Willis (1977), Marsh et al. (1978), and the articles in Woods (1980) and Hammersley and Woods (1984).

7 This had its most dramatic consequences in the sociology of science, see Barnes 1974 and Latour and Woolgar 1979.

In summary, then, the difficulty of understanding other people's points of view was emphasised by qualitative researchers, this difficulty being believed to arise both from the complexity of people's perspectives, and from the barriers to understanding created by those differences in assumption and orientation that frequently exist between researchers and researched. Central here was a rejection of the idea that societies operate on the basis of a widespread consensus – about either values or facts – in favour of an openness to at least the possibility that there can be heterogeneous (or even 'incommensurable') perspectives within a single society, organisation, or local community. Following from this, what was recommended in methodological terms was an attitude that allowed researchers to *learn* the cultural perspectives of the people being studied, this requiring quite lengthy contact and a relatively unstructured approach to data collection, along with forms of analysis that minimised researchers' prior assumptions and maximised their interpretative capacities.

Now, of course, a great deal of qualitative work has indeed sought to understand, or appreciate, perspectives and actions in this manner. And its contribution in this respect has undoubtedly been substantial in many fields. However, there are some respects, both methodological and theoretical, in which it has frequently failed to live up to this appreciative commitment.

One is that qualitative researchers have often been *selective* in seeking to understand the perspectives of the people they study. It is true that they have attempted to understand the views of people with whom they sympathised, for political or ethical reasons; and, laudably, these have often been those subordinated, devalued, discriminated against or oppressed by the wider society. However, qualitative researchers have been less ready to seek to understand, and to represent in their own terms, the perspectives of those they regard as playing a more central or dominant social role, and/or those with whom they have little sympathy. In this way, a radical methodological principle of early qualitative research – the commitment to understanding or appreciation – became compromised. In fact, what has resulted here is a process of distortion not unlike that which qualitative researchers complained about in quantitative work; in this case the attitudes of people 'in power', or those judged to support the status quo or to be politically incorrect, came to be treated as pathological.

This failing is exemplified by the common misinterpretation of Becker's influential article 'Whose side are we on?' (Becker 1967). This has frequently been treated as a call for partisanship, yet it was actually a demand for full commitment to objectivity, in the specific sense of being prepared to question dominant views when these are false (Hammersley 2000:ch 3 and 2004a). Becker argued that researchers must suspend the hierarchy of credibility, in terms of which those at the top of power and status structures are assumed to know more and better than those at the bottom. However, what many qualitative researchers have done is to *invert* this credibility hierarchy. While they have sought to appreciate the perspectives and actions of many people at the bottom of the heap, they have generally adopted a correctionalist stance towards those judged to be in power or in a privileged position. In relation to *them*, the usual devices of ideological analysis have been deployed.[8]

Sometimes, a more sophisticated version of this politically discriminating approach has been adopted, with elements of the perspectives of the marginalised being treated differentially, depending upon whether these are deemed rational or irrational by the – usually implicit – evaluative criteria of the analyst. An exemplar here, still much cited, is Willis's *Learning to Labour*, where he carefully selects out those aspects of the Lads' perspective which offend his political sensibilities and explains them away as ideological (Willis 1977). Subsequently, others have done much the same, for instance in interpreting the perspectives of black students (Mac an Ghaill 1988; see Hammersley 1998b).

What this reflects, I suggest, is a failure fully to grasp the nature of a commitment to appreciation. Setting out to understand the rationality of someone's beliefs and actions does not require accepting the validity or legitimacy of those beliefs and actions. All it requires is for us to find the conditions (for example, particular assumptions about the nature of the world or the situation faced) that made it rational for these people to come to the conclusions they did, or to engage in the kind of action they performed.[9] The analyst does not need to accept that the assumptions made were true, the conclusions correct, or the actions right. Indeed, whether or not the analyst does so is irrelevant to the process of understanding, except as a potential source of bias.

This error also explains an obverse failing. This is the tendency to protect at least *some* of the views of *some* people from assessment when they are being used as a source of information about the world. This is occasionally legitimated on the grounds that these people are in a privileged cognitive position, for example in terms of standpoint epistemology; or that questioning their views would be disrespectful. An example is the ruling out of any questioning of claims by black children, black parents or black teachers about the extent of racism in the British education system (see, for example, Connolly 1992). It is sometimes argued on epistemological or ethical grounds that their claims must be accepted at face value, and that not to do this is itself racist (see, for example, Gillborn 1995:ch 3). Here we can see inversion of the conventional credibility hierarchy in full-blown form. And it amounts to what Becker labelled as 'sentimentalism' in his article.

This leads me to another, closely related, point. In the past, it was frequently claimed that qualitative research would overcome reliance on the taken-for-granted assumptions that much discussion of social issues, and much quantitative research, had previously involved. Thus, the new approach was believed to

---

8  For one example see Ball (1990).

9  And here 'rational' does not mean 'logical' in the sense that there could only be one reasonable conclusion.

entail an explicit distancing from conventional assumptions: a making of the familiar strange. And this required a suspension of the researcher's political and ethical assumptions. Yet, in some ways, qualitative research has come to be more embroiled in political and ethical constraints than most quantitative research ever was. Indeed, some qualitative researchers argue that its very *purpose* is political or ethical, in the sense that this extends beyond a concern with the production of knowledge (see Denzin and Lincoln 2005). What this means is that, in many cases, the shift to qualitative research has amounted primarily to a change in political assumptions, rather than to an abandonment of correctionalism in favour of appreciation.

There are several reasons why this has happened. One is the close association between the emergence of qualitative research as a viable challenger to quantitative method, in the late 1960s and 1970s, and the rise of what has come to be called 'critical' research. The labelling theory of deviance was, in part, a political as well as a theoretical challenge to established views in criminology, one that was motivated by a radical liberalism (Pearson 1975; Downes and Rock 1979). On top of this, the emergence of student radicalism, in the late 1960s, shaped the development of sociology and of other social sciences. One aspect of this was a reinvigoration of Marxism after widespread disillusionment with it in the late 1950s. Moreover, Marxism was now seen by many very much in terms of the work of the young Marx, which was regarded as placing greater emphasis on agency: the active role that people can play in structuring social relations. The influence of Western Marxism (Merquior 1986a) was central here, and particularly the Critical Theory of the Frankfurt School. There were important parallels, as well as conflicts, between this and the interactionist and phenomenological ideas that surrounded qualitative research; and in a number of fields, notably deviance and education, there was a fusion of these different trends.[10] This was later reinforced by the influence of feminism and anti-racism, which introduced new political criteria to be used in critically evaluating the social phenomena under study. Later still, similar orientations developed around disability and sexual orientation.

From this 'critical' point of view, older forms of qualitative research came to be judged as insufficiently radical in political terms, on the alleged grounds that they neglected power differences and failed to recognise the researcher's responsibility to challenge dominant groups.[11] Yet, to repeat the point, what is involved here is a relapse from an early methodological radicalism centred on a commitment to appreciation back to a form of correctionalism; a reversion to the old evaluative orientation, albeit with changed political criteria.

It is worth noting that another important influence on qualitative inquiry in recent years, what has come to be put under the heading of 'postmodernism',

---

10  But not without dispute. See, for example, Downes and Rock (1979) and Hargreaves (1982).

11  For an early response to these criticisms, see Hargreaves (1978).

challenges the ethnographic commitment to understanding in an even more fundamental way. Several influences that strongly affected younger French intellectuals in the 1950s and 1960s, including Derrida and Foucault, played down or undercut the sort of interpretivism and hermeneutics that had influenced early qualitative research. Behind this post-structuralism lay the Nietzsche- and Durkheim-inspired ideas of Bataille and others, the resurgence of interest in psycho-analysis and Hegelian Marxism, as well as the influence of Russian formalism and structuralism in linguistics and literary study. These perspectives all focus, in one way or another, on the role of the unconscious: on how people's experience and actions are shaped by factors of which they are (perhaps necessarily) unaware. This has undercut the idea that in order to explain social actions and institutions a primary requirement is to understand the perspectives of those involved. Indeed, the very possibility of understanding others, and perhaps even the desirability of attempting to do so, is questioned. Thus, the emphasis on difference, on the Otherness of others, characteristic of much writing that is labelled as postmodernist, stresses the importance of what escapes any understanding. Another challenge derives from rejection of the notion of unitary selves: it is argued that the commitment to understanding others assumes a unitary self that can be comprehended, and also one that is actually doing the understanding.

However, rather than these ideas being subjected to critical evaluation, in the way that they are in the large secondary literature about post-structuralism, qualitative researchers have often used them in *ad hoc* ways. The fact that they conflict, not just with the initial commitments of qualitative inquiry but also with the notion of 'voice' and even with key elements of a 'critical' orientation, has usually been overlooked or neglected. In particular, what has *not* been addressed is the way that such 'postmodernism' challenges the constitutive assumptions of research as an activity. But my main point here is that it undermines what was one of the main bases on which the switch to a qualitative orientation was originally proposed.

### Process

A second important commitment of qualitative research, when it emerged as a distinctive approach in the 1960s and 1970s, was an emphasis on process: its advocates argued that, rather than patterns of human activity being pre-determined by some set of psychological or social variables, people ongoingly *build* courses of action over time. They do this on the basis of their goals and concerns, but these are adjusted or even transformed in response to the actions of others. As a result, human action is contextually variable, in terms of both what people say about themselves and their world, and what they do; and it is contingent in character – it can change in orientation, subtly or dramatically, even over relatively short periods of time.

An important methodological implication of this second commitment is recognition that in studying human behaviour there will often be a substantial element of reactivity, with people responding in various ways to the fact that they are being researched (procedural reactivity) and/or to the particular characteristics of the researcher (personal reactivity). The importance of this was highlighted by studies of the role of self-fulfilling and self-defeating expectations in human social life.[12]

On the basis of this commitment to the importance of process, quantitative research was criticised for failing to respect the very nature of human social life. For example, experimental investigations were dismissed as incapable of telling us anything about what goes on in the real world. Attitude surveys were also often rejected, on at least two grounds:

1  They involve the doubtful presupposition that people have stable attitudes which guide behaviour across all contexts as well as over substantial stretches of time; and
2  They assume that variation in attitude can be explained through causal analysis of social and psychological variables, treated as if these all operated independently and at the same point in time.

Against this, qualitative researchers emphasised the need for people's actions — including what people say about themselves and the world — to be *observed in situ*, and indeed across different contexts, as well as over relatively long periods of time. This was the sense in which Becker and Geer argued that participant observation provides the more complete form of data by contrast with interviews (Becker and Geer 1957).[13]

Qualitative researchers also criticised the commitment of most quantitative work to what Blumer referred to as 'variable analysis' (Blumer 1956). This was challenged for two reasons. First, much human behaviour is not sufficiently stable in its course to be explained in terms of a small set of key variables, in the way that the planets' movement in the solar system can (in gross terms at least) be accounted for. Secondly, processual complexity and change mean that, even more than in the exemplary case of evolutionary biology, the very phenomena whose character, causes, and consequences are to be understood do not fall neatly into natural kinds which can be characterised in terms of their essential features. Rather, at best, they form fuzzy sets having family resemblances; in other words, members of these sets do not all share a finite number of clearly demarcated characteristics in common.

---

12  See Merton (1948), and also Rosenthal and Jacobson (1968). The core idea here is to be found in the dictum of W. I. Thomas to the effect that what people treat as real is real in its consequences (see Merton 1995).

13  For a recent critique of this classic article, see Atkinson et al. (2002).

As with the first commitment I discussed, qualitative researchers have not lived up fully to this second one. Silverman and others have pointed out that a large proportion of qualitative research today relies entirely on interview data, and treats this as a window on people's stable perspectives and/or on their behaviour in other contexts (Silverman 1973, 1997 and 2007; Murphy et al. 1998; Seale 1998). While I would not go as far as some of these critics in challenging the value of interviews, it is not difficult to see that there are grave dangers in exclusive reliance on this source of data (see Chapter 5). Indeed, the older criticisms of interviews apply as much to qualitative researchers' use of them as to their employment in survey research:

- that interviews elicit responses in a distinctive context whose character is shaped through reactivity; and
- that, therefore, they do not provide a reliable basis – on their own – for inferring what people say and do in other contexts.

In other words, reliance on qualitative interviews as an exclusive, or even a primary, means of understanding people's behaviour suffers from some of the same problems as reliance on attitude inventories in survey research. In many cases, it assumes that behaviour is in large part a function of some stable orientation that directly expresses itself in the same way in diverse contexts. Here there is a neglect of contextual variation – of the way in which people respond to variation in socio-cultural context – and of the scope for change in people's orientations over time. Furthermore, there is often a failure to recognise the implications of the contextual sensitivity of what is said and done for what can be inferred from what people say in interviews about their experience of, and actions in, the world.

There are a number of possible reasons for this over-reliance on interviews. One arises from the first commitment I discussed, or rather the kinds of distortion that have been introduced into it. The emphasis that some qualitative researchers have come to place on capturing the 'voices', by implication the 'true' or 'authentic' voices, of the marginalised or oppressed has perhaps tended to privilege the use of interviews. So, too, probably, has the parallel concern with ideology critique of the views of those in dominant positions. Also significant is what has been referred to as the 'discursive turn' in social thought: the increased interest in detailed analysis of what people say or write. In particular, audio-recording and transcriptions have become the main kind of data employed in much qualitative work. While observation can generate discourse data, interviews are a more accessible source. It is often easier to gain agreement to carry out a few interviews than to negotiate access for a lengthy period of participant observation; and the scope for audio-recording is likely to be greater and the quality of the recording better. Increases in the time pressures under which researchers work may have exacerbated this trend towards reliance on interview data, since relatively large amounts can be generated quite quickly.

A similar neglect of the significance of process operates at the level of qualitative *analysis*. In practice, much of this is concerned with the ways in which variables, usually treated in a largely static way, shape perspectives and actions; or how particular types of orientation result in particular types of outcome. Moreover, many of the variables employed are those that are central to conventional social theory and/or everyday policy language – for example, social class, gender, and ethnicity, and outcomes such as criminal conviction or educational qualification – rather than variables whose significance has emerged from the particular study being carried out and/or which are distinctive to the local context being investigated. As a result, quite a lot of qualitative inquiry now takes a form that is not far from being old-style quantitative research without the numbers. A range of different attitudes or orientations may be identified, their distribution specified, albeit usually in qualitative rather than quantitative terms; and this is then explained as resulting from the operation of structural variables and/or as producing a certain pattern of outcome (for examples, see Gewirtz et al. 1995; Reay 1995; Reay et al. 2001).

One reason for this move back towards variable analysis is the influence of the 'critical' approaches mentioned earlier. These have generated pressure to 'locate' whatever is being studied in its 'macro context', and most recently in a global context (see, for example, Burawoy 2000). And it is this wider context, often introduced in a heavily pre-theorised fashion, which gives the researcher the structural variables that are to be the main focus. Here the arguments of interactionists and ethnomethodologists about the nature of context have been largely ignored, forgotten, or never properly understood (see Rock 1973; Watson and Seiler 1992). They have certainly not been refuted. More importantly, though, there has been a failure to recognise the importance of generating theory rigorously through the analysis of data, in the manner recommended, for example, by grounded theorising and analytic induction. While both these labels are used frequently, the considerable demands these approaches make on qualitative analysis are generally ignored. Instead, what seems to take place is a much weaker form of pattern-finding.[14]

### Summary

I have argued that in two significant respects – relating to the initial guiding themes of 'understanding' and of 'process' – qualitative research has failed to live up to its own initial commitments. Now, to some degree this may have

---

14 I am not suggesting that either grounded theorising or analytic induction are without problems. See Dey (1999) on the first, and Chapter 4 for the second. However, they both represent systematic approaches to the production of theory from qualitative data.

arisen from judgements to the effect that those commitments were ill-conceived or illegitimate. But, in large part, what seems to have occurred is a process of *ad hoc* and largely unconscious drift: back towards orientations that ignore the radical break represented by the principle of appreciation and a concern with taking process seriously.

At the same time, there has been little recognition of the extent to which this leads to a re-emergence of the standard methodological problems that have long preoccupied quantitative researchers. In the second half of the chapter, I want to discuss qualitative researchers' attitudes towards those traditional problems. Here, too, it seems to me that there has been a significant failure.

## Defensive failings

In my view, qualitative researchers have failed to defend their work effectively against quantitative criticisms; or, to put it less combatively, they have not addressed effectively the problems to which those criticisms point. In the early battles with quantitative researchers, qualitative inquiry was criticised in three main areas:

1   For failing rigorously to operationalise concepts and thereby to document measurable differences.
2   For being unable to rule out rival explanations through physical or statistical control.
3   For failing to produce generalisable findings.

Qualitative researchers' responses to these criticisms have varied, but the following are the main ones:

1   It is sometimes argued that qualitative work does not need to stand on its own, and if it is combined with quantitative work it can meet the requirements that lie behind these criticisms.
2   Alternatively, it may be argued that qualitative research has its own ways of documenting differences, identifying causal relations, and producing theoretical generalisations. Therefore, the strategies associated with quantitative work are not relevant to it, and the criticisms do not apply.
3   Finally, it is often argued that these criticisms of qualitative inquiry simply misconceive the nature of social research, since they derive from a positivistic paradigm that has been discredited and superseded.

Over the years, the latter two responses, and especially the third, have probably become the most common; though a revival in the fortunes of the first may be taking place, in the context of calls for mixed methods research. My own view is that there is an element of truth in all of these responses, but that none is adequate. Moreover, these three counter-arguments have tended to be used as shields to fend off criticisms rather than as starting points for the development of a sounder position.

Those putting forward the first defence have often appealed to the concept of triangulation as a way of dealing with the issues of measurement, causal validation, and perhaps even generalisability. Yet, this term is used in a variety of ways, often without much clarity about its meaning. Initially, it was employed to refer to the use of additional types of data in order to check the *validity* of inferences. The idea here is that by drawing data from sources that have divergent threats to validity it is possible to discount error built into the data (see, for example, Denzin 1970). And combining quantitative and qualitative data has frequently been regarded as the paradigm case of such triangulation.

In practice, however, even qualitative researchers who use the term 'triangulation' in this sense often do not apply the strategy in a rigorous fashion: they do not seek to identify the relevant validity threats and assess their impact. Instead, the term has come to refer more loosely to drawing on different sorts of data within the same study, irrespective of how these are used. Moreover, there has been a shift in the qualitative methodological literature away from this original interpretation of the term. Flick reports this move as follows: 'Triangulation was first conceptualized as a strategy for validating results obtained with the individual methods. The focus, however, has shifted increasingly towards further enriching and completing knowledge and towards transgressing the (always limited) epistemological potentials of the individual method'. From this latter point of view, as he remarks, 'triangulation is less a strategy for validating results and procedures than an alternative to validation [...]' (Flick 1998:230). This is probably an accurate account of how views have changed. However, it amounts to a move away from responding to quantitative researchers' criticisms, and the grounds for this move have not been presented very clearly, nor do they seem convincing (Hammersley 2008a).

So, in this respect at least, the first of the three responses to quantitative criticisms has not been developed effectively. And neither have the other two. Qualitative researchers' insistence that they operate on the basis of a quite different paradigm, one which either deals with the problems in a distinctive way or avoids those problems altogether, is seriously weakened, as a defence, by the fact that there has been a proliferation of alternative qualitative paradigms, none of which has gained a broad consensus. In the early stages of growth in qualitative inquiry, interpretivism was appealed to as a counter to the positivism that was held to underpin quantitative method. Even this took a number of different forms, captured at the philosophical level by the divergent positions of Schutz and Winch (Winch 1958; Schutz 1962; Thomason 1982). For the former, philosophical understanding was to provide a foundation on which social scientific work of relatively conventional kinds could be carried out. For the latter, philosophical understanding was a substitute for social science.[15] There was also the already-mentioned influence of 'Critical' Theory, which in its early forms insisted on the importance of a philosophical-cum-scientific grasp of the whole process of socio-historical development if the perspectives and actions of any particular group of people were to be properly understood. This then differentiated into forms concerned with other kinds of social inequality besides social class, centring on gender, ethnicity, sexual orientation, and disability. More recently still, all these approaches have been subjected to criticism and modification by post-structuralism and postmodernism, in various ways. The result is that, as noted earlier, the stances taken by qualitative researchers today often involve an unstable blend of different positions, with arguments that have potentially contradictory implications being used in an *ad hoc* fashion to respond to criticism, or to justify particular research strategies.[16]

In general terms, the predominant trend has been to move further and further into what we might call the constructionist cul-de-sac. There are various way-stations on this road. The starting point is a quite reasonable insistence that all accounts of the world are constructions – in the sense that they are produced by particular people in particular places with characteristic interests, attitudes and background assumptions – and that they are always constructed in terms of some set of cultural conventions, since otherwise they would be unintelligible. It may also be recognised that there are different genres in terms of which accounts can be formulated, and that multiple true accounts can be given of the same scene.

However, many are tempted to go beyond this first position to assume, wrongly, that researchers must recognise *contradictory* accounts produced by informants as all true, or at least as no more false than one another. This is often proposed on the grounds that these accounts represent the voices of diverse groups of people, or that the validity of no account can be 'legislated' by the researcher – that the task instead is, for example, to analyse the discursive practices which make them persuasive (see Potter 1996a). It should be noted, though, that this position is rarely applied across the board: there are some views, for example those regarded as sexist or racist, that are almost always subjected to implicit or even explicit critique.

---

15  There is some dispute about the relationship Schutz envisaged between his phenomenological investigation of the lifeworld and the conventional practice of social science (see Thomason 1982). Furthermore, Lyas has questioned the common interpretation of Winch's position I have presented here (see Lyas 1999). Nevertheless, my point is that these writers were treated as exemplifying contrasting orientations within the interpretive tradition.

16  In their introductions to successive editions of the *Handbook of Qualitative Research* (1994, 2000, and 2005), Denzin and Lincoln have sought to legitimise this by suggesting that the qualitative researcher should be a '*bricoleur*'. See Chapter 7.

Moreover, a few qualitative researchers go even further into the cul-de-sac, accepting that even their own accounts and those of other social scientists must themselves be treated as simply further 'versions of reality', constructed in particular ways and with no more claim to truth than any other, since all accounts actively constitute the reality they purport to represent. The implication of this radical epistemological constructionism is not simply a rejection of the methodological principles underlying quantitative work, or even of positivism, but an erosion of the fundamental commitments that are preconditions of *all* inquiry. These are replaced by a general scepticism about the very possibility of knowledge, or at least a denial that research knowledge can make any claim to knowledge which is superior to that from other sources. This undermines the viability of inquiry as a specialised activity that warrants effort or funding.[17] Thus, what we have here is not a defence of qualitative research but rather an abandonment of it in favour of some other activity: politics, literature, or art.

Under the influence of constructionism, the purpose of research is sometimes presented as simply raising questions or challenging taken-for-granted assumptions, and thereby unsettling existing positions (see, for example, Lather 1996; MacLure 2003). Yet, it is unclear why research would be necessary in order to achieve this; after all, it seems to come naturally to young children. At the same time, how could blanket questioning of assumptions be justified? Here, genuine recognition of the fallible nature of our knowledge has collapsed into a spurious scepticism. It is spurious, not least, because it cannot be maintained consistently: as has long been recognised, in order to doubt anything we always have to take something else for granted.

My basic point, then, is that no effective response to quantitative criticisms has been developed by qualitative researchers. Triangulation has been appealed to as a basis for combining quantitative and qualitative methods, but without this being properly theorised; and without much evidence in practical terms of the effective combination of different types of data to meet the demands for measurement and causal validation. More usually, qualitative researchers have discounted quantitative criticisms as based on an inappropriate or false paradigm, but they have not developed an effective consensus about the philosophical underpinnings of their work. Indeed, many have drifted into a denial that consensus is necessary or desirable, insisting on the celebration of 'difference'. But there is no such thing as difference in general, and the identification of any particular difference depends upon some assumption of underlying similarity. The situation we are faced with is methodological fragmentation in many fields of research, and this probably should not be tolerated, even less celebrated (Hammersley 2005b). Finally, some of the positions now adopted amount to the abandonment of inquiry, under the influence of an extreme version of constructionism.

---

17  At the same time, puzzlingly, this scepticism is often combined with an apparent belief that certain political, ethical or aesthetic values can be treated as absolute.

In my view, the quantitative criticisms of qualitative inquiry have some force and need to be properly addressed:

- *Measurement*: While often denying the need for quantification, qualitative researchers frequently make quantitative judgements about intensity of commitment or belief, about the distribution of perspectives across categories of actor, about the frequency of particular sorts of action or event, and so on. I am not suggesting that these must always be dealt with via counting, even less by formal measurement procedures, but this may sometimes be necessary (see Hammersley 1986). In particular, we need to address the well-known threats to the validity of frequency judgements – both our own as researchers and those of our informants (Phillips 1990:33). There are, of course, arguments to be developed here about what is meant by 'measurement', when it is and is not necessary to measure, what can and cannot be measured, and so on. But these have scarcely begun to be addressed by qualitative researchers. Instead, they have been largely ignored.

- *Causal analysis*: While qualitative researchers sometimes deny that they are engaged in causal analysis, most of their research reports are saturated with causal claims about how X affects, influences or shapes Y, about the consequences of various institutional practices, and so on. Moreover, this cannot be avoided without radically re-specifying the whole nature of the enterprise. There are, of course, examples of such re-specification. One is ethnomethodology, but only a relatively few qualitative researchers adopt this orientation consistently, and there are serious questions to be raised about it (see Chapter 6). Another sort of re-specification is the kind of constructionism, mentioned earlier, that attempts to be fully reflexive, continually undermining its own claims to knowledge. Yet few qualitative researchers adopt this radical re-specification either. Not unreasonably, they want to continue in the business of inquiry. But the price for doing this is finding some effective means of documenting what causes what (see Gomm et al. 2000: ch 12).

- *Generalisation*: Some qualitative researchers insist that they focus on the uniqueness of the cases they investigate. However, most cases studied by social scientists are of little general interest in themselves, and qualitative researchers, even when they deny that they are generalising, often go on to do just this. Of course, there are important arguments that have been developed about the *kinds* of generalisation that are possible on the basis of qualitative work, though some of these involve major problems. For example, there are writers who insist that they are not engaged in *empirical* generalisation but rather rely on *theoretical* generalisation. However, there is rarely much clarity about what is meant by 'theory' here, about how such inference is possible and can be checked, and so on (see Gomm et al. 2000: ch 5). Moreover, very little effort has been devoted to the systematic development and testing of theory by qualitative researchers.[18] Similar issues arise with generalisation from a sample to a finite population. Qualitative researchers often seek to do this in practice and it does not require the application of statistical sampling procedures; nor are these unproblematic. However, the task does need to be addressed explicitly, and the strategies used for doing it justified.[19]

So, the various defences that qualitative researchers use against the criticisms made by quantitative researchers have not been properly developed. And the problems these criticisms point to are genuine ones. Instead of addressing the criticisms effectively, stock defences have been treated as if they were magic symbols that can ward off positivist demons.

## Conclusion

In this chapter, I have identified two respects in which much recent qualitative research has failed to live up to the promises that were initially made on its behalf. First, there has been failure to satisfy the claims made for its superiority. Qualitative inquiry was supposed to provide genuine understanding of people's perspectives, rather than being biased by methodological preconceptions and conventional wisdom. However, this appreciative approach has been applied only selectively, and has sometimes been distorted into the idea of 'giving voice' or advocacy. Moreover, some influences on qualitative inquiry, notably 'critical' theory, postmodernism and constructionism, challenge the very possibility of, and/or desirability of seeking, such understanding.

Equally important, qualitative inquiry promised to take proper account of the processual character of human social life. Yet much qualitative research today relies primarily on interviews, and implicitly resorts to variable analysis, identifying what it claims are relatively stable orientations on the part of the people studied, explaining these in terms of structural variables, and treating them as having determinate effects. Once again, there seems to have been a collapse back into the sort of approach used by the quantitative work that was heavily criticised in the initial promotion of qualitative inquiry. Moreover, this has not been done in an explicit and reasoned fashion, but rather there seems to have been an unwitting slide back into old ways under the cover of adopting 'new' approaches.

---

18 For discussion of an exception, see Hammersley (1985).

19 For the most illuminating discussion of the problem of generalisation by a qualitative researcher, see Schofield (1989).

Secondly, I discussed what I referred to as defensive failings. I argued that qualitative researchers' various responses to the criticisms that quantitative researchers have made of their work are largely ineffective. Instead of engaging with these criticisms, stock arguments are often used as a way of trying to deflect them. Yet the problems are genuine ones that qualitative researchers cannot avoid. Furthermore, some of the positions taken involve a rejection not just of positivism and quantitative method but of the constitutive assumptions of any research: that there are phenomena that exist independently of our investigations of them, and that pursuing knowledge of these is a viable and worthwhile goal.

I am not arguing here that qualitative researchers must revert either to their original commitments or to positivism.[20] Nor am I suggesting that qualitative research is unsustainable and therefore must be incorporated into a quantitative approach; though I do believe that an integrated approach to social research would be desirable – one that takes proper account of the methodological arguments on both sides of the divide. For the moment, however, it seems to me that qualitative researchers need to become more reflective and open-minded, to recognise the contradictory methodological arguments that now inform their work, and to engage with the serious problems that remain unresolved.

---

20 I would not deny that there are aspects of positivism from which much could still be learned (Hammersley 1995:ch 1). But there is also much to be learned from the other perspectives that have shaped qualitative inquiry over the past fifty years, including postmodernism.

# 2

## Capturing Complexity? Examining a Commonly used Rationale for Qualitative Research

'There is no quality so universal in the appearance of things as their diversity and variety.' (Montaigne)[1]

Qualitative researchers have often argued for the superiority of their approach on the grounds that it respects the complexity of the social world. An influential example, many years ago, was David Matza's advocacy of naturalism, which he interpreted as an orientation 'that strives *to remain true to the nature of the phenomenon under study or scrutiny*' and which respects 'whatever measure of variety or universality happens to inhere in it' (Matza 1969:5). What is implied here is a contrast between, on the one hand, approaches to studying the social world which move very quickly to claims about what 'lies behind' (and generates) appearances and, on the other, those which (at the very least) start from the careful observation and description of appearances. In short, 'being true to phenomena' means refusing to accept statements about their nature which do not take full account of how they actually appear to us in experience.[2] Moreover, by their very nature, phenomena are diverse; as Montaigne points out in the quotation at the head of this chapter. Thus, naturalism involves an injunction to accept the complexity of the social world, at least as a starting point; rather than

---

1 This is from the translation by Cohen (1958); quoted in Lock and Gordon (1988:v).

2 The meaning of the term 'phenomenon' here is complex. In its Kantian sense it referred to appearance as against 'noumena', or 'things in themselves'. For Kant, the latter were formless, form (for example, causality) being imposed by the mind to create the world of distinct but interrelated 'phenomena' that is experienced. Subsequently, the distinction between phenomena and noumena came to be abandoned even by neo-Kantians; and, as a result, the former term came to be used in a manner that blended both meanings. Later, in the work of William James, the older empiricist view of experience as consisting of distinct elements was replaced by an image of it as a flow of by no means entirely determinate phenomena; an idea represented, for example, in the 'stream of consciousness' portrayed in novels like James Joyce's *Ulysses*.

immediately seeking to abstract away from it to some simpler underlying reality of laws, mechanisms, structures, or forms. Matza quotes the words of John Randall: 'the richness and variety of natural phenomena and human experience cannot be explained away and "reduced" to something else. The world is not really "nothing but" something other than it appears to be: it is what it is, in all its manifold variety, with all its distinctive kinds of activity' (Randall 1944:361; quoted in Matza 1969:5).

Building on Matza's work, Paul Rock contrasts 'phenomenalism and essentialism in the sociology of deviance' (Rock 1973:17). What he means by 'phenomenalism', in this context, is 'the need to faithfully reproduce the social world as it is known by its inhabitants' (1973:17). He quotes Blumer to the effect that: 'students of human society will have to face the question of whether their preoccupation with categories of structure and organisation can be squared with the interpretative process by means of which human beings [...] act in human society' (Blumer 1962:191).[3] By contrast, 'essentialism' refers to the search for 'the underlying properties of social order' (Rock 1973:17). Rock's proposed solution to the tension between these two orientations is to investigate the concepts about social structure which people use to construct their behaviour in particular contexts. In other words, as with ethnomethodology, the focus is on interpretative structures that are immanent in experience as a complex reality, rather than material structures which occupy some separate realm below, or above, that immediate reality.

These arguments for naturalism were strongly, if indirectly, influenced by nineteenth-century versions of historicism and hermeneutics, concerned with capturing 'lived experience' (see Hammersley 1989), and by the model of phenomenological description provided by the work of Husserl and his followers (see Moran 2005). Here, the study of human social life was still to be scientific, but it was believed to involve a different kind of science from that which had been so successful in gaining knowledge about the physical world (often, for example, it was to be descriptive rather than explanatory). However, more recently, under the stimulus of philosophical hermeneutics, radical forms of the philosophy and sociology of science, and postmodernism, a more wide-ranging rejection of essentialism has emerged. This often involves abandoning the commitment to a science of human social life, the idea that there can be a proper method of inquiry (Smith 1989), and perhaps even the whole notion of rationality (Thomas 1998). Still retained usually, though, is the injunction to respect complex appearances, albeit now often 'discursively constructed' rather than 'naturally occurring' (Lather 1996). For example, MacLure argues that a postmodern analytic 'preserves, and indeed intensifies, the complexity of the specific' (MacLure 2006:230).

---

3 This is part of what might be referred to as 'Blumer's dilemma' (see Hammersley 1989).

## Forms of complexity

In the past, qualitative researchers have emphasised complexity in reaction against two influential competing approaches: on the one hand, against general theoretical models of social processes, such as functionalism, Marxism, or rational choice theory; on the other hand, against quantitative studies employing highly structured forms of data, such as those produced by survey research questionnaires, 'systematic' or experimental observations. The first seeks to reduce complexity by selecting out what is most important on grounds pre-determined by the theory concerned, and formulating it in terms of some model of the social system, or of the actor, that guides the interpretation of data. A key issue for qualitative researchers here is how these approaches deal with what does not fit the model; not just what is not relevant but also data that might suggest a quite different interpretation of the phenomena being dealt with. In a parallel way, structured methods of data collection reduce complexity by physically shaping and/or by selectively focusing on and formulating data in terms of some pre-defined relevance structure: a set of pre-ordained categories. These sometimes derive from an explicit and systematic theory but often do not. Here, what troubles qualitative researchers is that simplifying inferences are built into the data via this structuring, and that these may need to be questioned.

The complexity that qualitative researchers have been preoccupied with is of at least two, related, kinds. First of all, they have often highlighted cultural diversity, not just across different societies but also *within* any large, modern society. They have argued that this kind of complexity is at odds with much social theory. For example: normative functionalism assumes consensus and social integration as the equilibrium state; Marxism and some kinds of 'critical' theory tend to reduce all cultural diversity to one form of social division; rational choice theory assumes a single concept of rationality as a cultural universal; and so on. More recently, cultural diversity has been interpreted in terms of conflicting discursive constructions of what counts as reality. And this approach even challenges those forms of social theory, concerned with understanding local cultural diversity within large complex societies, which had previously been treated as compatible with qualitative inquiry.

The idea of cultural diversity was also believed to undermine the rationale for highly structured methods of data collection. This rationale assumes that the stimuli these methods present to respondents or subjects will have a standard meaning, so that variation in response will be restricted to what is generated by the causal variable(s) under investigation. However, if the meaning of 'the same' question or experimental treatment varies according to the cultural or subcultural membership of subjects or respondents, or even depends on the discursive practices they employ on a particular occasion, this will be a source not just of considerable noise but perhaps even of systematic error. Furthermore, the structuring of data by means of a standard set of categories assumes that those categories capture all that is relevant about the actions or responses of the people being studied; an assumption on which cultural diversity throws doubt, in that what will be relevant for some will not be relevant for others. An even more radical challenge is introduced if cultural diversity is allowed to raise the possibility that the categories employed to structure the data are themselves the product of interpretative practices that reflect the cultural background or socio-cultural practices of the researcher.

In summary, then, complexity in the form of cultural diversity implies that theoretical models may often be unrealistic and/or ethnocentric: in other words, they fail to take account of the range of variation in orientation to be found even within a single society. And, in relation to the procedures employed by quantitative sociologists to structure their data, the commitment to cultural diversity suggests that these are not methodologically neutral in their effects: that, at the very least, those effects will vary according to the cultural backgrounds of the people being studied.

A second kind of complexity emphasised by qualitative researchers arises from the *processual* character of social life. This is perhaps more fundamental.[4] The argument is that, rather than the outcome of any sequence of events being a pre-determined or law-like result of some set of causal factors operating on it, the outcome is an emergent and contingent product, one which would not necessarily be produced in other similar cases.[5]

One source of this kind of complexity in social life, to which some qualitative researchers have given great emphasis, is the ability of human beings to suspend a line of action in which they are engaged, and to redirect it. As Rock points out, emphasis on 'the emergent and relational properties of interaction' (1973:18) is linked to a model of human behaviour that ascribes 'reflexivity' to the actor: actors reflect on courses of action in the process of engaging in them, and may adjust (or completely transform) their behaviour in light of these reflections. In fact, there is a sense in which judgement is built into even relatively automatic forms of human action, judgement that can go in different directions on different occasions.[6] All this suggests that social processes cannot be understood in terms of some immanent, fixed pattern of causal relations. Instead, the routes followed by social processes (and therefore the outcomes) are in an important sense contingent, though at the same time not simply inexplicable.

---

4  It is more fundamental because, in one of its forms, it generates cultural diversity.

5  This argument raises questions even about conditional laws.

6  See Dewey's discussion of habit (Dewey 1922:70–1 and 1938:31–3), and Ryle's account of 'knowing how', which 'is a disposition, but not a single track disposition' (Ryle 1949:46).

However, it is a mistake to see processual complexity as solely a product of human agency, as restricted to the social world, or even as necessarily indeterministic in character. Processual complexity is also to be found in the physical world, at least outside the laboratory (and, perhaps, to some degree within it as well). Any causal factor works on an existing situation, and the outcome is determined as much by that starting point as by the nature of the causal factor itself. Moreover, causal factors can operate on particular situations in various temporal orders or configurations, at different intervals of time, and for varying durations; and each combination may produce differences in outcome. In addition, what epidemiologists call induction time (Rothman 1986:14–15), the time it takes for factors to generate a particular type of outcome, may also vary. This means that even physical courses of events are frequently highly contingent and unpredictable. Those which are not are the exception rather than the rule.

This kind of processual complexity, as it occurs outside the realm of the human, was captured nicely many years ago by Hayek, as follows:

> If I watch and record the process by which a plot in my garden that I leave untouched for months is gradually covered with weeds, I am describing a process which in all its detail is no less unique than any event in human history. If I want to explain any particular configuration of different plants which may appear at any state of that process, I can do so only by giving an account of all the relevant influences which have affected different parts of my plot at different times. I shall have to consider what I can find out about the differences of the soil in different parts of the plot, about differences in the radiation of the sun, of moisture, of the air-currents etc., etc.; and in order to explain the effects of all these factors I shall have to use, apart from the knowledge of all these particular facts, various parts of the theory of physics, of chemistry, biology, meteorology, and so on. (Hayek 1955:66–7)

It is significant that, if one were to re-run the process that Hayek describes, somewhat different patterns of vegetation would be produced; though this is not to say that the variation in outcomes would be random or entirely unpredictable. Gould has made exactly the same point about the evolution of life forms on earth (Gould 1991).

In relation to the social world, processual complexity, whatever its source, raises problems for those forms of social theory which treat each national society, or even global society, as a closed system in which surface complexity is generated by eternal or even historically specific laws of operation (whether biological, psychological, or sociological). It also creates problems for methodological approaches which seek to structure and standardise the process of data collection so as to eliminate the effect of that process on the data produced – contingency and uncertainty cannot be eliminated. It may be possible to reduce them, but it is also easy simply to obscure them.

Moreover, it does seem that human social life is more processually complex than are physical phenomena, in that experimental control is more difficult to exercise, and the more closely it is achieved the greater the threat to the external validity of the findings. As has been pointed out many times, psychological and sociological experiments are social situations, and so too are survey interviews (see, for example, Orne 1962; Silverman 1973; Mishler 1986 and van den Berg et al. 2003). What people do in those situations will be affected by how they interpret them, and this may change over their course. Moreover, even the same person may interpret 'the same' situation in different ways on different occasions.

On the basis of the processual character of social situations, in the senses outlined above, qualitative researchers have often drawn the conclusion that the categories produced by social theorists are reifications, and that quantitative investigators' attempts to structure and standardise their research procedures are futile. There is much to be said for these arguments, but they are a starting point rather than a conclusion. A relevant question is: how well does, and can, qualitative research deal with these problems itself?

## Qualitative research as capturing complexity

It is important to emphasise that, despite their commitment to documenting the complexity of appearances, and their rejection of approaches which (as they see it) fail to do this, qualitative researchers nevertheless engage in processes of theoretical abstraction and data reduction; *and that they cannot avoid doing so*. In other words, they do not simply render reality, in the sense of capturing and displaying it, but rather they selectively collect and interpret data, formulating what is observed and organising it under categories. While some may wish to portray their approach as naturalistic or phenomenalist, in contrast to the essentialism or reductionism of social theorists and quantitative researchers, any kind of *pure* naturalism or phenomenalism is impossible. In fact, this is recognised, *en passant*, by the two writers whose work I relied on in outlining qualitative researchers' early commitment to capturing complexity. At the very beginning of his book *Becoming Deviant*, Matza writes:

> The aim of writing is to create coherence. The risk is that coherence will be imposed on an actual disorder and a forgery thus produced. No way of avoiding that risk exists, since to write is to take on the task of bringing together or organising materials. Thus, the only legitimate question about a work is the measure of imposition, or the amount of forgery, the only off-setting compensation the possibility of entertainment or illumination. (Matza 1969:1)

In this quotation, what begins as a risk of rendering as orderly what is disorderly turns into an inevitability, since 'organising materials' involves making them coherent. Matza seems to regret what is lost here, implying that minimising the amount of organisation might be a virtue, and that all that can be said for imposing order, aside from its inevitability, is that it may provide some compensations.[7]

Similarly, in presenting the distinction between phenomenalism and essentialism, Rock notes that the two ideal types to which these terms refer 'violate [...] somewhat ill-developed and open sets of ideas' by imposing on them 'rationality, coherence and discreteness' (Rock 1973:17). And it is a small step from this to suggesting that such 'violation' is also a necessary feature of qualitative researchers' attempts to document the perspectives of the people they study. As Rock correctly points out more generally: 'any intellectual analysis entails some abstraction and some movement away from the "purely" phenomenal' (Rock 1973:20). Again, though, the implication seems to be that this ought to be minimised.

Recognition of this tension between acknowledging complexity and the essential requirements of analysis has been given new life and emphasis by post-phenomenological and post-structuralist ideas about the 'dissemination' of meaning. Thus, for Derrida, the importance of what any account marginalises or leaves out is central, and he emphasises not just that accounts cannot capture everything but also that they are always unstable, that they can never achieve full coherence.

On the basis of this, any researcher is caught between equally impossible ideals: on the one hand, seeking to portray the world as it is in all its diversity and complexity; and, on the other, rendering it down into some coherent and stable representation. Stimulated by postmodernist and constructionist ideas, some qualitative researchers have argued that it is necessary to produce accounts which subvert any impression that they are exhaustively documenting reality, are entirely coherent in their theoretical assumptions, or are in fact actually 'representing' anything or anyone at all. This has produced a turn to modernist literary and artistic models, and a rejection of science.

Actually, there are two separate tensions involved here. The first is that which has already been highlighted: between, on the one hand, somehow capturing the complex nature of reality, and, on the other, producing a theoretical account which allows one to comprehend it. After all, comprehension always requires the account to be more simple than the reality. This tension can be illustrated by an extract from Lewis Carroll's *Sylvie and Bruno Concluded*:

'What a useful thing a pocket-map is!' I remarked.

'That's another thing we've learned from *your* Nation,' said Mein Herr, 'map-making. But we've carried it much further than *you*. What do you consider the *largest* map that would be really useful?'

---

7 As regards the inevitability of 'forgery', Matza here anticipates Clifford's (1986:6–7) postmodernist formulation. See Chapter 7.

'About six inches to the mile.'

'Only *six inches*!' exclaimed Mein Herr. 'We very soon got to six *yards* to the mile. Then we tried a *hundred* yards to the mile. And then came the grandest idea of all! We actually made a map of the country, on the scale of a *mile to a mile*!'

'Have you used it much?' I enquired.

'It has never been spread out, yet' said Mein Herr: 'the farmers objected: they said it would cover the whole country, and shut out the sunlight! So we now use the country itself, as its own map, and I assure you it does nearly as well. (Carroll 1939:556–7)

Given the tension between naturalism and the simplification necessarily involved in producing any account, it is not surprising that if we look at how qualitative data analysis is done, we find that even in its initial stages it is devoted to *reducing* complexity. Generally speaking, it involves categorising data under headings, and then identifying a relatively small number of interrelated categories which organise the data judged to be pertinent to the research focus. Moreover, ultimately at least, instances coded the same way are treated as homogeneous in the relevant aspects of their character. This is characteristic not just of grounded theorising, and associated kinds of ethnographic analysis, but also of much discourse or narrative analysis. What distinguishes the latter, in these terms, is simply that the categories tend to focus on discursive function, and the aim is often the explication of what is happening in particular stretches of text.

The second tension between representation and reality implicated in qualitative research arises if we interpret 'phenomena' as 'how the people studied see the world' – in the way that Rock does, allegedly following Blumer. One question is: what 'news' can a scientific analysis provide which does not in some sense go 'behind' or 'beyond' participants' perspectives, in all their diversity and complexity? Theoreticians and quantitative researchers have not usually had qualms about employing abstraction, simplification, reduction, etc. in order to achieve this aim. Qualitative researchers, by contrast, *have* sometimes hesitated over doing this. This is evidenced, for example, in a nervousness about using theoretical terms that are different from those employed by the people whose behaviour is being studied. More recently, in some quarters, the concern has been ethical rather than methodological; to the extent that any such distinction is recognised. Here, the preoccupation has been with preserving and amplifying the 'voices' of particular categories of people, along with a rejection of 'speaking on their behalf'. And, as already noted, some qualitative researchers have argued that, in order to avoid abstraction and reduction, the mode of presenting research findings should be more 'literary' than 'scientific'. It is argued that the former is closer to 'natural' (for instance, narrative) ways of thinking and speaking about the social world, and therefore does not distort it in the way that scientific analysis threatens to do.

In line with the reaction against science, an influential emphasis among qualitative researchers in recent years has been on capturing 'lived experience'. In a prescient comment which seems to apply to some versions of recent postmodernist–influenced qualitative research, Rock wrote in 1973 that phenomenalism could lead to the adoption of 'a literary posture in which all explicit analysis will be foregone' (Rock 1973:19). At the same time, we should note that even a literary account will involve *implicit* analysis. Indeed, it is not clear in what way, or in what sense, someone's 'lived experience' could ever be reproduced. Nor would most forms of post-structuralism imply that it can be.

Furthermore, in practice, many recent qualitative researchers have routinely produced accounts which employ concepts – such as social class, gender, and ethnicity – in ways that refer to properties of social structure whose character is potentially independent of whether, or how, actors actually experience them; and sometimes these concepts are at odds with actors' perceptions, opening the way for analytic use of concepts like ideology and false consciousness. Yet these concepts are in conflict with any notion of research as simply rendering complex appearances explicit.

As already noted, one radical response to this problem is to re-specify the focus of qualitative inquiry as 'giving voice' to marginalised groups, where what representatives of these groups say is to be treated as expressive of a particular 'epistemological' standpoint, and therefore as immune to assessment by the researcher, being treated as true in its own terms. However, this raises questions about the 'essentialism' built into the identification of categories of person, the assumption of homogeneity of perspective across such categories, and what 'representation' means in this context, as well as whether it is legitimate. It also prompts doubts about whether there is a distinctive role for the researcher, as against that of advocate or politician. A move to so-called auto-ethnography, where the voice represented is that of the ethnographer her or himself, avoids some, but not the most fundamental, of these problems.[8]

What all this makes clear, it seems to me, is that the key issue is not phenomenalism versus essentialism, but rather what *mix of*, or *orientation to*, these equally unrealisable polarities is required. What is needed is an approach that analyses, but nevertheless respects the relevant complexity of, the social world.[9] However, standing in the way of developing this are some fundamental

---

8 For the rationale for auto-ethnography, see Ellis and Bochner (2000). For useful discussion of some of the problems, see Anderson (2006) and Atkinson (2006).

9 As already noted, Rock proposes a means by which 'a phenomenological analysis of social structure can be built up. For instance [the sociologist] will be able to explore the import of such phenomena as social class without [commitment] to the belief that social class is an autonomous or "real" entity' (Rock 1973:19). But, in relation to Rock's own framework, the question is: why is this any less of an 'imposition' and any less of a 'distortion' than other kinds of essentialism?

questions that need to be addressed, relating to the way in which qualitative researchers have thought about appearance and reality. The first problem, already touched on indirectly, concerns exactly what are to count as 'appearances' or 'phenomena' in the social world. The second is about whether appearances are the 'reality' which it is the task of researchers to 'capture'; and, if not, what going beyond these means and how it is to be achieved.

## Appearance versus reality?

As regards the first issue, I have already noted that naturalists or phenomenalists sometimes regard the 'phenomena' or 'appearances' to be described in all their complexity as 'the lived experience' of others. Yet, unless some sort of internally homogeneous collective subject can be presumed, to which both researcher and those studied belong, what is given to the researcher as experience will not be how the world appears to *everyone*. Even less is the *process* by which the world appears to the people they study given directly to researchers. So, if the aim is to capture how the world appears to the people being studied, then the researcher must find a way of seeing *through* the world as it appears to him or her, in order to capture how *others* experience it. Here, then, another form of essentialism seems to be implied: an attempt to penetrate through how things appear to the researcher to the reality beyond. What must be assumed is both that there is such a reality, consisting of determinate features, and that there is a method, or some means, by which it can be grasped.

Moreover, even if the task is restricted to researchers documenting the world as it appears to them, as in the case of some kinds of auto-ethnography, can they produce descriptions that simply reproduce their experience? To formulate experience in linguistic terms is surely in some sense to structure it, rather than to capture or reproduce it. And the 'same' experience can be formulated in different ways (not only via different languages but, for example, by means of different genres within the same language). Of course, for many social scientists today, this is taken for granted: language is regarded as *constitutive* of experience, and the use of language is seen as 'performative' – it is designed to bring about certain effects, rather than simply to represent the world.[10] But if we accept this, in any strong form, what is left of naturalism or phenomenalism? Are we not reduced simply to producing accounts which cannot claim

---

10 Here the term 'performative' (is being used in a broader sense) than Austin (1962) originally intended. This compounds the problems involved in analysing the accounts people provide of their lives as a way of capturing their lived experience. To the extent that people's accounts of their experience cannot be regarded as simply embodying that experience, but rather involve 'working it up' for particular purposes on particular occasions in order to do particular things, the idea that studying accounts can give access to social phenomena as experienced by the people studied becomes open to question. This is one element of the 'radical critique of interviews', see Chapter 5.

any correspondence to phenomena existing independently of them? The very *possibility* of naturalism or phenomenalism seems to have been lost here. This is spelt out by Thomas, using the example of interview data:

> What is said in an interview is coded in intonation, in personal history. It is coded in what Oakeshott (1989) called 'historic languages of feelings, senti-ments, imaginings, fancies, desires, recognitions, moral and religious beliefs, intellectual and practical enterprises, customs, conventions, procedures and practice, canons, maxims and principles of conduct' (p. 65). Its expression through language is infinitely complex. Literally infinitely: there will be an infi-nite set of meanings built into a complex utterance, resting in the 'language games' which a speaker is using – meaning hidden in what Giroux (1988) calls the 'shifting, changing relations of difference that characterise the referential play of language' (p. 20). (Thomas 1998:144–5)

Here, it seems, the complexity of social life is no longer something that can be represented in any way at all; at best it can only be continually alluded to as something forever beyond any representation.

One attempt to avoid this problem can be found in various forms of discourse analysis. Here, the phenomena being investigated can be rendered in researchers' accounts because they are already in discursive form. In other words, if the world is assumed to be discursive, then we are not faced by any contradiction in seeking to render its discursive character in our accounts of it. However, this is to assume that discursive phenomena are discursive through and through, and that they are self-displaying or transparent in character. Doubts can be raised about both these assumptions (see Chapter 6).

The second fundamental issue is whether the set of phenomena to be cap-tured, in the sense of how the world appears to the researcher or how it appears to others, is the primary or the only reality that social research *should* be concerned with capturing or representing. As Bhaskar and others have pointed out, treating reality as what is experienced is a form of empiricism, and one that is open to serious question (Bhaskar 1975 and 1989; see also Rescher 1998:ch 2). Some have argued that the very origin of modern natural science lay in getting behind the way the physical world appears to us, dressed up in 'secondary' qualities, in order to identify those qualities which are 'primary' or intrinsic to it. In the early twentieth century this led to a dispute about whether tables are solid objects, with all the characteristics we normally assign to them, or whether they are systems of fundamental particles in dynamic ten-sion (see Stebbing 1958). However, even if we do not adopt a physicalist reduc-tionism, we may still be forced to conclude that natural science has been concerned with getting behind naturally-occurring appearances by means of experimental method, so as to be able to identify the generative mechanisms which produced those complex appearances, these mechanisms being obscured by normal appearances most of the time. From this point of view, the idea that any analysis involves a distortion of reality, or creates a 'forgery', in Matza's

terms, is an empiricist error. It is precisely treating appearances as if they are
reality that amounts, if not to distortion, at least to an obfuscation of reality.
This argument has an additional twist in the case of Marxism and critical
theory, where appearances, in the form of commonsense understandings, are
treated as ideological; in other words, as *systematically misleading* – their
misleading character is a design feature generated by the underlying causal
mechanisms.

Now it is, of course, reasonable to complain about oversimplified accounts
of the nature of social phenomena without denying that analysis necessarily
involves some simplification. But what is urgently required is to address the
question of what counts as *over*simplification. Furthermore, we must abandon
the rationale which purports to claim that we are simply presenting reality as
it is. One part of this is to recognise that research is concerned with answering
questions not with 'capturing' reality. Of course, there are still issues here about
what should, and should not, be treated as worthwhile questions. And we need
to distinguish between different types of question, for example descriptive,
explanatory and theoretical (Hammersley 1997a). We must be much clearer
about the nature of the accounts we are producing, rather than presenting them
as capturing complex reality, as documenting our own (or someone else's)
experience of reality, or as demonstrating the impossibility of representation of
any kind.

## Conclusion

As I noted, an influential rationale for qualitative approaches, when they were
challenging the supremacy of quantitative method, was to argue that the primary commitment of research should be to be 'true to the phenomena'. This
was often contrasted with the positivist commitment to method. Closely associated with this rationale, in fact built into it, was the argument that what is
required is to capture the complexity of the real world, rather than seeking to
reduce it to some theoretical model or to a set of variables and measurement
procedures. In this chapter, I have tried to show that while this commitment
signals something important, it is not a sound basis for qualitative research. It is
not possible to grasp complexity fully, nor is it desirable to attempt this. Rather,
producing knowledge necessarily involves selection and abstraction. The task
of research is not to reproduce reality, or even to represent it – in the sense of
capturing its likeness. Rather, the task is always to answer some specific set of
questions about it. The questions need not be fixed from the start: they can be
open to change during the course of inquiry. Indeed, leaving them open is
often desirable, since we may need to discover what are good questions to ask.
But, however tentatively, we always have to rely upon some framework of
assumptions built into the question(s) we are currently addressing, in order to

select and work on data. And we will have to simplify and reduce those data in order to produce answers, however exploratory and uncertain in validity.

The issue for me is: how can we find ways of doing this without forcing reality into categories that do not fit? This is a question to which, I suggest, qualitative researchers have not given sufficient attention. This is partly because the rhetoric of capturing complexity implies that it does not arise. But the issue is also occluded by those who see research as construction rather than discovery. I have tried to show that the problem is a genuine, and difficult, one; though I do not believe it is impossible to resolve.

One traditional way of conceptualising this issue is to say that we need to 'cut nature at the joints': in other words, our categories must mark out those types of phenomenon that are different from one another in significant and relevant ways. This is characteristic, for example, of the critical realist focus on causal powers or mechanisms. However, there are problems with this way of thinking. For me, these do not lie in the fact that they assume that distinct types of social phenomenon exist independently of the researcher. I take that as given (Hammersley 2004b). I have in mind two other problems. First, there is the fact that the imagery of the social world as naturally divided up into separate objects in fixed relations with one another, so that our categories must be devised to capture these, neglects a point made earlier: that all knowledge consists of answers to questions, and that different questions will produce different answers (all of which can be true, so long as they are not contradictory). There is a kind of perspectivism here that this realist imagery does not seem to be able to accommodate. The second problem is a practical one: if we have to discover natural kinds, how do we go about doing this? This seems to me to be a much more important problem, and one that it is by no means obvious how to resolve. In the next two chapters I examine two contrasting approaches that are designed to recognise the complexity of human social life while at the same time producing theoretical accounts of social phenomena: these approaches are centred on the notions of thick description and analytic induction.

# 3

# On Thick Description: Interpreting Clifford Geertz

The term 'thick description' is often used as a way to characterise the distinctiveness of qualitative research, in terms of both process and product. Like some other terms – such as 'grounded theory' – it serves as a technical label deployed by many qualitative researchers in marking their work off from quantitative inquiry. Yet what this phrase means is usually taken for granted. It is clear that, in this context, thick is good while thin is bad – but why? And there are important questions to be asked about exactly what it means for description to be thick. In this chapter I will explore these issues, in order to assess how sound a rationale the concept of thick description provides for qualitative inquiry.

The most influential source of this term is, of course, the work of the anthropologist Clifford Geertz (1973b). In a famous essay 'Thick description: toward an interpretive theory of culture', he argues for a form of anthropology which employs a 'semiotic' conception of culture, albeit one modelled on Weber more than on Saussure. However, Geertz reports that he borrowed the phrase 'thick description' from the work of the philosopher Gilbert Ryle, one of the key figures (along with Wittgenstein) in the development of what has sometimes been referred to as 'ordinary language philosophy' (Hacker 1996). Given this, Ryle's work is a necessary starting point.

## Ryle on thick description

As a philosopher, Ryle was primarily concerned with explicating the logical geography of concepts, by which he meant determining their mutual semantic relations within conventional usage. In particular, he points to cases where the superficial form of expressions obscures the underlying grammar of the concepts employed, and can thereby lead to misconceptions. The concept of thick description appears in two articles where Ryle is trying to unravel the logical grammar of 'thinking' (1971a and b).[1]

In *The Concept of Mind,* Ryle had argued against the idea that thinking is a covert event or private cognitive act of some kind which then produces spoken or written expressions or other kinds of observable action. Here he was rejecting the Cartesian picture of a material process that is accompanied, or stimulated, by some spiritual shadow that we can label 'thought'. Thus, to think about an abstract idea is not to have in one's head some image which is then made explicit through language; and what is said cannot therefore be explained in terms of internal brain processes. Rather, having an idea is no more and no less than the capacity to outline and explain it, or perhaps the ability to act on it (Ryle 1949).

In a later discussion, Ryle focuses on those cases where the term 'thinking' refers to 'such activities as pondering, musing and calculating' (Ryle 1971a:258). He is interested in the nature of these categories of action, and is particularly concerned to reject any treatment of them which takes thinking to have a single set of always-present features. In other words, he denies that it is unitary in character. In one place, he suggests that it is a loose collection of activities that have mutually overlapping characteristics, rather than a set of necessary and sufficient features shared in common. He draws the parallel with 'game', the example used by Wittgenstein to make a similar point; though he denies that he is appealing to 'the now over-hallowed "family likeness" device' – on the grounds that this should only be used as a last resort. Indeed, he questions Wittgenstein's analysis of 'game' (see Kolenda 1979:6; Ryle 1979:20).

Elsewhere, he argues that the various words used to denote thinking are adverbial in character (Ryle 1971b). In other words, they do not refer even to a distinctive set of activities but rather to *the ways in which various activities can be performed.* This is where the concept of thick description comes in. To say that someone made a move in chess *thoughtfully* is to describe the act in a way that tells us about *how* it was performed. What is provided here is a thick description in the sense that it does not just tell us *what* was done but *how* it was done.

In these terms, then, it might be concluded that a 'thick description' is a description of an action that involves at least one adverb. However, it may go beyond this; though there are some uncertainties and problems with Ryle's discussion, partly deriving from the fact that he engaged in this 'thinking about thinking' on several occasions over many years (see Sibley 1970; Kolenda 1979; Lyons 1980:ch 3; Coulter 2003). The key illustration that Geertz draws from Ryle is a discussion of the difference between a twitch, a conspiratorial wink, a parody of winking, and practising winking (Ryle 1971c). Here, first of all, Ryle is arguing for a difference between 'contracting the eyelid' and 'winking' (that is, between a physical description and description of an action), *and*

---

1 The concept of 'thick description' was not central to Ryle's work, in the way that, for example, 'systematically misleading expression' and 'category mistake' were.

between 'twitching' and 'winking' (two types of action, albeit with only the second referring to intended meaning):

> To wink is to try to signal to someone in particular, without the cognisance of others, a definite message according to an already understood code. It has very complex success-versus-failure conditions. The wink is a failure if its intended recipient does not see it; or sees it but does not know or forgets the code; or misconstrues it; or disobeys or disbelieves it; or if anyone else spots it. A mere twitch, on the other hand, is neither a failure nor a success, it has no intended recipient; it is not meant to be unwitnessed by anybody; it carries no message. It may be a symptom but it is not a signal. The winker could not *not* know that he was winking; but the victim of the twitch might be quite unaware of his twitch. The winker can tell what he was trying to do; the twitcher will deny that he was trying to do anything. (Ryle 1971c:480)

Ryle emphasises that while 'there are five or more ways in which [a person's] winking attempt might have been a failure', the person 'was not attempting to do five things', only one (Ryle 1971c:481). Moreover, the success conditions for conspiratorial winking, parodying winking, and practising parodying winking are rather different; though each activity in the series depends upon the actor's capacity to do the earlier ones; and all depend, of course, upon being able to contract one eyelid on its own.

Here, Ryle seems to wish to ground the notion of meaning in terms of success conditions in much the same manner that Austin specifies the felicitous conditions required for some performative utterance to be successful (Austin 1962). Thus, discussing the example of someone saying 'Today is the 3rd of February', Ryle argues that 'our natural and probably correct thick description of what the utterer of the noises was up to in uttering them has to indicate success-versus-failure conditions additional to and quite different from the purely phonetic success-conditions to which the mere vocal uttering was subject' (Ryle 1971c:484). But there is the further idea that some action descriptions involve at least implicit reference to other action descriptions. For example, one cannot describe someone as parodying an action without also referring to the type of action being parodied, and presumably the success conditions associated with it. So, Ryle's use of the notion of 'adverb' in analysing 'thinking' is metaphorical. He writes of 'constitutionally adverbial verbs – active verbs that are not verbs for separately do–able, lowest-level doings' (Ryle 1971c:486). He seems to mean that we sometimes discriminate various forms of action that are at the same time related to one another in something like an adverbial fashion: so that parodying is always parodying *some other activity*, and the verb 'practising' has the same character.

## Geertz's elaboration

Geertz defines the task of anthropology as 'explication', in other words the interpretation of 'social expressions' that at face value are enigmatic or unclear

(Geertz 1973a:5). And he goes on to define 'ethnography' as 'an elaborate venture in [...] "thick description"' (1973a:6). What Geertz takes from Ryle's discussion is that an action is not a physical movement *plus* a meaning, in other words a material movement plus a spiritual accompaniment. For example, a wink is not the closing of one eye plus the intention to convey a message. Geertz concludes from this that what an action actually *is* implies a whole context in terms of which it can be the sort of thing it is described as being.

What are being rejected here are physicalism and psychological behaviourism: the idea that physical events in the world are more fundamental in ontological status than human actions; and the assumption that actions can be reduced to, or translated into, physical behaviour. Interestingly, any form of idealism – the idea that meaning should be treated as operating in some distinct non-material realm – is also simultaneously rejected. What is involved, in other words, is an expansion of the notion of the material or observable world beyond what is allowed by physicalism and behaviourism, or, for that matter, by idealism.

It is perhaps for this reason that Geertz contrasts his approach with the idea that what happens in human social relations is a calculable product of underlying semiotic structures, whether those of Lévi-Strauss or of proponents of ethnosemantics/componential analysis. His rejection of this idea means that while anthropology is necessarily concerned with semiotic codes, it does not aim at producing an abstract account of those codes. Rather, what are to be produced are descriptions of the realisation and interweaving of codes in particular situations, this being regarded as a contingent process rather than as in any way logically derivable from the codes themselves. So, he is rejecting both any notion of mechanical causality and any account which appeals solely to the internal logic of ideas or of cognitive structures.

While there are strong parallels between the orientations of Geertz and Ryle, in some respects Ryle's position is closer to componential analysis and speech act theory. As we have seen, for Ryle, thick descriptions of human actions are structured by what he calls the latter's success conditions. In other words, Ryle is concerned with identifying and differentiating forms of action in terms of the conditions of success in 'bringing them off'. It is those conditions that determine what is relevant for inclusion in the thick description of an action, and thereby determine what is 'the thickest possible description' (Ryle 1971c:487).[2] By contrast, Geertz treats thick descriptions as documenting the way in which

---

2 After describing several possible candidates for someone engaging in thinking, in the manner of *le Penseur*, Ryle writes: 'Note that in each case there is a thinnest description of what the person is doing, e.g. pencilling a line or dot on paper, and that this thinnest description requires a thickening, often a multiple thickening, *of a perfectly specific kind* before it amounts to an account of what the person is trying to accomplish, e.g. design a new rigging for his yacht' (Ryle 1971c:489–90, emphasis added). Geertz's position is also at odds with the way that conversation analysts deal with context (see Chapter 6).

symbolic codes shape the behaviour of, or are used by, individuals and groups involved in some event. These codes do not just relate to what is required to perform action X in culture A, but also to motives for engaging in action X on this occasion, responding to it with action Y, and so on. One of the effects of this shift in the meaning of 'thick description' is that we move from what is probably a self-limiting notion to one that is indeterminately open-ended; since many codes could be overlaid on one another in any particular thick description of a series of events, and could be being used in ways intended to extend beyond those events. The result is that it seems likely that different interpreters could, and often would, deploy different ranges of context in order to characterise the processes involved, thereby producing rather different, perhaps even conflicting, descriptions.

The central point for Geertz is that interpretation 'goes all the way down'. So, understanding what people are doing, and why, requires us to take account of the cultural context in which they are acting. And it follows from this that, if we are to convey the nature of their actions and why they do what they do, we must provide a description of that context. This is the sense in which anthropological description must be thick. But there is some ambiguity here about the nature of this context. Is it the context that is in some sense implied by the action, in other words the context assumed by the person who is acting? Or is it a context which provides us with a way of understanding the action in a broader sense than this; indeed, perhaps one that indicates why the person comes to define the context in the way that he or she does, why they select and classify some features of the situation in particular ways, why these imply one sort of action rather than another, what consequences this has, and so on? The answer seems to be: both.

Geertz argues that reliance on interpretation, and the focus on producing thick descriptions, does not make anthropology any less a science than physics or chemistry. However, it does make it a different *kind* of science. Indeed, he compares the task of the anthropologist with that of the literary scholar. In an often-quoted statement, he suggests that ethnography is analogous to trying to construct a reading of a manuscript that is 'foreign, faded, and full of ellipses, incoherencies, suspicious emendations and tendentious commentaries' (Geertz 1973a:10). Furthermore, the nature of the task means that validating interpretations is more difficult than it is in other sciences.

However, the task is not just to produce a reading of a particular 'text' but also to use this to illuminate general issues about human social life. Geertz argues that the production of broader conclusions does not take place through studies building on one another, in the sense of starting from where previous ones left off, but rather by their using the theoretical resources previous work provides in order to try to deepen our understanding of universal human themes. He criticises two ways in which social scientists have often sought to generalise from single cases: the 'Jonesville-is-the-USA' model, where the case studied is treated as a microcosm of the whole society; and the 'Easter Island as a test case' approach, where a case is selected in order to assess the validity of some theoretical idea. Instead, Geertz argues for a distinction between the locus and the focus of study. Anthropologists study *in* villages, he argues, rather than simply studying villages. And what they study in villages are social processes that will be found elsewhere; or, at least, their work provides knowledge about particulars that can be used to think more deeply about general social processes.

Part of the argument here seems to be that theories are tools rather than representations, and that the main product of anthropological work is not theories but rather depictions of exemplary cases highlighting processes in which the 'structures' or 'codes' to which theories point are implicated.

## Ambiguities in Geertz

Geertz's position is notoriously elusive on some key points.[3] As Shankman has commented: '[He] seems more concerned with suggesting a science of interpretation than with developing it in a systematic, rigorous fashion' (Shankman 1984:264). Certainly, there are important ambiguities or obscurities in his work. These relate to fundamental tensions that have long characterised the history of social science. In many cases, Geertz does not make his position on these clear, and the range of authors to whom he appeals in support of his approach could be taken to suggest that he does not have a specific position. For example, early on in the Introduction to his book *Local Knowledge*, he cites 'philosophers such as Heidegger, Wittgenstein, Gadamer, or Ricœur, such critics as Burke, Frye, Jameson, or Fish, and such all-purpose subversives as Foucault' (Geertz 1983: 3–4). Within the same paragraph there are also implicitly approving references to Freud and Collingwood. While most of these writers share an opposition to any 'laws-and-causes social physics' (1983:3), it is equally obvious that they differ fundamentally in all manner of other relevant ways. However, for the most part, Geertz does not address those differences. This perhaps reflects the fact that he was, by character, an essayist;[4] but its consequence is that there are a lot of uncertainties surrounding his notion of thick description.

---

3 Interestingly, a similar criticism has been made of Ryle. What Lyons (1980:xi) says of Ryle could equally be applied to Geertz: '[...] while Ryle writes with literary fluency, he also writes with a deliberately allusive style which all too often makes his arguments and conclusions elusive as well. When one has read through a paper, a chapter, or even a whole book of his, one is puzzled, provoked, and usually charmed by the epigrams and analogies, yet, on reflection, one is not able easily to say exactly what his arguments have been and what conclusions one should draw from them.'

4 See his own comments on the essay form and its advantages (Geertz 1983:6).

### From Ryle to Geertz and the tensions within contextualisation

Geertz picks up one part of Ryle's discussion and contrasts 'the "thin description" of what someone rehearsing a parody of a wink [is doing]', namely 'rapidly contracting his right eyelid', with 'the "thick description" of what he is doing ("practicing a burlesque of a friend faking a wink to deceive an innocent into thinking a conspiracy is in motion") [...]' (Geertz 1973a:7). What is involved, he suggests, is 'a stratified hierarchy of meaningful structures in terms of which twitches, winks, fake-winks, parodies, rehearsals of parodies are produced, perceived, and interpreted, and without which they would not (not even the zero-form twitches, which, *as a cultural category*, are as much nonwinks as winks are nontwitches) in fact exist, no matter what anyone did or didn't do with his eyelids' (1973a:7). In some ways, this seems close to Ryle's discussion of the way in which variations on the act of winking are related, and how none of them can be reduced to the act of shutting one eye. However, it becomes clear as the discussion progresses that Geertz is not following Ryle closely.

After discussing the case of winking, which he suggests 'may seem a bit artificial' (1973b:7), Geertz provides what he sees as a more realistic example. This is an account of an incident in Morocco, which started with Cohen, a Jewish trader, being robbed, attacked and nearly killed by members of a Berber tribe. Cohen appeals to the French authorities for permission to seek the reparation to which, under traditional rules (outlawed by the French), he is entitled. The local French commander cannot do this officially, but grants permission informally. Cohen and his supporters from local tribes steal some sheep from the Berber group that had attacked him, and he then negotiates compensation from them. However, when he returns he is imprisoned by the French and the sheep he had received in compensation are confiscated.[5] Geertz seems to see a direct parallel between what is involved here and Ryle's example of a wink and a parody of a wink. This hinges on the idea that what Cohen carried out was not a sheep raid but a parody of a sheep raid that was designed to communicate a cultural message to the Berber tribe: that they should honour the traditional rules and provide compensation. Similarly, the French authorities' agreeing to the 'raid' but then apparently reneging on this, amounts to a failed communication, just as a wink does not always come off. Indeed, one suspects that the parallel Geertz saw here hangs partly on the idea that the covert French agreement to Cohen's mounting a 'raid' could have been conveyed by a wink. However, despite the parallel, if we look more closely, it becomes clear that the meaning of 'thick description' has changed considerably in the course of Geertz's discussion.

---

5 It might be argued that what I have provided here is a rather 'thin' version of the 'thicker' account that Geertz presents. However, the issue is precisely what these terms mean.

While it is certainly true that what Geertz provides here is not a 'thin' description of physical behaviour, and that no such description could serve as a substitute, what 'thickness' amounts to in this example seems to be different from what Ryle had in mind. For one thing, it involves a lengthy narrative of a complex incident, not an account of a single, relatively brief act. So, at least in part, the 'thickness' of this 'description' arises from its quite complex narrative structure. Furthermore, what Geertz provides is an extract from his fieldnotes, and these in turn are based on accounts from at least one informant. The events recounted were not observed by Geertz, they took place long before he arrived in Morocco. And Geertz adds another layer in his commentary on the fieldnote extract. He specifically refers to this multiple layering of accounts as producing 'thickness': 'what we call our data are really our own constructions of other people's constructions of what they and their compatriots are up to' (1973b:9).

Geertz also points to the role of background information in allowing us to comprehend what is going on, or in determining our understanding of it: it is clear that he believes we need to know about the ethnic identities of the several participants involved in the events he describes, and the socio-cultural relations operating among them. This seems to be another kind of 'thickness' again. Furthermore, Geertz argues that multiple 'frames of interpretation' are involved because the participants in the events described belong to different cultures: some are Jewish, some are Berber, some are French. And he generalises this point to suggest that 'what the ethnographer is in fact faced with […] is a multiplicity of complex conceptual structures, many of them superimposed upon or knotted into one another, which are at once strange, irregular, and inexplicit, and which he must contrive somehow first to grasp and then to render'. So 'thickness' here seems to mean identifying the semiotic structures, associated with different cultural identities, that are involved in producing the pattern of events being studied.

Geertz is aware that there is at least one tension in his conception of the goal of ethnographic analysis. For example, he writes:

The whole point of a semiotic approach to culture is [...] to aid us in gaining access to the conceptual world in which our subjects live so that we can, in some extended sense of the term, converse with them. The tension between the pull of this need to penetrate an unfamiliar universe of symbolic action and the requirements of technical advance in the theory of culture, between the need to grasp and the need to analyze, is, as a result, both necessarily great and essentially irremovable. Indeed, the further theoretical development goes, the deeper the tension gets. This is the first condition for cultural theory: it is not its own master. As it is unseverable from the immediacies thick description presents, its freedom to shape itself in terms of its own internal logic is rather limited. What generality it contrives to achieve grows out of the delicacy of its distinctions, not the sweep of its abstractions. (1973b:24–5)

While Geertz recognises that there is a problem, and suggests that it is unavoidable, he does not discuss how to cope with it. The last sentence of this quotation is characteristic of the engaging, but at the same time frustrating, mode of writing he employs. In fact, it is in large part the absence of clear, delicate distinctions in his work that makes interpreting his position so difficult. Elsewhere, of course, he writes of the 'blurring of genres' (Geertz 1983), and this perhaps provides a better characterisation of his style.

Even though he continues to discuss this issue in the course of his essay on thick description in *The Interpretation of Cultures* (1973b), in effect the same point about the inevitability and depth of the tension is simply repeated, rather than its character clarified and strategies for dealing with it assessed. For example, at a later point he writes:

> The major theoretical contributions not only lie in specific studies – that is true in almost any field – but they are very difficult to abstract from such studies and integrate into anything one might call 'culture theory' as such. Theoretical formulations hover so low over the interpretations they govern that they don't make much sense or hold much interest apart from them. This is so, not because they are not general (if they are not general, they are not theoretical), but because, stated independently of their applications, they seem either commonplace or vacant. One can, and this in fact is how the field progresses conceptually, take a line of theoretical attack developed in connection with one exercise in ethnographic interpretation and employ it in another, pushing it forward to greater precision and broader relevance; but one cannot write a 'General Theory of Cultural Interpretation'. Or, rather, one can, but there appears to be little profit in it, because the essential task of theory building here is not to codify abstract regularities but to make thick description possible, not to generalize across cases but to generalize within them. (1973b:25–6)

There also seem to be two rather different views in Geertz's writing about the scope of thick description. Much of what he says implies that producing such descriptions is the whole task of ethnography. However, there is at least one place where he seems to use a narrower definition, in which thick description is only part of the ethnographic task, so that 'explanation' now becomes a separate sub-task (namely, 'specification' or 'diagnosis'):

> [...] the distinction, relative in any case, that appears in the experimental or observational sciences between 'description' and 'explanation' appears here as one, even more relative, between 'inscription' ('thick description') and 'specification' ('diagnosis') – between setting down the meaning particular social actions have for the actors whose actions they are, and stating, as explicitly as we can manage, what the knowledge thus attained demonstrates about the society in which it is found, and, beyond that, about social life as such. Our double task is to uncover the conceptual structures that inform our subjects' acts, the 'said' of social discourse, and to construct a system of analysis in whose terms what is generic to those structures, what belongs to them because they are what they are, will stand out against the other determinants of human

behavior. In ethnography, the office of theory is to provide a vocabulary in which what symbolic action has to say about itself – that is, about the role of culture in human life – can be expressed. (1973b:27)[6]

Later, Geertz talks of ethnography as presenting 'the sociological mind with bodied stuff on which to feed' (1973b:23), which could be read as suggesting a division of labour along the above lines between anthropology and sociology. And the subsequent discussion reinforces this interpretation of his conception of the role of anthropology in relation to the social sciences generally. Yet, almost immediately after the above quotation, Geertz returns to a broader concept of thick description in which description and explanation are combined:

A repertoire of very general, made-in-the-academy concepts and systems of concepts [...] is woven into the body of thick-description ethnography in the hope of rendering mere occurrences scientifically eloquent. The aim is to draw large conclusions from small, but very densely textured facts; to support broad assertions about the role of culture in the construction of collective life by engaging them exactly with complex specifics. (1973b:28)

The various tensions within Geertz's account of thick description reflect some endemic conflicts within the history of the human sciences, and it is worth separating these out.

### *Understanding versus explanation*

One tension is between understanding the perspectives of those involved in the situations or events being studied in their own terms, and the researcher developing her or his own scientific explanations for features of those situations and/or the actions taken to deal with them; explanations which may, of course, be at odds with participants' understandings.[7] Geertz seems to accept the need to take account of how participants see their world but he does not treat their perceptions and interpretations as sufficient for the purposes of ethnographic analysis. Given this, 'thickness' seems to involve both describing the perspectives of the participants *and* providing information about the context that is defined as relevant by the researcher's theoretical interpretation of what is

---

6 The formulation is unfortunate here, it seems to me: people's symbolic action is not concerned with saying things about the role of culture in human life, it is concerned with getting various things done. There is almost the idea of a collective subject speaking through texts in Geertz's discussion at this point. Note too that 'setting down the meaning that particular social actions have for the actors [...]' is not the same as uncovering 'the conceptual structures that inform our subjects' acts'.

7 Crapanzano (1986) criticises the rhetorical strategies Geertz employs in his influential article 'Deep play: notes on a Balinese cockfight' (Geertz 1973b) in these terms. See also Kuper's (1999:ch 3, especially pp. 105–14) critique of Geertz's argument, which parallels my discussion in this chapter in some key respects.

going on. In other words, participants themselves produce thick descriptions, and the anthropologist then provides a description that in some way builds a theoretical interpretation on top of these. A key problem arises here in relation to both of these tasks, concerning how we determine what is relevant: whose thick descriptions are taken as the basis for ethnographic analysis, and by means of what theoretical framework should these be elaborated? A second problem concerns how to deal with conflicts among participants' thick descriptions and between these and the interpretations of the ethnographer.

Also involved here, of course, is the question of causation. Geertz seems to reject the idea that the task of ethnography is to identify causal relations, insisting that it is concerned with the explication of meanings. As noted earlier, the model he adopts is the interpretation of communications which are not immediately meaningful; in other words, the model is hermeneutics. Yet, at the same time, he wishes to show how various semiotic codes shape situations and events, leading to identifiable forms of cultural variation across different societies. In addition, he insists that actors are not simply bearers of particular codes, and denies that what occurs is completely beyond their influence. Instead, they are portrayed as, perhaps unconsciously, using these codes in making sense of and dealing with the contingent situations they face. But this means that the task of ethnography is not simply explication of intended messages, it is also, in important part, to explain why people do what they do. Here a key question that arises concerns how competing candidate explanations are to be assessed. For instance, how can we know whether Cohen mounted his raid in order to send a message to the Berbers rather than in order to gain recompense directly; or whether the Berbers agreed to give him compensation because that was the traditional rule or because they were afraid of the French? In broad terms, at least, these are causal questions.

### Nomothetic versus idiographic orientations

Probably the most obvious tension in Geertz's notion of thick description is that between a nomothetic and an idiographic orientation: between searching for general types of mechanism or process that produce social phenomena, on the one hand, and seeking to capture the unique character of a particular situation, organisation, or society, on the other. Like many other qualitative researchers, Geertz wishes to combine these two orientations: he wants to produce accounts of the social world that are focused on particular cases but that also provide more general insight into social processes. He sees anthropological understanding of specific situations as enabling us to think more productively about the general questions surrounding human social life.

In its original form, the distinction between a nomothetic and an idiographic focus involved a contrast between two approaches to studying the world: one which broadly conformed to what was seen as the proper orientation for natural science, and one that was judged to be more appropriate to the social and cultural sciences (see Hammersley 1989:ch 1). The differentiating axis here was the intended product of inquiry: is the aim to generate knowledge about universal laws, general causal mechanisms, etc.; or is it to understand the character and history of a particular situation (including relatively large-scale ones, for example the current state of a national society)? While some commentators saw this difference in orientation between the natural and social sciences as stemming from a fundamental contrast in the character of the phenomena being investigated, for others it was a matter of different purposes and their relative value in the two realms. For these latter writers, notably the Heidelberg school of neo-Kantians, it was not that a nomothetic science of human social life was impossible but rather that it was of little practical value or human interest; and much the same was taken to be true of an idiographic approach to natural phenomena. At the same time, there was some dispute about the source, nature, and role of general ideas in idiographic social inquiry. Some saw nomothetic inquiry as being necessary to provide these, while others viewed them as quite different in character from universal laws: for example, Max Weber argued that they are ideal types constructed for particular purposes by the analyst (see Bruun 2007).

Geertz clearly rejects a nomothetic orientation, to the extent that this involves the pursuit of laws on the model of natural science. Indeed, his work spearheaded a challenge to those who sought to apply this approach in anthropology. At the same time, he does not believe that this discipline's task is simply to describe every situation in its own unique terms. As we have seen, he treats general, theoretical ideas as facilitating description of particular contexts in illuminating ways; and ways that provide general understanding and not just insight into the particular situation. Indeed, the thick descriptions that this sort of work produces are regarded as enabling us to think in a clearer way about the nature of human social life more widely. Unfortunately, though, Geertz does not address the debates that have taken place around the nomothetic/idiographic distinction in any depth; nor does he indicate clearly his own position in relation to them. He obviously believes that it is possible to study the general through the particular as well as to use the general to illuminate the particular, but it remains unclear how he believes that this can be done, or how his own work does it.[8]

As I noted one strategy at which he sometimes hints is the idea that theories must not be seen as representing the world but rather as tools that we can use to understand particular situations. The implication is that we should judge them simply in terms of their usefulness. But, we might ask, what determines usefulness, and how are we to judge good and bad uses of them? Is there no such thing as theory abuse? A similar question arises on the other side: given that our descriptions are thick in the sense of incorporating theory, where and how do

---

8 This is a criticism that others have made of Geertz (see, for example, Yoshida 2007:293–4).

we draw the line between speculation and well-grounded analysis, especially if it is true that 'interpretation goes all the way down'?

Ironically, here there is an at least partial parallel with Lévi-Strauss's characterisation of the 'science of the concrete', the mode of thought by which myths are generated. This, too, involves a refusal to go much beyond or beneath appearances. In describing Lévi-Strauss's account of the 'science of the concrete', Geertz notes that it involves a reluctance to sacrifice 'the vividness of perceived particulars for the explanatory power of generalized conceptual systems'. Instead, the task becomes the 'ordering of perceived particulars into immediately intelligible wholes'. Geertz continues: 'the science of the concrete arranges directly sensed realities [...] These become structural models representing the underlying order of reality as it were analogically' (Geertz 1973b:352). We must surely ask: in what ways does thick description differ from myth-making, as described here? Geertz does not give us the resources to answer that question.

In summary, then, it is fairly clear that the aim of Geertz's interpretive anthropology is to produce thick descriptions, and in the process to improve the theoretical resources available for making even better thick descriptions of new phenomena in the future. While some theorising is involved in those descriptions, it is to stay close to the surface complexity of what happens in particular places at particular times. Nevertheless, thick descriptions are to carry 'broad assertions about the role of culture' (Geertz 1973b:28) in collective life. Here, then, we have an approach which seeks to operate fairly close to the pole of capturing complex particularity, denying that theory – in the sense of laws or rules – is an appropriate aim for ethnography, yet at the same time insisting that thick descriptions carry general implications.

But even if the aim is reasonably clear, how Geertz believes it can be achieved is obscure. At one point he writes that 'the methodological problem which the microscopic nature of ethnography presents is both real and critical', but that it is:

> to be resolved – or, anyway, decently kept at bay – by realizing that social actions are comments on more than themselves; that where an interpretation comes from does not determine where it can be impelled to go. Small facts speak to large issues, winks to epistemology, or sheep raids to revolution, because they are made to. (Geertz 1973a:23)

What we are not told, here or elsewhere, is how researchers should go about producing thick descriptions, and how they (and readers) should assess their work in this respect. This is not to ask for some set of fully explicit rules in terms of which thick descriptions can be produced and evaluated: that seems unlikely to be possible. But we do need at least some characterisation of what would be involved. And it seems likely that our judgement of any candidate thick description would vary depending upon whether we were primarily concerned with how well it represented the situation being described or how illuminating it was in general terms. Moreover, if the task is to draw general conclusions, or to indicate general truths, from studying the particular, various questions arise. How can we study the general through the particular without abstracting from those aspects of the latter that are specific to the particular 'village' being studied? If such abstraction is legitimate, what is the nature of the abstraction process involved? How does the researcher identify what is general and what is distinctive?

There is a significant tension here. Indeed, it can be argued that the project of producing thick descriptions, as formulated by Geertz, amounts to a futile attempt to combine two activities that, while they are complementary, are very different in character from one another: theorising about the types of mechanism or process that operate in the social world, and describing and explaining what happened in particular situations. It can be argued that both tasks are important, and that each can serve the other. What is not clear is how they could be combined. As Geertz himself seems to recognise, they place contradictory demands upon the researcher. In more specific terms: how can the ethnographer simultaneously assess the validity of both theoretical ideas about symbolic codes *and* interpretations of what is going on and why in particular situations? Each clearly relies upon the other, so by what means do we determine whether the theoretical ideas are sound in their own terms, and whether they apply to the particular situation being investigated in the ways that are claimed?

## Geertz's alternative models

As a challenge to the influence of physics as a methodological model, Geertz puts forward two models from other disciplines. The predominant one he recommends, as already noted, is that of hermeneutics and the interpretation of texts; and there is an initial difficulty here that has already been touched on. This is that, in its narrowest sense, interpretation of this kind is concerned with identifying an intended, or at least an embedded, message. Knowledge of the context in which the text was produced is only used to try to clarify the content of that message. So, this model applies quite well to Ryle's original example: is it a twitch, a wink, a parody of a wink, or someone practising a parody of a wink? By contrast, Geertz's example of the sheep raid does not seem to fit so well. Of course, various communications are reported as part of this story, but Geertz does not focus on understanding what his informant was trying to tell him by recounting this story. Nor does he approach the story in the way that Lévi-Strauss would in explicating the meaning of myths; or in the manner of a discourse analyst. Rather, Geertz wishes to understand what was going on – why the various participants did what they did, how this related to the various cultural codes on which they drew, etc. – and what lesson might be drawn from this about human social life more generally. And, in doing this, it seems that any thick description would necessarily rely on general theoretical ideas about, for example, Jewish traders as mediators between cultures, the nature of Berber society, the character of French colonialism in North Africa, and so on.

This goes a long way beyond the analogy with hermeneutics as explicating initially obscure messages. Of course, much nineteenth- and twentieth-century work under that heading has been aimed at a broader form of cultural interpretation that is not dissimilar to what Geertz recommends and practices. However, the character of and rationale for this has been subject to fundamental dispute, as for example in Gadamer's influential critique of nineteenth-century hermeneutics. This is, then, a far from unproblematic model; and the problems need addressing.[9]

At one point in his essay on thick description, Geertz appeals to a second paradigm that is, at least at first sight, rather different in character from hermeneutics: clinical inference. He writes:

> To generalize within cases is usually called, at least in medicine and depth psychology, clinical inference. Rather than beginning with a set of observations and attempting to subsume them under a governing law, such inference begins with a set of (presumptive) signifiers and attempts to place them within an intelligible frame. Measures are matched to theoretical predictions, but symptoms (even when they are measured) are scanned for theoretical peculiarities – that is, they are diagnosed. In the study of culture the signifiers are not symptoms or clusters of symptoms, but symbolic acts or clusters of symbolic acts, and the aim is not therapy but the analysis of social discourse. But the way in which theory is used – to ferret out the unapparent import of things – is the same. (1973a:25–6)

Once again it is not clear how this model resolves the problems. At the very least, we can reasonably ask whether clinical inference does not rely on knowledge of something like underlying laws, or at least the general idea that there are respects in which each case is essentially similar to all other members of the class to which it belongs? Indeed, Geertz seems to reinforce this assumption when he insists that: 'the theoretical framework in terms of which such an interpretation is made must be capable of continuing to yield defensible interpretations as new social phenomena swim into view' (1973a:27).

One interpretation of Geertz here is that he is proposing an instrumentalist view of theory. He claims at one point that anthropological theories are rarely decisively disproved. Rather, 'if they cease being useful with respect to [new interpretative] problems, they tend to stop being used and are more or less abandoned. If they continue being useful, throwing up new understandings,

---

9 For the disputes around hermeneutics, see Palmer (1969), Caputo (1987), Dostal (2002) and Harrington (2000 and 2001).

they are further elaborated and go on being used' ( 1973a:27). However, this instrumentalism raises questions about the ontological status of the structures or codes that Geertz sees theories as identifying. Are these simply fictions? And, if so, whose fictions are they: those of the people concerned or the researcher?

While both these models may provide some illumination when we are thinking about the forms of inference that ought to be employed in qualitative research, they raise as many questions as they resolve. Furthermore, there is a danger with use of the term 'thick description': that it can be interpreted as implying that the task is to capture or reproduce the phenomenon being described. And much the same problem arises with the notion of culture, where cultures are treated as objects existing in the world that can be represented. While Geertz certainly rejects any idea that there are distinct, internally homogeneous and self-sustaining cultures, he nevertheless seems to retain a notion of cultural description which assumes that the task is to capture what is there, both as it occurs in very specific situations and in more general terms. It seems to me that this is an impossible task: any inquiry is an attempt to answer some specific set of questions; and there are always different questions that could be asked about the same phenomena, which would produce different answers. It is the set of questions being addressed that indicates what should (and, at least as importantly, what should not) be included in any description or explanation. In other words, it is *this* which provides the guide as to how thick a description should be, or rather where a description needs to be thick and where it does not.[10] Furthermore both hermeneutics (in its least problematic form) and clinical inference address practical problems, yet Geertz's thick description is concerned with developing disciplinary knowledge about sociocultural phenomena. In other words, it is aimed at answering a very different type of question.

There is clearly a tension between the imaginative 'reading' of social life to make sense of what is initially puzzling, and/or to draw lessons about human social life, and the formulation and investigation of particular questions, along with the testing out of candidate answers. This links to the relationship between the humanities and the sciences, a major theme in Geertz's writings. More specifically, it concerns the kind of science that he believes anthropology, and social or cultural inquiry more generally, is (or ought to be). He wishes to open up and loosen social scientists' ideas about how to go about their work. In the earlier period when he was writing, this was undoubtedly of great value, but there is much less need for it today.

---

10 At one point, Geertz seems to come close to this point of view, arguing that different things can be studied in the same place, and the same sort of thing in different places (see 1973a:22). However, he does not draw any implications from this about thickness of description. Indeed, he seems to neglect the implications, as for example in his comment, in relation to the story of the sheep raid he has provided, that 'a really good ethnographer would have gone into what kind of sheep they were' (1973a:23). This seems to imply an open-ended valuing of detail, rather than a concern with what is and is not relevant given the particular set of questions to be answered.

## Conclusion

In this chapter I have examined Clifford Geertz's notion of 'thick description', which is widely appealed to as marking the distinctiveness of qualitative inquiry, as against quantitative research. I have suggested that there are some serious ambiguities in how Geertz discusses this concept, and that it does not provide a sound foundation for thinking about how qualitative research can produce knowledge about the social world, and what kind of knowledge it offers.

There is no doubt about the stimulating and illuminating character of Geertz's work. Nothing I have written here denies this, or suggests that his writings are of no value. My point is that the concept of thick description does not provide an adequate specification of the goal of social inquiry or an effective rationale for how it should be pursued.

# 4

# The Critical Case of Analytic Induction

One of the distinctive features often attributed to qualitative inquiry, as compared with quantitative method, is that it adopts an inductive (or, sometimes, the word used is 'abductive') rather than a hypothetico-deductive approach. To put the point in brief, crude, but only partly misleading, terms: it starts from the data rather than from a hypothesis to be tested, or even from a fixed research question. While some qualitative work *does* begin from within a specific theoretical framework, or even has a starting hypothesis, and while some quantitative work is exploratory rather than hypothesis-testing in character, there is no doubt that there is significant variation in typical orientations here.

What is less clear is the exact nature of this difference. After all, it is impossible to begin research without prior assumptions of some kind. A more useful approach is, perhaps, to think about this difference in orientation as relating to what is fixed and what is allowed to change during the course of inquiry. All activities, including research, must make some background assumptions. However, there can be variation in *how much* is assumed, and in how what is assumed is *treated* – for example, whether it is treated as beyond all doubt or as a set of working assumptions open to subsequent revision.

There is also, of course, the question of *why* it is believed advantageous to minimise prior assumptions and/or to treat some of them as open to change. One argument is that this allows the researcher to escape the blinkers of her or his own cultural background, or at least to minimise the effect of these, and thereby to appreciate the perspectives of those who are the focus of the research. A second, related but separate, argument is that it opens up to challenge at least some of the assumptions built into the initial formulation of the research question; on the grounds that these may be wrong. It is this second argument, rather than the first, which underpins the notion of analytic induction.

The idea of analytic induction has been widely appealed to by qualitative researchers, though more in the past than today. The term has been used within social science methodology, on and off, since its introduction by Florian Znaniecki in 1934; though some later usage of it does not correspond closely to Znaniecki's original sense of the term and the intentions behind it.[1] At the same time, there are some accounts of the logic of social inquiry that are close in character to Znaniecki's original but which make little use of the term 'analytic induction', notably the writings of Lindesmith (1937, 1952 and 1968). Furthermore, as we shall see, exactly what is involved in analytic induction, and what its assumptions are about the nature of human social life and how we can understand it, are not straightforward matters – even if we stick to what Znaniecki and Lindesmith had in mind. Given this, I will discuss each of what I take to be the major contributions to the theory of analytic induction in some detail. This is an essential preface to any assessment of its value.

## Znaniecki

Znaniecki contrasted analytic induction with enumerative induction. The latter involves trying to discover the essential characteristics of phenomena belonging to a particular pre-defined class by studying a large sample of them and looking for what they have in common. Znaniecki points to what he regards as a vicious circle involved in this approach: if one does not know the essential features of a class of phenomena beforehand, it is impossible to identify what are and are not instances of it for study. So, there is a procedural problem. But this also relates to a more fundamental issue: the class of phenomena taken for study is unlikely to be one that is well-formed, in other words one which contains phenomena, *and only those phenomena*, that share a single set of features that are essential to the relevant type – in other words that are produced by the same cause. The result is that, at best, any characterisation of the category can only operate in terms of features that members of it *tend* to have, rather than features that they *all* have. In other words, characterisation of the features of the category will be probabilistic rather than universalistic. Yet, for Znaniecki, it is essential to science that it searches for universal laws – relations of causality or functional dependence – not statistical generalisations. From this, he draws the conclusion that enumerative induction is not a scientific procedure.

---

1 There is room for reasonable disagreement about what should count under the heading of 'analytic induction'. Becker (1998), for example, distinguishes between 'rigorous' and 'not-so-rigorous' versions. See also Manning (1982).

Instead, what is required, he insists, is analytic, rather than enumerative, induction. His argument for this is as follows:

1. All concrete objects are descriptively inexhaustible, and therefore all description must be selective.
2. The selection criteria that should govern description are provided by the way in which phenomena are involved in semi-closed systems of various kinds.
3. The essential characteristics of a category of phenomena involved in such systems can be identified neither deductively, *a priori*, nor by enumerative induction.
4. They can only be identified by in-depth study of one or a small number of cases, aimed at identifying the functional relations among the features belonging to the type of phenomenon concerned.

It is an important feature of Znaniecki's formulation of analytic induction that it explicitly involves abstraction from 'the concreteness of pure empirical reality as given in unprejudiced observation' (1934:252). This is because he specifically rejects reliance by the social scientist on commonsense categories – as already noted, he believes that these are unlikely to gather together all, and only, those phenomena belonging to a specific causal type. He sees this problem as arising from the pragmatic function of commonsense knowledge, as against the theoretical function of scientific knowledge. Moreover, it is quite clear from Znaniecki's account that the aim of social science is to identify the universal laws which generate social phenomena.

Znaniecki's account does not make entirely clear how analytic induction overcomes the procedural problem that he identified with enumerative induction. After all, those adopting this approach still have to select cases for study, and there is no obvious guarantee that what they select will turn out to form part of a semi-closed system. What he perhaps has in mind is that having selected a case for investigation, necessarily in terms of commonsense categories and/or on the basis of observation, the process of analysis will lead to reconceptualisation of its character (and presumably also of its boundaries) so as to discover the scientific category to which the reconstructed case belongs.

It is worth noting Znaniecki's belief that, if universal laws are to be discovered, it is essential to study closed, or at least semi-closed, systems. In natural science, to a large extent, this closure is achieved by experimental method, but Znaniecki does not recommend this method in the social sciences. He seems to believe that semi-closed systems can be identified within social life, *if we find the right way of approaching and conceptualising it.* The nature of those systems is not very clear in his account, however.

Later versions of analytic induction depart from Znaniecki in various ways. For example, where he treats lawlike relations as *essential* features of particular types of object, they tend not to speak in terms of 'essences'. And where he argues that analytic induction can operate via the study of a single case, reject-ing comparative method as a means of identifying the essential features of phenomena, they endorse the value of comparative method in discovering law-like relationships among types of social phenomenon. Despite these dif-ferences, later versions of analytic induction put forward by Lindesmith, Cressey, and Becker do all share with Znaniecki the idea that its distinctive fea-ture is that it produces theories or explanations (no distinction is usually drawn between the two) that are universal or deterministic, rather than probabilistic, in character.

In most of these later versions, analytic induction involves investigating a small number of cases of the phenomenon to be explained, as initially defined. From this a hypothesis is generated about what it is that explains the occur-rence of the phenomenon. This hypothesis is then tested by studying further cases. On the basis of the evidence generated, the hypothesis is usually refor-mulated or abandoned; or *the conceptualisation of what is to be explained is rede-fined*. This process continues until no further refinement or reconceptualisation is judged to be required, in that new cases seem to fit the theory.

## Lindesmith, Cressey, and then Lindesmith again

Alfred Lindesmith provided one of the most influential formulations of analytic induction, albeit preferring the term 'casual analysis' (Lindesmith 1937 and 1968). The substantive theory that he produced, relating to drug addiction, maps a process by which people may move from an initial experience with a drug, by stages, to a position where they are addicted to it. The latter involves their being aware that they are taking the drug, that the symptoms they experience when they stop taking it are a result of withdrawal, and that those symptoms can be eradicated by taking the drug again.

Lindesmith presents his method as that of science, drawing on the logic of the experiment. He mentions, though in practice does not emphasise, the search for negative cases as part of this. He begins with a definition of the phe-nomenon he seeks to explain, which he restricts to opiate addiction on the grounds that other forms of addiction seem likely to be produced by different causes. He interviewed a considerable number of individuals suffering from opiate addiction, this addiction often arising as a result of hospital treatment. And, in the course of the study, he formulates and reformulates his hypothesis until the data coming from the cases no longer seem to challenge it. At that point he declares that the validity of his hypothesis is established, though he recognises that evidence could appear later which would force modification.

In a second classic study, Cressey, a student of Lindesmith, set out to study embezzlement. He took over Lewin's distinction between systematic and genetic causation (Lewin 1936), a distinction that runs parallel with Znaniecki's contrast between closed and open systems. He treats analytic induction as concerned with systematic causation, with causal relations occurring within semi-closed systems, rather than with external factors that bring such systems into existence or affect their operation.

Cressey's approach was very similar to that of Lindesmith. However, an important feature was that, unlike the latter, he was forced to reformulate the phenomenon he was seeking to explain. He found that legal usage of the term 'embezzlement' was not consistent, and that it seemed to include cases whose causal origin was unlikely to be the same, and excluded others that were likely to have similar causes. He therefore produced his own concept of 'financial trust violation', which he defined as occurring when a person had accepted a position of financial trust in good faith but later exploited that position. This term covered only some of the people convicted of embezzlement, and also included people convicted of other offences. Cressey interviewed all inmates in a particular prison who met the criteria of his new definition in order to identify causal factors in their lives that were necessary and sufficient to lead to their committing the offence. As with Lindesmith's work, there came a point where additional cases were no longer forcing changes either in the hypothetical explanation or in the definition of the phenomenon to be explained, signalling at least temporary completion of the investigation. Cressey's theory of financial trust violation portrayed it as occurring when someone has a 'non-shareable problem', recognises that it can be solved secretly by illicitly drawing money from funds over which they have control, and can rationalise this action to themselves, for example, as 'borrowing'.

In an article published in 1981, Lindesmith returned to the issue of analytic induction, exploring the nature of causality in the social world. He explains that he began by trying to think of it in terms of necessary and sufficient conditions, but later abandoned this in favour of treating it 'as a process – not as a condition, variable, thing or event'.[2] Following Dewey, he argues that 'a cause is a set of interactional processes which in their later stages produce or become the effect. What is called effect and what is called cause depends upon the particular stage or aspect of the total process that is taken as the problem' (Lindesmith 1981:88). Lindesmith uses as an example one that Dewey had also employed: the causation of malarial infection in humans. He summarises this as follows:

> [...] the causal process ordinarily begins in the human body when one is bitten by an infected female mosquito and forms of the parasite enter the blood stream. Within about half an hour or so the parasites enter the liver and vanish from the blood. In about 9, 10, or more days they reappear in the blood stream in large numbers where they invade red corpuscles and multiply within them by subdivision, destroying the corpuscles in the process. (1981: 91)

---

2 In fact, it is not entirely clear that he does abandon his original conception of causal relations completely.

Lindesmith points out that while the presence of the parasite is a necessary condition in both these processes, it is not a sufficient condition for disease. In the mosquito, it does not interfere with the insect's life cycle or reduce its longevity. Moreover, even within the human body, 'the parasite may continue to live and reproduce within the cells of the liver for many years without producing symptoms of the disease, although it may trigger recurrences. In addition, there are persons who, because of acquired immunity or protective genetic mutations, may be carriers without themselves having the disease' (1981:91).

What Lindesmith recommends, then, is that we think of the cause of the disease 'as a unique, complex set of interactional processes involving very large numbers of essential conditions, factors or variables'. The cause 'is not simply an antecedent item in a sequence of events. There is no precise point at which one can say with assurance that the cause has given way to the effect' (1981:91).

He argues that the universal form of generalisation – 'If A, then, and only then, B' – matches the uniqueness of causal processes, and has logical advantages. It indicates how the hypothesis might be falsified by a single negative instance. He comments that 'the uniqueness of the causal process frees us from the intellectual chaos that comes from assuming that all effects have multiple and numerous causes and that all causes have multiple and numerous effects'. He argues that to adopt the latter assumption violates:

> the principle of limited inquiry or of closed systems – a principle that restricts scientific explanations in a field to influences and processes within that field. Thus, the explanation of malaria does not include the earth's rotation on its axis as a causal factor despite the fact that the disease is spread mainly during the night and the hours of dusk. Similarly, while common sense might conclude that the atomic explosions in Nagasaki and Hiroshima were caused by political events in Washington, such an assertion makes no sense in physics. (1981:91)

What seems to be implied here is that different disciplines, and perhaps even different theories, are focused on different systems that can be treated as more or less self-enclosed, and which provide the basis for identifying determinate laws of operation.

Lindesmith uses the case of malaria to point out that the very definition of the phenomenon to be explained may need to be revised during the course of investigation (as Cressey had discovered). He comments: 'a statistician seeking a representative sample of instances of the "ague"' [a term, used in the English-speaking world prior to the nineteenth century, which covered malaria and various other diseases that involve fever] would probably have reached the conclusion that it 'manifests great variability in its symptoms, causes, and modes of infection and that no simple generalization can be made that applies to all the instances' (1981:92). He continues: 'Today, such conclusions abound in our field (sociology) and are often taken as confirmation of the idea that no two events are ever exactly alike and we therefore are unable to demonstrate causality in the real world'. The conclusion he draws is that 'we are too prone to use the ready-made, prefabricated classifications or kinds that are presented to us by our society [...]' (1981:92). In other words, the message seems to be that we are too inclined to accept appearances, including the conceptualisations of the people we study. There is a close parallel here with Znaniecki's position.

It is worth underlining that for Lindesmith, as for Znaniecki, what analytic induction is contrasted with is statistical method (primarily, as developed from the 1920s through to the 1950s or 1960s). He sees the latter as being concerned to map the complex surface of immediately given 'facts', rather than to identify underlying causal relations. He writes: 'It is often argued that the complex forms of human behavior that distinguish human beings from other animals are too subtle, complex and variable to be subject to scientific analysis and generalization of the usual type. Equating statistical correlation with genuine causality and the statistical method in general with the scientific one, is one response to this problem' (1981:94). He continues: 'A more plausible response perhaps, and a more optimistic one [...] is to observe that throughout the history of modern science this has been the contention in all fields that [scientific methods] had not yet successfully invaded' (1981:94).

There are some problems of apparent contradiction within Lindesmith's discussion that I will try to clarify here. One is that there seems to be a conflict between his claim that the distinction between cause and effect is functional, and the idea that the goal of science is to identify determinate laws operating in closed systems. After all, these laws must hold between clearly distinguished causes and effects. However, it may be that Lindesmith is simply arguing that the distinction between cause and effect is functional by contrast with being built into nature. In other words, there may be an element of perspectivism involved here, where what counts as cause and effect depends upon the question one is attempting to answer and therefore would certainly vary between disciplines.

A second apparent problem is that his talk of causation as a unique process might be interpreted in concrete terms: as asserting the uniqueness of the actual paths which events follow on particular occasions. This implies that those paths are not constrained by closed systems, and therefore will not display the kind of determinate patterns that Lindesmith sees as definitive of scientific laws. However, this second problem arises from misinterpretation. When Lindesmith uses the word 'unique', he does not refer to what is particular, to a one-off sequence of events. Rather, he means that the relationship between cause and effect is a unique one: in other words, it is the only relationship between the two types of thing or event which it connects; nothing else produces the same effect, and nothing else is produced by the same cause. This is an essential feature of what he means by a closed system; and it is another formulation of the idea that theoretical laws specify conditions that are both necessary and sufficient for the production of the type of effect with which they are concerned.

## Turner

A third account of what is involved in analytic induction was provided by Ralph Turner in two key papers of 1948 and 1953. He compares the theories of Lindesmith and Cressey, about drug addiction and embezzlement respectively, and relates them back to the work of Znaniecki. Furthermore, he takes over a point from Robinson's influential critique of analytic induction (Robinson 1951): that neither Lindesmith's nor Cressey's theory provides a basis for empirical prediction. For example, Lindesmith does not tell us who will and will not engage in rationalisation, take the drug to reduce the withdrawal symptoms, etc., and therefore become addicted. In other words, in practice, both he and Cressey focus on identifying necessary, rather than both necessary and sufficient, conditions; and there is no basis built into either of the theories they produce for determining beforehand whether the conditions specified as necessary will exist in a particular instance. Turner also agrees with Robinson that any remedying of this second defect would turn these two theories into 'relationships of statistical probability rather than absolute determination' (Turner 1953:609).

However, Turner argues that to criticise analytic induction for its focus on necessary conditions is to misunderstand what it was designed to produce, and indeed to misconstrue the nature of causality. He adopts the view of Thomas and Znaniecki, quoting them as follows:

> [a statement] of causal influences which hold true 'on the average', 'in the majority of cases' – is a flat self-contradiction, for, if something is a cause, it must by its very definition, always and necessarily have *the same effect*, otherwise it is not a cause at all. (Thomas and Znaniecki 1918, Vol. 1:39; quoted in Turner 1948:697)

What Thomas and Znaniecki, and Turner following them, are insisting on here is that causes specify necessary and sufficient conditions. In the words of Lindesmith, quoted earlier, they identify unique relationships: the cause always has only one effect, and the effect always has only one cause.

On this view, the aim of analytic induction is to identify such causal relationships, and this requires specifying a closed system within which relationships of absolute determination operate. Moreover, it is an essential feature of any such system, Turner argues, that it 'is not activatable from within but only from outside' (Turner 1953:609). In these terms, 'empirical prediction always concerns the way in which one closed system is activated by various intrusive factors' (Turner 1953:610). As a result, the theory of that closed system cannot, in itself, provide a basis for sound prediction (in other words, it cannot specify when the processes it describes will be activated).

Moreover, 'external variables operating upon any closed system do not have a uniform effect because they have to be assimilated to the receiving system in order to become effective as causes'. In other words, outside variables have to be 'translated' into causes relevant to the receiving system. This means that prediction always takes the form of statistical or probability statements, because there is 'uncertainty or lack of uniformity in the way in which the intrusive factors will activate the causal system and even in whether they will activate the system' (Turner 1953:610). Thus, in relation to Cressey's study, 'the situation in which a man finds himself [...] can only activate the closed system of the embezzlement process when it becomes translated into a non-shareable problem. Cressey finds no type of problem, phenomenologically speaking, which necessarily and uniformly becomes a non-shareable problem'. Turner summarises his argument as follows: 'the utility of defining universals within closed systems lies in the translation of variables into concepts. A variable is any category which can be measured or identified and correlated with something else. A concept is a variable which is part of a theoretical system, implying causal relations' (Turner 1953:610). And it is, perhaps, necessary to reiterate that what Turner means by 'causal relations' here is relations of absolute determination, in which (in Lindesmith's terms) the relationship between cause and effect is unique.

One way of formulating Turner's argument, very much in line with Znaniecki's original statement, is that what analytic induction provides are *definitions* of the phenomena to be explained. And these are real, not nominal or stipulative, definitions.[3] In other words, they identify a class of phenomena that is always produced in the same way. And the operation of analytic induction in practice involves alternation 'back and forth between tentative cause and tentative definition, each modifying the other, so that in a sense closure is achieved when a complete and integral relation between the two is established. Once the generalizations become self-evident from the definition of the phenomenon being explained, the task is complete' (Turner 1953:609).

Turner argues that 'analytic induction fails to carry us beyond identifying a number of closed systems, and enumerative induction fails to go beyond the measurement of associations'. He claims that: 'the functions of the two methods are not only distinct; they are complementary. When the two

---

3 See Robinson (1954) for an excellent discussion of these distinctions.

methods are used together in the right combination, they produce the type of findings which satisfies the canons of scientific method'. Thus, 'what the identification of closed systems does is to provide a basis for organizing and interpreting observed statistical associations'(Turner 1953:610). In other words, 'it is through conceiving the "essential" conditions in a closed system as the avenues through which correlated factors can operate as causes, that generalizations about closed systems can escape their self-containment, and probability associations may be organized into meaningful patterns' (Turner 1953:611).

The argument is, then, that on the basis of a theory we can show why there is an association between some variables outside the theory and the causal outcome with which the theory is concerned, by showing how those variables can set in motion the closed system of causal relations which the theory documents.[4] For example, there may be a relationship between gambling and embezzlement, but it is only an association, rather than a causal relation proper: it will sometimes, but only sometimes, activate the causal process when it produces non-shareable problems, these being part of the necessary and sufficient conditions that result in 'financial trust violation', as defined by Cressey.

Identification of closed systems also gives guidance about significant variables; in other words, indicating which correlations would be worthy of test. For example, Cressey's and Lindesmith's theories highlight the importance of such things as the kinds of situation which most often become non-shareable problems, characteristics correlated with the ability to rationalise what would normally be regarded as contrary to the mores of society, the personal and social motivations associated with taking opiates sufficiently to experience withdrawal symptoms, and so on.

At one point, Turner considers whether statistical information about an aggregate can yield causal information about the individuals who belong to that aggregate. He argues that it can only do this where causal homogeneity can be assumed in the aggregate. He uses the example of throwing 6,000 dice once each, pointing out that if each number, one to six, appears approximately 1,000 times we can conclude that the dice were not loaded, but that this is only because causally relevant features have not been varied between dice: they all had six sides and are properly balanced. He summarises the point as follows: 'the number of sides and the balance constitute the causal system determining the dice's behaviour, and no statement concerning individuals can be made from statistics unless the causal system is alike in each case' (Turner 1948:700-1). He concludes:

---

4  Under Lindesmith's influence, Sutherland adopted a similar position in explaining crime, arguing that differential association is the specific causal process through which other factors must operate. Therefore, poverty and other factors only facilitate criminal behaviour by bringing people into contact with others from whom they can learn a mode of criminal behaviour. See Laub and Sampson (1991).

The approximateness of the statistical frame of reference needs to be stressed in order to counteract the appearance of precision given by exact mathematical methods and by generalizations stated in terms of probable degree of error. Granted precise conclusions about the aggregate, conclusions about the unit remain approximate under most circumstances. On the other hand, the fact that the framework is approximate is no justification for abandoning or depreciating it. Probably every framework that has been devised has failed to fit nature completely, but scientific advancement has proceeded from one imprecise framework to another. Improvement can come within an approximate framework if the nature of its approximateness is recognized and constant attempts are made during its use to approach the ideal requirements. It is the thesis of this paper that sounder results can be secured through keeping this limitation of statistical inference in mind and through making all possible efforts to approach the required homogeneity. (Turner 1948:701)

Turner goes on to identify four means by which homogeneity can often be increased. The first is through careful scrutiny and redefinition of the boundaries of the universe of data being studied. As we saw, this was identified by Lindesmith as an essential feature of analytic induction, and led Cressey to redefine the phenomenon he was seeking to explain. The second method, rather more obvious, is redefinition of the independent or causal variables. In relation to this Turner comments: 'The tendency for statisticians [that is, researchers using the statistical method] to be satisfied with correlating variables on which simple data happen to be at hand and to avoid logical and common-sense analysis of their variables severely restricts the usefulness of many a study. Indices, rather than causes, are yielded by such methods' (Turner 1948:702–3). And he adds: 'As in redefining universes, there is no short-cut in finding the best variables. In nearly every instance it will be necessary to seek out new data to make a useful analysis' (Turner 1948:703). The third strategy seems to me to be essentially the same as the first: 'redefinition of the dependent or resultant variable' (Turner 1948:703). The final strategy is reducing the interference of other variables. As Turner comments: 'In most instances the effect of one variable is so confused by the influence of other variables that it is impossible to see a consistent relationship of any sort' (Turner 1948:703). He summarises what would be required in the new approach he is suggesting as follows:

The study cannot be limited by the simple data made available from census tables or standardized scales. The form in which the hypothesis is stated (universe and variables) must be subject to change in the light of early findings. Statistical manipulation must be complemented with a great amount of imagination and insight, which comes from intimate acquaintance with the subject matter. And there must be detailed examination of the individual cases to which statistical generalizations do not fully apply. The customary practice of showing that the findings apply significantly to some aggregate must be complemented, as a step toward making new generalizations, by a study of why the generalizations do not apply to [every] unit. (Turner 1948:704)[5]

---

5 For an approach within survey research that recognises the value of studying deviant cases, see Kendall and Wolf (1949). See the discussion of this in Becker (1998).

In summary, then, Turner insists on the distinction between analytic and enumerative induction, and believes that only the former identifies causes. However, unlike the other authors whose work I have considered, he believes that these two methods are complementary, rather than the first alone being the true method of science. He insists that they are both necessary – especially if the aim is to produce empirical predictions.

## Becker

Finally, I want to look at the writings of Howard S. Becker on analytic induction and other related matters. Many years ago, in *Outsiders*, Becker presented an example of this research strategy in his account of how people learn to enjoy smoking marihuana (Becker 1963). More recently, in his book *Tricks of the Trade*, he argued that it is superior to other forms of analysis because it allows us to make the most effective use of negative cases to correct our understanding of causal relationships. However, Becker distinguishes between what he calls 'classical' or 'rigorous' analytic induction, as exemplified in the studies by Lindesmith and Cressey, and his own earlier work, and what he calls 'not-so-rigorous analytic induction' (Becker 1998:195-212). The latter involves looking for or thinking up exceptions to generalisations and insisting on the need for reformulation in order to take account of these. Here the focus can be on 'how' questions, such as 'How do these people do X?' (1998:196) as well as on the explanatory 'why' questions that analytic induction typically addresses.

Becker also argues for what he calls a narrative account of causation. He criticises the approach to causality taken in much quantitative research for ignoring temporality: for assuming that the various causal factors identified all operate at the same point in time, or at least that the sequence and periodicity of their operation does not affect outcomes (Becker 1998:chs 2 and 5; see also 1992). Instead, he argues that social causation is a *process* in which there is *contingency*, in the sense that it can lead down different paths to a variety of possible outcomes. Conversely, the same outcomes can sometimes be reached by very different routes. He points out how difficult it can often be to explain an outcome without understanding the path by which it was reached over time. He uses the example of someone's decision to have a sex-change operation: what may not seem a likely outcome at an early point in the process becomes much more likely towards the end (Becker 1998:26-8).

Another example, drawing on Becker's own early work, is provided by the labelling theory of deviance. This argues that labelling can amplify deviance in two ways. First, it may change the circumstances of the offender's life, for example by making it more difficult to earn a living by legal means. Secondly, it could change his or her sense of self. Following punishment, the idea of being a 'criminal', or of being a deviant of a particular kind, often becomes much more central to a person's identity than it was before. For both these reasons, the chances of engagement in further deviance may be increased rather than reduced. Moreover, this process of deviance amplification often involves the creation of a subculture which valorises a particular form of deviance; and this subculture may draw others into deviance, thereby producing amplification at the collective not just the individual level. The novelty of labelling theory is not simply that it treats the identification and punishment of deviance as part of its causation, rather than simply as a response to it, but that it emphasises the temporal and contingent processes by which some people become committed to deviance of particular kinds while others do not.

So what labelling theory proposes is not that identification and punishment of deviance *always* amplify it, only that they *can* do so. Much depends on the temporally structured complex of events through which these processes take place. What we have here is an intervention – labelling deviance – that under different circumstances can send people down different paths to diverse outcomes. It may result in a reduction of deviance, through a process of deterrence, or it could amplify deviance; and this holds both in relation to the person labelled and to others, these effects being at least partially independent. As a result, the same act of labelling can generate both deterrence and amplification on the part of different people, or even for the same person on different occasions or in different contexts.

In another article, Becker elaborates on the concept of contingency. He addresses our experience of chance in everyday life, and notes how this is at odds with most social scientific notions of causation. He writes:

> When we talk as professional social scientists, we talk about 'causes' in a way we don't recognise in daily life. That disparity would not bother a lot of sociologists, but it bothers me. And I think it ought to bother all of us. Herbert Blumer used to give his students (of whom I was one) the following exercise: Apply any of the current theories of social psychology to any ten minutes of your own experience. What we found out doing this exercise was that the theories we learned in other courses were totally useless for this mundane purpose. We were left with the question: if these theories couldn't deal with something as simple as how I make breakfast, how could they deal with the nature of urbanism, class conflict, and the rest of it. (Becker 1994:185)

As a further illustration, Becker uses the example of the coincidences which led up to his meeting his wife, and also those which resulted in him starting to think about the issue of coincidence on a trip to Brazil. He comments: 'I wanted to be able to talk about all the elements that had to be present for some event to occur as it did. That made me keenly aware that many of those elements need not have been there at all. It was not their presence I wanted explained, but the way events depended on the copresence of all these elements, however likely or unlikely that might be' (1994:187).

In the course of his article, Becker reports how the philosopher of science Stephen Toulmin pointed out to him that the usual model for a theory in natural science is Newton's explanation of planetary motion, in other words a theory about a virtually closed system in which a very small number of variables can explain nearly everything. And he reports Toulmin as saying: 'determinism may be formally correct but it can only be an empty formalism, since the required degree of knowledge can't be achieved'. From this, Becker concludes that 'the kind of analysis called for by the view of social life I'm putting forward here demands something beyond the simple causal determinism my generation grew up with. If this view is correct, you can never produce laws of the "If A, then B" type, no matter how complicated you make A, B, and all their kin' (1994:188). What is needed instead, he suggests, 'is a way to talk about how things became possible, how a variety of conditions had to be met in order that the phenomenon I care enough about to want to explain actually happened'. And he adds: 'But this way of talking has to preserve the chancy character of what happened, the sense that it might not have happened at all' (1994:188). He sees this as leading:

> to the idea that things don't just happen, but rather occur in a series of steps, which we social scientists are inclined to call 'processes', but which could just as well be called 'stories'. A well constructed story can satisfy us as an explanation of an event. The story tells how something happened – how this happened first and led, in a way that is reasonable to see, to that happening, and then those things led to the next thing [...] and right on to the end. And how, if all that hadn't happened, the event we're interested in wouldn't have happened either. We could describe the necessary conditions for an event (call it *It*) to occur as the story of how one thing after another happened until it was almost certain that *It* would happen. (1994:188–9).

In the course of this discussion, Becker introduces the concept of 'contingencies', which he attributes to the influence of Everett Hughes. What he means by 'contingent' is the following:

> When event A happens, the people involved are now in a situation where any of several things could happen next. If I graduate high school I can go to college, to the Army, to trade school, to jail [...] those are among the possible next steps. There are a large number of possible next steps, but not an infinite number, and usually only a relatively small number are more or less likely (though the unlikely ones can happen too). Which path is taken at such a juncture depends on many things. We can call the things that the next step depends on 'contingencies', and say that event A being followed by B, rather than C or D, is contingent on something else, X. My going to college is contingent on my getting sufficiently high test scores to get into the college I want, on my having enough money, on having a sufficient desire to go to college to put up with some of the associated inconveniences, and so on. (1994:189)

He concludes: 'So the pathway that leads to any event can be seen as a succession of events that are contingent on each other in this way. You might envision it as a tree diagram in which, instead of the probability of getting to a particular end point getting smaller the farther you get from the starting point, the probability of reaching point X increases the nearer you get to it' (1994:189).[6]

In some respects, this seems to be very close to Lindesmith's view in his 1981 article. Once again the focus is on a causal *process*. Becker recognises the contingent character of the steps within this process, but also that they may eventually lead to a determinate outcome. Determinism only comes into play, as it were, once the final element identified by the explanation occurs. At that point, the effect is immediately caused: there are no mediating factors, so that there is a sense in which there is continuity between cause and effect. While they do not allow prediction, such explanations show how it was that a particular event came to be virtually inevitable, as a result of a long chain of contingent events. Becker comments that this view of the nature of explanation 'conceives of events as neither random nor determined' (1994:190). Like Lindesmith, he seems to be both denying that causation involves deterministic laws of an 'If A, then B' kind, yet at the same time seeking to develop theories that explain what always happens when certain conditions are met.

Becker points out the significance here of how our lives are intertwined, so that what one person does affects the contingencies in another's life. He refers to this as 'intercontingency'. He notes that biographers sometimes have the kind of detailed knowledge about people's lives necessary to provide this kind of explanation, but that sociologists do not usually have it about the lives of the people they study: for reasons of cost, if for no others, sociologists cannot get hold of such information. Thus, 'we must content ourselves, for the foreseeable future, with less than perfect data', but we need to be reminded 'of what we are missing in precision of data' (1994:192).

Becker notes the objection that: 'all these problems only arise if one insists on understanding the occurrence of unique individual events'. He responds: 'I suppose that's true, but it's also true that we often want to explain just such things, perhaps because we are interested in historical cases of great interest (e.g. the French Revolution) or for a variety of other reasons. And it is also true that even statements of mass probabilities suppose some underlying process which produces those regularities and that, eventually, we should like to understand that process' (1994:192–3). He concludes that hypertext is a literary form that 'is peculiarly suited to the presentation of an analysis of social life which contains so many possibilities and so many branching paths' (1994:193).

---

6 There is an apparent ambiguity in the meaning of the word 'contingent' here: it implies both that a result is uncertain and yet also that it is dependent upon some other condition.

Becker's narrative conception of causation represents a fundamental challenge to traditional kinds of variable analysis, which tend to assume that variables all operate at the same time. If we see factors as operating at different times on a developing situation, then the task of explanation becomes much more difficult than variable analysis assumes it to be: we need to take into account the sequencing and perhaps even the spacing of the impact of different factors. In other words, we have to recognise the different temporal ways in which factors operate on or in causal processes. This is, of course, very much the kind of explanation with which historians have long been concerned.

But Becker seeks to link this emphasis on the importance of narrative causation with analytic induction as the proper mode of social scientific analysis. He focuses on the way in which over time, following various paths, the conditions necessary for producing an outcome may emerge, thereby bringing it about. Unlike most of the other commentators whose accounts I have discussed, he is primarily concerned with explaining particular events, not with producing a theory about a category of event. Narrative accounts are important, he suggests, because, often, we can only understand how someone came to do what they have done, or to be the kind of person they now are, by tracing the path by which they reached this point. At face value, at least, this is very different from Lindesmith and Cressey seeking to identify the features that all cases of opiate addiction or financial trust violation have in common, and thereby specifying necessary conditions for those outcomes.

It is not clear how great the differences are between Becker and other advocates of analytic induction. Comparing his position with that of Turner may be fruitful. The latter is also interested in explaining particular events; or rather, what is equivalent in this context, predicting outcomes; whereas the other advocates of analytic induction I have discussed are concerned with developing theories about what type of cause produces, always and only, what type of effect. However, Turner distinguishes between the causal relationships that define the relevant closed system and the external contingencies that set that system in operation; whereas Becker makes no such distinction.

## Assessing analytic induction

Analytic induction, interpreted in what Becker refers to as 'rigorous' terms, is at odds with the theory and practice of most qualitative research as it is generally practised today, in several respects. For example, it involves an explicit commitment to science, and indeed to the aim of producing theories whose character is that of universal laws: in other words, conditional statements about causal processes that operate wherever the conditions are met. Furthermore, it is at odds not just with recent work influenced by constructionism but also with older types of qualitative and ethnographic research, where the focus was on documenting and explaining patterns of belief and action in particular communities, work settings, and so on.[7]

In my view, there is much to be said for analytic induction as a conceptualisation of the process of scientific inquiry. It is superior to the various philosophical attempts to find a logical or probabilistic rationale for induction; and also to Popper's argument that the source of theoretical ideas is irrelevant, that only the deduction of hypotheses and their testing is part of scientific method. What analytic induction proposes is that inquiry must start from some sort of puzzle about why a particular type of event occurs, followed by the abduction of hypothetical causal principles – in other words, theoretical ideas – from study of a few cases. There is then an iterative process in which, through examination of further cases and careful reflection, the theoretical hypothesis and/or the initial formulation of the type of event to be explained may be refined or transformed. The aim is to produce a theory that conceptualises a process of systematic causation that will operate whenever particular conditions are met.[8]

The most significant feature of analytic induction, in comparison with many other accounts of scientific method, is that it is not just the explanatory principle being developed that is open to revision but also the conceptualisation of the phenomenon to be explained. This is an idea that is absent from most discussions of statistical analysis, where it often seems to be assumed that any variable will be a cause of something and an effect of something else. It is therefore believed that its relative causal contribution can be discovered, along with the effects of various factors on it. On this view, there is little need to refine our understanding of the dependent variable, apart from making it more precise and operationalisable. And neither is this option given much emphasis in other accounts of qualitative analysis, including grounded theorising. Yet it is surely a crucial element of any process of theory development.

Despite the considerable value of analytic induction as a model for social scientific inquiry, there are a number of problems that can be raised about it; some are perhaps not serious, while others seem more likely to be.

1. There are questions concerning the meaning of the word 'induction'. This term is often seen as referring to an illegitimate form of logical inference – one that aims to move from the particular to the universal – and that also assumes a false regularity model of causation. In fact, none of the authors discussed here (with the possible exception of Znaniecki) believed that analytic induction is a logical procedure that guarantees valid conclusions. Instead, they were fallibilists who recognised that it is always possible that evidence may arise later that will force a revised estimation of the likely validity of a

---

7 However, Becker portrays some of this work as employing 'not-so-rigorous' analytic induction.

8 In its basic structure, analytic induction is very much in line with the model of inquiry outlined by Peirce (see Almeder 1980).

theory, and demand a reconstruction of it. Furthermore, none of them sees causal relations as normally visible in what Bhaskar (1975 and 1989) calls the domain of actuality. They emphasise the conceptual and investigative effort required to discover the theoretical categories by means of which causal relations can be detected. As a result, the theories they put forward are conditional universals, not claims about inevitable regularities. So, while the term 'induction' is potentially misleading, there is no fundamental problem here.

2.  Turning to the procedure outlined by advocates of analytic induction, it has to be said that, as a form of comparative analysis, it is underdeveloped. For one thing, such analysis requires investigating cases where the conditions specified by the target theory hold, in order to discover whether or not the expected effect occurs. This does not seem to have been done by most users of analytic induction. Having said that, it is by no means incompatible with the logic of the approach. A second requirement of comparative analysis is also given little attention in accounts of analytic induction, though Turner mentions it. This is the selection of cases in such a way as to control for confounding factors. This is required so as to minimise the danger of overlooking the role of one of these in bringing about the hypothesised effect. However, once again, while discussions of analytic induction tend to overlook this requirement, there is no reason, in principle, why it cannot be added.

3.  Some questions can be raised about whether we should define 'causality' as involving universal, deterministic relations that can be specified in terms of necessary and sufficient conditions. The work of Becker, in particular, raises some difficult questions about whether the notion of a closed system can be applied to the social realm, and what the implications are if it cannot. The model Becker outlines, of different paths leading to the same outcome and much the same path leading to different outcomes, is at odds with the idea of discovering deterministic relations; or, at the very least, it indicates that we should investigate the possibility that different combinations of factors may lead to different varieties of the same outcome, in the manner of Ragin's comparative qualitative analysis (Ragin 1987). While Becker retains the idea that there is what we might call a determinism of the last factor – so that once the final element is in place the outcome is determined – he seems to see this in temporal terms, which is closer in some ways to the notion of stochastic models or to Popper's (1990) individual propensity theory of probability.[9] There are very difficult philosophical issues involved here. A common complaint, relevant in this context, is that the theories produced by analytic induction are tautological. In part this issue concerns

---

9  On which see Williams (1999).

the nature of scientific theories; but also involved are questions about the character of social reality. Turner's distinction between the sort of relations that operate within and outside closed systems, and how knowledge of both is required if we are to produce knowledge of the social world, seems promising in many ways. But can this sharp distinction between systematic causation and other sorts of weaker, probabilistic relations be sustained? For example, might not the kinds of social system that sociologists are generally interested in studying be open rather than closed or even semi-closed in character? If this were true it could have major implications for the process of inquiry: it might mean, for instance, that we would need to look for trends across many cases, rather than being able to rely upon a single exception forcing revision of a theory.

4. There are some practical questions about the use of analytic induction as well. One concerns whether and how we can find closed systems to study 'in the wild', in other words without exercising experimental control. We can use the comparative method in relation to naturally occurring cases, but this will rarely enable us to separate out the operation of a particular closed system from that of all the other processes in which it is involved. An even more practical matter concerns the considerable demands that analytic induction makes on any qualitative researcher. These tend to narrow the potential topics that could be investigated to a specific type of easily defined outcome, where the process leading to it can be accessed through interviews with people who are relatively easy to find. And, generally speaking, this approach can only be used where the phenomena investigated are relatively small-scale, so that it is practicable to study a sufficiently large number of cases in the necessary depth. Where the phenomena are large-scale, the task of producing the relevant data will be greater and, given fixed resources, it will usually not be possible to study very many cases; and, anyway, there may be only a few cases available for investigation, as for example with studies of socio-political revolutions (Lieberson 1992). Moreover, the practical demands are considerably increased if analytic induction needs to be developed in the ways suggested in point 2 above: so as to check the various combinations of factors that could produce the outcome, to search for negative cases, and to control confounding variables. The practical demands would be further exacerbated if only *tendencies* can be detected, not universals, since, as already noted, the number of cases needing to be investigated would be greatly increased.

## Conclusion

Analytic induction remains a very promising model for social inquiry that is concerned with developing and testing theories. It is superior, in key respects, to other conceptualisations of qualitative research aimed at this goal, as well as to the logic behind most quantitative analysis. Furthermore, the work of Znaniecki, Lindesmith, Cressey, Turner and Becker has grappled with some important issues that have been largely ignored elsewhere in the methodological literature. At the same time, analytic induction involves some major problems that need attention if it is to provide a sound methodological basis for the persuit of theory in social science. Furthermore, studies using this method have tended to rely on interviews, a source of data whose value has been subjected to serious question by some qualitative researchers in recent times. These criticisms are the focus of the next chapter.

# 5

## Assessing the Radical Critique of Interviews

### *(Written with Roger Gomm)*

Interviewing has long been one of the methods of data collection most widely used by social researchers; and, today, a great number of qualitative studies rely entirely, or primarily, on interview data. Moreover, this has attracted criticism, stimulating what has been labelled 'the radical critique of interviews' (Murphy et al. 1998:120–3).[1] This chapter outlines and evaluates this critique, and then considers its implications for the use of interviews in qualitative inquiry.

The radical critique does not just raise questions about over-reliance on interview data. What makes it radical is that it challenges the use of these data *as a window into the minds of informants* and/or *as giving access to information about the social worlds in which informants live* (Dingwall 1997; Silverman 1997, 2007:125–30; Atkinson and Coffey 2002; Potter and Hepburn 2005). In other words, the critics throw doubt on the idea that interviews can tap stable attitudes or perspectives that govern people's behaviour beyond the interview situation, or that they can be a sound source of witness information about what happens in particular settings, or in the world more generally. Indeed, some of the critics seem to imply that interview data can only tell us what goes on in interviews, or perhaps even just what went on in a particular interview.

It has been claimed that the increasing reliance placed by researchers on interview material reflects a wider social trend: the emergence of 'the interview society' (Atkinson and Silverman 1997; Gubrium and Holstein 2002). This term is evaluative, indicating an obsession, on the part of the mass media and their audiences, with uncovering 'secrets and lies' – personal realities behind public façades. The critics also challenge what they regard as the 'romantic impulse' lying behind the idea that open-ended interviews capture the 'genuine voices' of interviewees. Instead, they argue that any 'voice' is 'not an

---

1  As Dingwall has pointed out, an influential early source of this is the chapter on interviews in Cicourel's *Method and Measurement* (Dingwall 1997:56; Cicourel 1964).

experientially authentic truth. It is itself a methodically constructed social product that emerges from its reflexive communicative practices' (Gubrium and Holstein 2002:11).

Concern over the status and use of interview data in social research is by no means new, of course. However, the grounds for this concern, and the conclusions drawn on the basis of it, have changed. In the past, the focus of criticism was on issues like:

- 'how do we know the informant is telling the truth' (Dean and Whyte 1958);
- the 'incompleteness' of interview data as compared with what can be gained from participant observation (Becker and Geer 1957); and
- the difference between what people say and what they do (Deutscher 1973).

To a large extent, these issues were practical, methodological ones concerned with what interviews could and could not provide, and with how best to conduct them in order to gain the information needed. By contrast, as we have indicated, the radical critique involves a more fundamental scepticism about the capacity of interviews to provide the basis for accurate representations of anything beyond the interview situation itself: either of the interviewee's general orientation or of the world in which he or she lives. On this basis, some critics insist that researchers should avoid the use of interviews altogether and restrict their analyses to 'naturally occurring' data. Others argue that we should only analyse interview data for what these data can tell us about interviews as sites for discursive meaning-making.

Along these latter lines, Atkinson and Coffey suggest that a recognition of the *performative* character of interview talk 'removes the temptation to deal with such data as if they give us access to personal or private "experiences"' (Atkinson and Coffey 2002:811). Similarly, Murphy et al. report that recent criticism has questioned the role of interviews 'as a means of collecting data about external reality (whether biographical information, beliefs, ideas about what should be done, reports of present or past behaviour, or conscious reasons for acting or thinking in particular ways) [...]'. And they note that such doubts are seen as following logically from the fact that interviews 'are essentially contextually situated social interactions' (Murphy et al. 1998:120).

So, the implication of the radical critique is that interviews must be viewed as social occasions, and what is said there should be treated both as socially constructed and as reflecting the particularities of the context (see Silverman 1973; Briggs 1986; Mishler 1986). Another argument is that what people say in interviews is driven by a preoccupation with self-presentation and/or with persuading others, rather than being concerned primarily with presenting facts about the world or about the informant him- or herself (which, it is claimed, previous use of interviews had assumed). Furthermore, alongside emergence of the radical critique there has been a growth in research which uses interview data to examine the context-sensitive 'work' that interviewees do, and the discursive resources on which they draw (see Stimson and Webb 1975; Voysey 1975; Gilbert and Mulkay 1980; Baruch 1981; Baker 1984 and 1997; Potter and Wetherell 1987; Riessman 1990; Hester and Francis 1994; Miller and Glassner 1997; Baker and Johnson 1998; van den Berg et al. 2003; see also West 1990).

## The target of the critique and its grounds

Looking at the history of social research, we can identify four main ways in which interview data have been used, with the balance among them varying across different disciplines and changing over time under the influence of various methodological approaches:

1. Interviews have often been employed as a source of witness accounts about events and settings in the social world. The information sought here may be about informants' own biographies, about some situations or incidents they have observed, about stable features of situations they are familiar with, and/or about the frequency of one or more types of event in such situations.

2. Interviews have also been used as a source of self-analyses by informants. Here, interviewees are asked to reflect on their behaviour, attitudes, beliefs, character, and personality; and their interpretations are used, albeit subject to critical assessment, as components of explanations for what they (and perhaps others) do or have done.

3. Interview data may also be employed as an indirect source of evidence about informants' orientations. Here, rather than treating informants' own accounts of their experiences or orientations as more or less true, the researcher analyses what they say in interviews as behaviour evidencing their characteristic motives, preoccupations, preferences, perspectives, attitudes, beliefs, and so on. It is usually assumed that what can be detected here are stable orientations that generate behaviour in other contexts besides the interview.

4. Finally, interviews may be used as a source of evidence about the constructional or discursive work engaged in by informants (and perhaps also by the interviewer) through which interview data are produced. Here, the focus is on the interview as an interactional site for various sorts of discursive practice, or for the use of particular discursive resources; and these may or may not be assumed to operate elsewhere.

There is a fundamental distinction to be drawn among these different uses of interview data. In the first and second, what is said by informants is treated as a direct source of information that can be relied upon if it survives an assessment of its likely validity. In effect, the informant is being used as surrogate researcher, supplying data that the actual researcher would not otherwise have access to, or triangulating with data that he or she *can* collect. By contrast, the third and fourth uses of interviews treat them as a source of observational data to be subjected to analysis by the researcher. Of course, in much research the same interview data are employed in both these broad ways: as a direct source of information and as an indirect means of gaining data about informants' orientations.

What is distinctive about the radical critique is that, in its most extreme form at least, it rules out all but the fourth use of interviews listed above – if it does not rule out interviews as a research method completely. The rationale for this restriction draws on one or other, or both, of two main theoretical approaches – ethnomethodology and social constructionism – and on forms of research stemming from these, specifically conversation and discourse analysis.[2]

Ethnomethodology analyses the social world as ongoingly constituted in-and-through participants' displaying what they are doing as intelligible – in other words, as orderly – in multifarious ways. It thus involves a re-specification of earlier sociological concern with the problem of order, patterns of inst itutional life, and so on; indeed, the focus is fundamentally transformed, so that what was previously treated as a resource – commonsense methods of making sense of the world – now becomes the sole topic for analytical inquiry (see Zimmerman and Pollner 1971; Heritage 1984; Lynch 1993). In other words, the topic is the 'accounting practices' (verbal and non-verbal) through which people, from one moment to the next, constitute the social world as an orderly place that has stable and recognisable features of particular kinds.

Constructionism also has radical implications for sociological work if applied consistently. As with ethnomethodology, the focus of inquiry can no longer be stable attitudes or patterns of behaviour, institutional structures, and so on – at least not if these are conceived as phenomena that exist independently of the discursive activities of the actors involved (in the sense of shaping them and being part of the environment in which those activities operate). Instead, the focus must be on the discourse practices through which people

---

2 Elsewhere in this book I have used a broad sense of the term 'constructionism' that incorporates ethnomethodology, and a broad interpretation of 'discourse analysis' that includes conversation analysis. However, in this chapter and the next I will define the meaning of these terms more narrowly, so that constructionism and ethnomethodology, discourse analysis and conversation analysis are distinct from one another. Different interpretations of these terms are to be found in the literature, reflecting imperfect agreement about their meaning.

construct the world – thereby presenting it as taking one form rather than another (see Potter and Wetherell 1987). Indeed, often, the very fact that phenomena are portrayed as having an independent existence is treated as itself a product of the rhetorical strategies employed (see, for example, Potter 1996a).

Drawing on ethnomethodology, conversation analysis has generally ruled out any use of interview data, insisting on the importance of employing data from 'naturally occurring talk'; in other words, talk unaffected by the researcher.[3] By contrast, under the influence of constructionism, discourse analysts *have* used interviews, but simply as a convenient way of generating data for analysis. Strictly speaking, in neither case should what people say be used as grounds for inferring what they think or feel, or what they and others do in other contexts. In this respect, both approaches abandon what were previously the main uses of interview data among social scientists.

## Assessing the critique

There are four analytically distinct components of the radical critique and these vary in cogency:

1. First, there is rejection of the idea that what people say somehow represents, or simply derives from, what goes on inside their heads. This is part of a general philosophical argument that insists on viewing mind as behaviour, and therefore as publicly available – rather than as a matter of internal, private experience beyond public representations. From this point of view, accounts of 'subjective' phenomena – of beliefs, attitudes, past experience, etc. – are treated not as more or less accurate representations of cognitive activity or of internal events but instead as public displays through which subjectivities are actively constituted and displayed. In this spirit, Dingwall argues that 'the private account is not the product of a more intimate understanding between interviewer and respondent. Private experience can be expressed only through a social medium in a social setting where the expression will immediately be evaluated for its fit to the range of versions of the self that are sanctioned in that environment' (Dingwall 1997:59–60). Here, then, the emphasis is on the social and discursive nature of psychological phenomena like beliefs, motives, intentions, personality, etc. As a useful shorthand phrase, we will call this first argument 'discursive psychology' (see Edwards 1997).

2. A second line of argument supporting the radical critique is scepticism about the idea that accounts can ever *represent* reality at all, whether this is 'external' or 'internal' reality. Here, even accounts of what happened in

---

3  For recent critiques of this kind of naturalism within conversation analysis, see Speer 2002, Speer and Hutchby (2002).

some public setting are treated not as true or false, but rather as constitutive –
as themselves producing one of many possible versions of events. Thus,
reality is constructed in and through the telling, rather than having characteristics that are independent of this. As with the first argument, such
epistemological scepticism often leads to an abandonment of any concern
with what information interviews might supply, in favour of a focus on the
work that the accounts produced in interviews do, and perhaps also on the
cultural resources which they employ.

3.    The radical critique is also often supported by a rather different line of
      argument, representing what we might call severe methodological caution.
      This relies on a contrast drawn between the results of scientific observa-
      tion and the ordinary accounts provided by informants in interviews. It is
      pointed out that informants' accounts – of situations, of themselves, or of
      their own past – are not usually based on rigorous data collection. They
      will not usually have employed audio- or video-recording plus full tran-
      scription, or even careful note-taking. Nor will they usually have been
      based on systematic observation for exclusively scientific purposes. Given
      this, it is suggested that interview data cannot be used as a substitute for
      observation by the researcher.

4.    Finally, there is the argument that a person's responses in interviews are so
      heavily shaped by the context, and especially by the influence of the inter-
      viewer, that reliable inferences about their attitudes or behaviour in other
      situations are impossible. Here the focus is on a high level of assumed reac-
      tivity, treated as characteristic of interviews and as an irremediable matter.
      It is argued that interview data are so contaminated by the features of the
      interview situation as to make them useless for analytic purposes, or at least
      for studying anything other than behaviour in interviews.

It should be clear that, at the very least, these various supporting arguments
for the radical critique are in some tension with one another. Taken literally,
the second argument – epistemological scepticism – denies the possibility that
*any* account represents reality, whereas the first one – what we referred to as
discursive psychology – treats accounts of public behaviour as capable of this.
Similarly, the second argument is also at odds with the third – methodological
caution – since the latter implies that accounts produced in a rigorous way *can*
represent reality. The fourth point is more limited in its implications than the
others: it is a methodological, rather than an ontological or epistemological,
argument; and the threat to validity it highlights – reactivity – is intrinsically a
matter of degree.

As a result of reliance on one or more of these arguments, many presenta-
tions of the radical critique seem to move back and forth between fundamental epistemological doubt and a more moderate methodological caution. To use
the example of Dingwall again, at one point he comments: '[W]hat parents

with a handicapped child say in an interview does not tell us what it is like to live in such a family. Ultimately, that experience is unknowable. What they do tell us quite a lot about is the work of doing being a normal family' (Dingwall 1997:60). Yet, later in the same paragraph, he seems to qualify this claim:

> It may also be that some aspects of the respondent's reality can be glimpsed through the accounts: the selection of details, the choice of 'facts' in the narrative, perhaps. In real life we recognize that the accounts we receive every day contain some mix of the real and the representation, and there seems no good reason why the accounts we receive as sociologists should be essentially different. My point is merely that interview data are fraught with problems because of the activity of the interviewer in producing them. At the same time, data are never merely accounts or versions, such that any reading is as good as any other. (Dingwall 1997:60)

Aside from the tensions among the four arguments, they also vary considerably in their persuasiveness. The first tells us something important about the nature of any accounts that informants might provide about their own experiences. This is that these will be formulated in language that is by its nature a collective resource; and moreover they will be shaped by notions of who can say what, when and to whom; what is an appropriate genre in the circumstances; what metaphors should and should not be employed; what are the usual narrative or other discursive forms in talking about the issues concerned; and so on. In short, there are socio-cultural conventions surrounding the accounts people give, and what they say in interviews will be structured by use of these conventions.

While all this is true, it does not automatically carry the implications that some radical critics assume. First, acknowledging the role of discursive conventions does not require us to deny that people have unique personal experiences that they can talk about, or that they have distinctive sources of information that may not be immediately accessible to others. All that the discursive psychology argument should be allowed to deny, is that individuals' experience is a stream of inner events that is given to them in a direct manner, without the mediation of language and culture; and that they have, or are able to gain, complete knowledge of their own thoughts and feelings. To take it beyond this, in such a way as to rule out the idea that individual people have distinctive experiences to which they have potentially superior access, and which they can convey to others, ends in absurdity. It distorts the character of social research, threatening important sources of information, and requires researchers to act in ways that make little sense. To use an analogy, imagine that someone told an optician that he experienced pains above the eyes from wearing the spectacles she had prescribed, but the optician insisted on treating what he had said as a conventional portrayal of himself as a victim of life's woes and/or as demanding a refund. If people were *routinely* to interpret one another's utterances in these ways, social life would be impossible. Nor is there any point in restricting researchers to this approach. While this first argument rightly challenges the naïve idea that interviews allow people to express themselves in uniquely authentic voices, it should not be taken to rule out researchers using interviews to gain information about what people think and what they have experienced – information that people might not disclose 'in public' yet which could help us to understand their behaviour.

As Price has pointed out, the dispositional account of belief, on which discursive psychology draws, does not deny that belief can sometimes be a mental occurrence – even less that thoughts, feelings, etc. are not mental occurrences (Price 1969). It is also important to recognise that conventions are *enabling* rather than simply constraining. Reality, even 'inner reality', is not something that exists as a self-displaying manifold which is open to view if only we can get into the right position, or acquire the right spectacles, to see it. Rather, it is something that we have to make sense of through concepts. At the same time, these concepts do not create something out of nothing but capture the nature of some aspect of reality more or less adequately. So, what people say – in interviews and elsewhere – can help us to understand their dispositions, even though they do not have complete, direct or definitive knowledge of these. Ironically, in effect, the radical critics implicitly take over an assumption from the position they are opposing: that we can only truly voice who we are, how we feel, etc. by means of some asocial, uniquely personal language. They deny, quite rightly, that any such language is available, and this is why they reject the idea of subjective reality. But there is no need to assume that such a language is required for people to provide accurate accounts of their experiences and attitudes. Indeed, we engage in identifying people's dispositions routinely in everyday life, and have built up skills for doing this on which research necessarily relies; which is not to deny that sometimes we may need to learn distinctive conventions if we are to interpret what other people say or do, nor is it to suggest that how social scientists go about identifying dispositions is exactly the same, or *should be* exactly the same, as how we all do it in ordinary life.

Some of the radical critics would reject any such reliance on commonsense capabilities. This, however, derives not from the first argument we identified but from either the second one, epistemological scepticism, or the third, methodological caution. As regards the former, little needs to be said; indeed, in one sense little *can* be said about the validity of such scepticism, since it is self-refuting. As has been recognised for over two millennia, we cannot claim that it is impossible to know anything without simultaneously implying that we can know at least one thing, namely that no knowledge is possible. Moreover, it is impossible to engage in any form of action, to live one's life or even to do empirical research, if one treats epistemological scepticism as valid (see Hammersley 1998a).

There is more to be said for the third argument, what we referred to as severe methodological caution. It is a key requirement of research that some caution is exercised in interpreting data. However, the level of caution seems excessive in the radical critique, and this reflects its reliance on some forms of ethnomethodology – particularly conversation analysis – where there is an emphasis on the need for data to be mechanically recorded and transcribed, and all interpretations to be grounded in what is 'observable' in the data.[4] It is true that informants' accounts will rarely be generated in exactly the same way as observational accounts produced by researchers, and that this introduces potential error. But the existence of threats to validity does not in itself undermine the validity of an account. If it did, we would have to conclude that all research findings are invalid, since they are always open to at least *some* threats to validity.

It may be true that, on balance, interviewees' accounts are more likely to be affected by error and bias than researchers' own observational reports, because interviewees have many other concerns besides providing sound information, because they are not always trained observers, and so on. However, this does not mean that all interview accounts are completely inaccurate, even less that they are fictions; though, of course, some may be. It is worth noting that a concern with accuracy is not restricted to researchers, nor is a commitment to honest reporting. Furthermore, the danger of inadvertent error will depend upon whether informants' accounts relate to features that are likely to be reliably reportable by witnesses, or whether they involve complex inferences that would require painstaking investigation.

Similarly, the fact that every informant has background assumptions, preferences, interests, etc. does not automatically mean that their accounts are biased, even less that they are simply expressions of these characteristics. At least occasionally, such assumptions, preferences, or interests may even encourage accurate representation, for example because they involve relevant local knowledge or cultural experience. Even where they do have a negative effect, this may not be significant for the purposes for which the researcher wants to use the account. And, even where it *is* significant, it may still be possible to detect and discount the bias through methodological assessment. Nor does the fact that interview accounts are always constructions mean that they cannot be accurate representations; any more than the fact that research reports are constructions rules out their claim to represent the world.

What is required as regards methodological caution, then, is a matter of degree. Furthermore, it is not clear that we must adopt some across-the-board standard that completely rules out interview accounts as a source of information. What is required, instead, is that we assess them in ways that take account

---

4 Methodological caution is only one of the arguments to be found within the ethnomethodological literature. It also draws on what we have referred to here as the discursive psychology argument and on a more fundamental philosophical conception of the nature of reality that can be seen as a variant of phenomenology (see Chapter 6).

of likely threats to validity; and that, where necessary, we draw on other sources of information to check them.

Much the same attitude needs to be adopted towards the fourth argument, concerned with reactivity. This certainly points to an important methodological problem. However, it is wrong to assume that the very existence of reactivity undermines all inferences that could be drawn from interview data; and, once again, it may be possible to allow for any error found. Moreover, ecological validity, which is what reactivity threatens, is by no means guaranteed even when a researcher relies on observation in natural settings. Inferences drawn from what happens in one natural setting to what happens in others are always in danger of misleading us, as a result of natural variation among settings (see Hammersley and Atkinson 2007:ch 1). So, this is not a problem that is restricted to interviews. And, once again, it is a matter of degree, and is rarely a complete barrier to gaining knowledge. In other words, the fact that interviews are a distinctive type of situation does not necessarily mean that what happens in them carries no reliable implications about people's attitudes, perspectives, etc., and thereby about their behaviour in other situations. Nor does it automatically indicate that the accounts they give in interviews about what goes on in the world are false as regards those matters in which a researcher is interested.

## Conclusion

It should be clear from our arguments here that the radical critique is unconvincing. The arguments it presents are not always sound and therefore do not undermine the first three uses of interview data we identified earlier: all four uses are legitimate. However, while we do not accept its full force, we *do* think that the radical critique is of some value, and we agree with its proponents' criticisms of the tendency for much recent qualitative research to rely exclusively on interview data. In other words, what is important about the radical critique, above all, is that it forces us to think more carefully about how we use data from this source. And, in recent times, interview material does seem to have been employed in ways that are relatively unreflective. There has been an increasing tendency to treat what people say in interviews as obvious in its meaning and its implications; at least where it does not conflict with what the researcher already takes to be true or justified (see Hammersley 1998b).

So, the proper conclusion to be drawn from the radical critique, we suggest, is that researchers must exercise greater caution in their use of interview material, *not* that they should abandon all, or even the more orthodox, uses of it. This critique reminds us that, like other sources of data, interviews are far from unproblematic. As a source of direct information, we cannot treat them as automatically giving us the low-down on what has happened, even less on what typically happens, in particular situations. Nor can we assume that what informants tell us about themselves is a direct representation of how they think and feel about things – even when we can assume that they are being honest. In everyday life when people tell us things, we tend to take what they say on trust unless it conflicts with what we already believe, or unless we have some reason to doubt what they say. By contrast, the researcher must be less 'charitable' in this sense; in other words, he or she must adopt a more sceptical attitude towards the information provided by informants.[5] This is not just a matter of taking precautions against deliberate misrepresentation, though that is certainly part of it, but also recognising that people do not necessarily know what they think they know, that interpreting what they say is not always straightforward, and so on. Above all, we need to recognise how both informants' accounts and researchers' interpretations of those accounts always depend on assumptions, some of which may turn out to be false. Scepticism, in the sense of a generally heightened level of methodological caution, rather than sustained epistemological doubt, is therefore always required.

Furthermore, because they are quite familiar to most of us, we tend to forget how peculiar interview situations are, as compared with other kinds of context. And, therefore, we forget that what is said in them will be shaped in various ways by the character of the situation. For instance, one of the peculiarities of interviews is that interviewers usually offer no comment on the answers provided, at most only asking for clarification or elaboration. By contrast, in ordinary conversations we generally do comment on what people say, if only for the sake of politeness. And, because of this, in interviews informants may read the behaviour of interviewers, or what they say, as implying an evaluation, despite efforts on the part of the interviewer to appear neutral. So, for this and other reasons, we need to take account of the interactional dynamics of any interview in interpreting the data from it.

It follows from this that there are some important questions to consider when we are dealing with interview data. When we are using them as a source of witness information, we need to ask: Are people in a position to know what we are asking them? Are they in a position to tell us, and are they likely to be willing to tell us, what they know? Finally, even if they are able and willing to tell us in principle, will they be able to do this immediately, or will they need to reflect and deliberate, to put their thoughts in order? On the other hand, if we allow them time to do this, does this bring in a potential source of bias, does it introduce a screen of reflection between us as researchers and what our informants know unreflectively that might be useful to us?

Also, we need to think very carefully about the nature of the questions we ask informants. Sometimes, these may be quite complicated, and they may even

---

5  Of course, even in everyday life people may question the information others provide, at least privately, if much hangs on its validity. However, a norm of charity does usually operate whereby openly questioning what people say is regarded as impolite at best, if not downright insulting. Indeed, it may be interpreted as intentionally snubbing the person concerned.

be impossible for informants to answer with any validity. For example, they may require the informant to generalise over time or across people in ways that cannot be more than speculative. Equally, sometimes we ask people to provide explanations for things. Yet, explaining something is a difficult business, and the requirements placed on the validity of explanations are different in research from those appropriate in everyday life. Given this, we must consider how reliable informants' explanations are likely to be. It is not that we can always assume that people's accounts will be inferior in validity to researchers' observations and analyses, sometimes they will be superior. However, we always need to subject them to careful assessment, rather than accepting them at face value. And this is true even, in fact especially, when they fit our preconceptions.

Similar problems arise with employing interview data as evidence about people's perspectives. We need to remember that what people say in an interview will indeed be shaped, to some degree, by the questions they are asked; by conventions about what can be spoken about, by whom and to whom, and so on; by what they think the interviewer wants; by what they believe he or she would approve or disapprove of; by the setting in which the interview is carried out; by the timing of the interview; by how it has developed over time; and so on. All of this is well known, but there is little sign of it being taken into account in much qualitative analysis of interview data. We should look for any signs that these factors have operated to shape the data in such a way as to lead us astray. We may need to compare what a person says at one point in an interview with what he or she says at others, taking account of the different contexts. Or it may be necessary to carry out second, or even third, interviews with them in order to make further checks. Also, comparing what one informant says with what others say may enable us to detect error in our interpretations. Equally, we may have observational or documentary data that provides an opportunity to check our analyses. We must assess likely threats to validity, and use comparisons with information from other sources in order to facilitate this. In analysing interview data in order to identify perspectives, we need to be aware that what we are trying to detect are dispositions: tendencies to act in particular ways in particular types of circumstance, including responses to interview questions. And given that dispositions can be complex and context-sensitive, relying on interviews alone is rarely advisable.

In summary, then, the arguments underlying the radical critique of interviews are not as powerful as some of the critics believe. Certainly, they do not rule out all use of interviews, nor even the use of interviews as a source of information about the settings in which people participate or about their experiences, attitudes, perspectives, and so on. However, the radical critique can serve an important function in forcing us to be more circumspect in what inferences we draw from interview data. It should also discourage any tendency to rely exclusively upon interviews: it reinforces the need for triangulation of data from diverse sources.

# 6

## Conversation Analysis and Discourse Analysis: Self-Sufficient Paradigms?

There are many different approaches to the study of discourse. Here I want to focus on just two: ethnomethodological conversation analysis (CA) and the kind of discourse analysis pioneered by Potter and Wetherell (DA).[1] In my view, both of these make important contributions towards understanding human social life. CA, in particular, represents one of the few examples in the social sciences of a genuinely cumulative empirical research programme. However, my particular interest is in whether these forms of analysis amount to *paradigms* – in the sense of being exclusive and self-sufficient approaches to investigating the social world. The proponents of both kinds of analysis treat them as paradigms in this sense, and as superior to available alternatives. CA seems to be viewed this way by most of its practitioners; even though there are occasional suggestions even from the most radical exponents that it might provide the foundation for other kinds of work (see, for example, Schegloff 1997 and 1998). Similarly, while in some places Potter and Wetherell explicitly deny that they see DA as replacing other forms of social psychology, they introduce it as breaking with traditional approaches, and as avoiding what they regard as the fundamental problems these face. Furthermore, in practice, they have employed it largely on its own, and they do not appear to have selected it as the most appropriate method for studying particular topics, but rather on the basis of what they take to be its general advantages.[2]

---

1 Since their seminal publication of 1987, Potter's and Wetherell's work has diverged in important respects, but much discourse analysis continues to follow their original model in respects relevant to my argument here. For an attempt at a bibliographical 'map' of the diverse forms of discourse analysis, see Hammersley (2001). There is a huge literature on CA, but Hutchby and Wooffitt (1998) and ten Have (1999) provide useful introductions. As regards DA, some of the more recent developments in this field have been under the heading of 'discursive psychology'; on which see, for example, Edwards (1997).

2 In one place, Potter describes it as 'not just a method but a whole perspective on social life and research into it [...]' (Potter 1996b:130). Furthermore, in their work on racism, Wetherell and Potter suggest that other kinds of social psychology have often sustained 'some of the ideological practices of racist discourse' (Wetherell and Potter 1992:2). This suggests political as well as methodological grounds for rejection of at least some other approaches.

My specific focus here will be on two basic methodological commitments shared by CA and DA that are central to their presentation as self-sufficient approaches. These commitments are negative in character:

1. A refusal to attribute to particular categories of actor distinctive, substantive psycho-social features – ones that are relatively stable across time and/or social context – as a basis for explaining their behaviour.
2. A refusal to treat what the people studied say about the social world as a source of information about it.

What I mean by the first of these commitments is an unwillingness to view actors as controlled, or even as guided in their behaviour, by substantive, distinctive, and stable mental characteristics such as 'attitudes', 'personalities', 'perspectives', 'strategic orientations', etc. Rather, actors are treated as *employing* cultural resources that are *publicly available*, and doing so in *contextually variable* ways. As a result, what they do is not seen as relying on anything specific about *them*: what they do is what any 'member' could, or perhaps would, do.

The meaning of, if not the rationale for, the second commitment is more obvious: it rules out the content of what people say about the world as a source of analytically usable witness information. The grounds for this are not entirely technical – what is involved is not simply a denial that what this source produces can ever reach an appropriate level of likely validity. Rather, there is an insistence that such everyday accounts must be included within the analytic focus; in other words, treated as topic not resource. They must be examined for the ways they are *constructed*, and thereby for the way the social phenomena they portray are *constituted* through these accounts. The interest here is in what this can tell us about the cultural resources available to members and/or about the practices in which they participate.

I will begin by exploring the rationales which underpin these two commitments – as will become clear, I believe that these differ significantly between CA and DA. I will then assess the cogency of those rationales. Finally, I will consider whether CA and DA abide by these methodological commitments in practice.

## Conversation analysis

In the case of CA, I take it that the justification for these two negative commitments arises out of Garfinkel's ethnomethodology.[3] Garfinkel started from

---

3 It is worth noting that the relationship between CA and ethnomethodology, and the nature of both, are contested matters. On the relationship between the two, see the discussion and references in Watson and Seiler (1992:introduction) and in Clayman and Maynard (1995).

a problem which he detected in efforts to create a theoretically-informed scientific sociology in America in the late 1940s and early 1950s. The dominant theoretical framework at this time was Parsons' social theory, and Garfinkel has often expressed his respect for, and debt to, it. Parsons' focus was on 'the problem of order', and he explained the orderliness of social action in terms of the socialisation of actors into the values and norms characteristic of their society. However, Garfinkel raised questions about this theory by arguing that every application of a norm requires *interpretation*; in the sense that it involves identifying a situation as being of a kind that is relevant to a norm, or to one norm rather than another, and recognising what the implications of the norm are for action in that situation.[4] The implication of this is that particular values and norms, being members' constructs which they *use* in making sense of and acting in the world, cannot be taken as adequate descriptions of behaviour nor treated as analytic devices for explaining behaviour, since they do not include instructions for their own interpretation. Moreover, this is not just a problem of a missing element in Parsons' theory, it is a basic flaw. This is because there is no scientific or general way of remedying the indexicality of any formulation of a value or norm: that is, how it is to be applied has to be 'determined' on each and every occasion. For example, if the analyst tried to specify the interpretative rules by which values and norms are applied, the problem would arise again at this level, since these rules too would not include instructions for their own application. The implication drawn from this is that the process of interpretation involved in applying norms, or rules of any kind, depends upon practical rather than scientific rationality (see Sharrock 1977:558–9 and *passim*).

Garfinkel treats this difficulty as pointing to a more fundamental one about the very way in which Parsons had formulated the problem of social order. Parsons took this problem over from Hobbes, even while rejecting the Hobbesian solution to it. And implicit in Parsons' approach is the idea that social order is something whose existence (and non-existence) can be scientifically explained. However, in setting out to do this, he conflates two quite different conceptions of order: Hobbes' political sense of order, which refers to the absence, or minimisation, of conflict and violence; and the kind of order whose existence is required if scientific understanding is even to be possible. The latter refers to intelligibility or explainability; and, of course, social conflicts are not disorderly in *this* sense. While they may involve much uncertainty, their causation, temporal course, and consequences can be understood to the same extent and in much the same ways as can social harmony. By contrast, if human social life were disorderly in the fundamental sense of being unintelligible, we could have no knowledge or understanding

---

4 This argument was not new. It is to be found, for instance, in Kant and Aristotle. However, Garfinkel has explored its implications for sociological analysis further than anyone else (see Heritage 1984). Note that 'interpretation' here does not necessarily imply conscious deliberation.

of it. This conflation of two different meanings of 'order' arises because Parsons' conception of social order is a pragmatic or political one, yet also claims to be scientific. In this way, Garfinkel's critique suggests, his project of a scientific sociology is vitiated.

Contrary to the way in which ethnomethodology is sometimes understood, Garfinkel's response to this problem was to try to find a more rigorous, scientific basis for the study of human social life. He did this by re-specifying the focus of the sociological project, drawing on phenomenology. The work of Husserl, Schutz, and other phenomenologists emphasises that we inhabit a lifeworld which is experienced as orderly *in the sense of being intelligible*: any problems in understanding particular events or actions are framed in terms of, indeed are only problems *in the light of*, our general sense of orderliness. Moreover, these authors see this orderliness as something which is a product of the constitutive activity of human beings. Phenomenological philosophy treats our experience of the world not as a passive matter of sense *impression*, but as constituted through pre-predicative activity. Thus, to use one of Husserl's well-worn examples, our perception of a cube involves going beyond immediate appearances, anticipating other features of this object, including what we would see if we were to look at it from other points of view. We experience it, in other words, not simply as a collection of edges and planes but as a three-dimensional object of a particular kind; and in doing so we draw on memories of previous encounters with similar objects, and expectations about how it might appear or behave in the future. Husserl regarded these memories and anticipations as based upon our access to an essential notion of a cube; and he saw such essences as underlying all perception and cognition.

Garfinkel follows Schutz and many later phenomenological philosophers, rather than Husserl, in keeping his focus on the lifeworld rather than on underlying essences; and this is also in line with his commitment to doing sociology rather than philosophy.[5] He argues that the orderliness of social life must be a product of collective human activity: of our ability to interpret situations and to act on those interpretations. However, this is not a matter of everyone automatically understanding a situation in the same way. There are always many different ways of interpreting any scene. Rather, what is involved is that we have the ability to understand how others are defining a situation, not just (or so much) from their explicit communications about it but primarily from what they *do*. We 'read' the behaviour of others for what it tells us about how they understand a situation, and we act on the basis of those 'readings'. Furthermore, in acting we indicate to them *our* understandings, and

---

5 According to Lynch (1993:ch 4), there are other respects in which Garfinkel was closer to Husserl than to Schutz.

they will in turn act on the basis of *their* understanding of *us*; and so on. This capacity to make intelligible sense of situations, actions, etc. is fundamental to human social life.

In this way, social situations are self-organising: their character is created ongoingly in and through the actions that make them up. But how is it possible for actors to read one another's behaviour in this way and thereby to coordinate their actions? Garfinkel's answer to this question is that, in making sense of the situations they face, ordinary people engage in practical reasoning that is *methodical* (or *accountable*) in character. If it were not, others would not be able to follow it. He was drawn to this conclusion through empirical work: in particular, as a result of looking at how jury members went about determining 'the facts' in the legal cases with which they were dealing. Thus, he argues that it is the availability of shared methods for sensemaking, rather than the existence of stable substantive meanings, which makes social coordination and communication (and social order of this kind) possible. It follows from this that what we should be focusing on as social scientists, if we are interested in the problem of social order, are the methods employed by actors in the practical reasoning through which they continuously constitute, and thereby display the orderliness of, the social world. This is his re-specified focus for sociological inquiry. Like Parsons, he sees the problem of order as central, but he reformulates that problem and provides a different methodological strategy for addressing it. For Garfinkel, what is to be explained is not why there is order rather than conflict, but how it is that social processes are orderly in the sense of being intelligible. Moreover, he takes over from Schutz the insight that the social world's intelligible orderliness is reflexive: it is produced in and through social action, and is recognisable to those involved in such action. In this crucial respect, it contrasts with the orderliness of the natural world.[6]

Going back to the two negative commitments I identified earlier, in part at least conversation analysts reject them because they breach the analytic orientation which ethnomethodology suggests is necessary for a science of social life. Both the attribution of substantive, distinctive, and stable psycho–social characteristics to actors, and the use of what people say as a source of information about the world, treat commonsense methods and understandings (which are involved in constituting an intelligible world) as a *resource* rather than as a *topic*. By contrast, what is demanded of social *science*, ethnomethodology and CA argue, is that it document the processes by which social life is constituted. Social phenomena are not to be treated as given objects in the world, but rather

---

6  Indeed, it could be argued to be more fundamental than the orderliness of the physical world, since the latter can only be recognised through the former.

as phenomena that are constituted within ongoing social practices. This does not amount to denying the independent existence of social phenomena (in relation to the researcher), only to arguing that they are constituted in and through the ordinary actions of the people involved in them.[7] But, the argument runs, if documentation of the practices by which social phenomena are constituted is to be scientific, it must not itself rely on those practices in an unexplicated way. Thus, for conversation analysts, all the data must be presented in research reports, and the analysis should only appeal for evidence to what is observable in those data. If these requirements are not met, the conclusions will be a *product of* the practices that constitute the human social world, rather than being a scientific *analysis of* them.[8]

So, the problem with attributing substantive and distinctive orientations to actors is that it relies on commonsense methods of interpretation in an unexplicated way. Furthermore, it implies a causal analysis of human behaviour rather than one focusing on constitutive, methodical practices. Thus, it cannot deal with the contingent and reflexive relationship between the ascription of orientation (of commitment to norms and values, or to goals, interests, etc.) and the behaviour this is used to explain. As noted earlier, the argument is that values, norms, rules, etc. cannot be employed as explanatory factors in social science accounts of human behaviour because they are actually resources that are used by participants; and they always have to be interpreted in particular contexts in order to lead to any course of action. In short, they cannot form the first part of stable law-like statements which can then be employed to explain people's behaviour. They must be treated as part of the social world, and as matters for study, rather than being taken into the analytic machinery of sociology.

Even more obviously, relying on informants' accounts of the world trades on these people's exercise of members' methods in making sense of this world, and

---

7 The relation between account and object for ethnomethodology is much the same as that between the act of experiencing and what is experienced (*noesis* and *noema*) for phenomenology. On the role of this distinction in Husserl, see Hammond et al. (1991:ch 2). It is also worth pointing out that this does not imply that social phenomena are products of freely exercised will on the part of actors; rather, from the point of view of analysis, they can only be treated as self-constituting, with the characteristics of the agents involved, including their agency and responsibility, being generated along with everything else. While, unlike Husserl, Garfinkel does not assume a transcendental subjectivity, or for that matter a transcendental collectivity, his sociological approach is closer to Durkheim than to Weber. For this reason, the term 'practices' may be more appropriate than 'methods', given that the latter implies an agent who uses them. However, I will continue to use the two terms interchangeably.

8 Ethnomethodologists and conversation analysts sometimes deny that their work is based on, or implies, criticism of conventional sociology. What certainly *is* implied, though, is criticism of any claim to scientific status on the part of that sociology. Later, I will raise some questions about the conception of science involved here.

in a way that leaves those methods unexplicated. It also implies a focus on the substantive features of the world rather than on the way in which such features are constituted in and through social interaction.[9]

## Discourse analysis

Let me turn now to discourse analysis, of the kind developed by Potter and Wetherell (1987) and the large body of work that has been influenced by this. These authors drew in part on conversation analysis and ethnomethodology. From these sources are derived a primary reliance on transcribed audio-recordings as data and a central concern with discourse as action. However, other influences have also been important, including the ethnography of communication, ordinary language philosophy, semiology, and post-structuralism (Potter and Wetherell 1987; Potter 1996b; Wetherell et al. 2001). And these led to some important departures from the ethnomethodological approach of conversation analysis. Crucial here is the adoption of a distinctive form of constructionism.[10]

Like conversation analysts, Potter and Wetherell are particularly impressed by the fact that language-use involves engaging in action, and on this basis they specifically reject the representational model of language, whereby statements are held to correspond to phenomena that exist independently of them. However, whereas ethnomethodologists and conversation analysts generally adopt something like the Husserlian position that the objects to which language-use refers exist in correlation with it, Potter and Wetherell place most emphasis on the generative power of discursive acts. In other words, the constructed character of social phenomena is taken to indicate that those phenomena do not have the kind of objective reality normally ascribed to them by everyday social actors and by most social scientists. In other words, a distinction is drawn between how social phenomena appear to people, as objective things existing in the world, and their true nature, which is that they are discursively constructed – and

---

9 Not all those expressly committed to ethnomethodology and conversation analysis adopt these two negative principles. For example, Moerman (1988) argues for 'culturally contexted conversation analysis' which draws on conventional ethnographic work. For general discussions of the issue, see Button (1978), Atkinson (1988), Watson and Seiler (1992), Nelson (1994), and Pollner and Emerson (2001).

10 In this chapter, like the previous one, I am using narrower definitions of 'discourse analysis' and 'constructionism' than those employed in the Introduction and some other chapters, one which involves a contrast with conversational analysis and ethnomethodology. For accounts of the contrast between constructionism and ethnomethodology, see Button and Sharrock (1993) and Watson (1994). For an account of constructionism from the point of view of DA, see Potter (1996a). Note that there is variation within DA about what constructionism entails, arising from differential emphasis on the disparate sources on which it has drawn (see Wetherell 1998).

constructed precisely in such a way as to appear to be objective features of the world. Central here, then, is the notion of reification: the question of how social phenomena are discursively constructed to appear as non-discursively *given*.

Also distinctive is that discourse analysts of this kind see their approach as opening up a new way of studying issues that have long preoccupied social psychologists and sociologists, one which avoids the problems that other approaches face; rather than radically re-specifying the very focus of inquiry in the manner of ethnomethodology. A clear indication of this is discourse analytic work on racism and sexism (for example, Wetherell and Potter 1992; Edley and Wetherell 1995 and 1997). However, it is also true of a more recent development out of DA: 'discursive social psychology' (see, for example, Edwards 1997). Potter and Edwards describe this as 'an approach to social psychology that takes the action-orientated and reality-constructing features of discourse as fundamental', rather than being 'a social psychology of language' (Potter and Edwards 2001:2). Thus, attitudes are treated not as 'inner entities that drive behaviour' but as evaluations that are part of discourse practices; in other words, they are seen as constituted in and through participants' ways of talking.

What is involved here is a difference in view, from ethnomethodology, about the ontological status of social phenomena: these are now to be treated as discursive products, and the focus of inquiry becomes how and why they are constructed in the particular ways they are on particular occasions (see Coulter 1999; Potter and Edwards 2003; Coulter 2004). Moreover, in some DA, this is done against the background of a view of social life in which individuals and groups employ discursive strategies in pursuit of various interests, and this is held to explain why the world is currently constructed how it is. Here the discursive constitution of the world comes to be located within a wider social philosophy or social theory, often largely implicit, that provides the background in terms of which discursive strategies gain their significance. Following on from this, there is a concern with how reifying accounts can be undermined; and this implies a link with 'critical' approaches to social research. It is argued that the world can always be constructed differently. Thus, the mission of some discourse analysts is constantly to remind readers of this fact, and thereby to facilitate the process of change.[11]

While the sources of constructionism include phenomenology – which, as we saw, was a key influence on ethnomethodology – they extend well beyond this. One way to understand it is as a linguistic transformation of Kantianism. Kant argued that our experience of the world does not simply reflect its nature. Rather, mind plays an active role in constituting 'the world as it appears' in our experience. Thus, some features of experience – notably spatial, temporal, and

---

11  At this point, DA comes close to critical discourse analysis (see, for example, Chouliaraki and Fairclough 1999).

causal relations – derive from the constitutive activity of the mind rather than from things-in-themselves. Post-Kantian philosophy, in its various forms, involved several moves away from Kant's position, while accepting his starting point. Discourse analysts, like many other post-Kantians, abandon Kant's distinction between reality and appearances; so that it is reality that is constituted, not appearances. Secondly, where the constituting mind for Kant was transcendental in character, though modelled on the individual ego, for social constructionists it is the individual-as-social-actor, or social interaction as a process, or Discourse, or even Power, which is the constituting agent. In other words, the constitution of reality is a socio-cultural process. Thirdly, the range of what is constituted is greatly expanded: it is not just space, time, and causality but the whole of the world as given to us in experience; though usually, of course, the focus of inquiry is on some particular aspect of that world.

DA also differs from CA in placing less emphasis on the distinction between an analytic and a practical orientation; in other words, they disagree about what is involved in a commitment to science. Whereas CA can be seen as relying on phenomenology in this respect as in many others, or even on a form of 'logical empiricism' (Lynch 1993:ch 6; Lynch and Bogen 1994), Potter and Wetherell appeal to recent developments in the philosophy and sociology of science to justify their approach. These developments question not only older views about scientific method but also any claim that there is a fundamental difference in orientation between science and other social activities.[12] This move is sometimes reinforced by the influence of post-structuralism, which is taken to undermine any claim to scientific authority; such authority is treated as a strategy used in the exercise of power, one that is of particular significance in contemporary societies.

A further difference from CA is that discourse analysts' arguments for their focus on discourse are sometimes ethical or political in character. For constructionists, the attribution of substantive psycho-social characteristics to people must be avoided because those characteristics are discursive products rather than ontologically given properties of the people concerned. To ignore this, it is suggested, is to collude in essentialism: to take as fixed and beyond human control what is actually a product of human activity. Similarly, constructionists believe that reliance on people's accounts about themselves, or about social situations they have experienced, ignores the fact that these accounts are actually constructs; and that quite different accounts could have been provided. Behind this is a commitment to recognising, and perhaps even celebrating, the diversity or creativity of interpretation.[13] So, from the constructionist point of view,

---

12 This is also questioned by some ethnomethodologists (see Lynch 1988 and 1993).

13 Not all interpretations are celebrated, of course; in particular, not those deemed racist or sexist (see, for example, Wetherell and Potter 1992; and Wetherell 1998).

discourse analysis not only captures something important about the social world but also plays a key ethical and political role in showing how social phenomena are discursively constituted: it demonstrates *how* things come to be as they are, that they could be *different*, and thereby that they can be *changed*.

DA, like CA, involves a reflective turning back on our experience of the world; but in the case of DA this is not done from a separate analytic standpoint, it is done as a participant rather than as a spectator.[14] Implicit here is a notion of ethical or political authenticity: the implication is that we must always remain aware that the world is a discursive construction, that we are ourselves constantly engaged in constituting it, and of the ethical obligations which are held to follow from this. In some respects, we could say that constructionism is existentialism to ethnomethodology's phenomenology.

## Assessing the two rationales

In my view, the rationales for treating CA or DA as self-sufficient and superior paradigms are not convincing. I will discuss each of them in turn.

### Ethnomethodology and CA

The problems with ethnomethodology as a rationale for CA can be highlighted by comparing it with phenomenology. One concerns the nature of the data CA employs. The slogan of phenomenology was 'Back to the Phenomena!'. And what was meant by 'phenomena' here were the mundane appearances of things as they are 'given' in our experience. These were the data from which investigation was to start. It is less clear, however, what the phenomena or data are in the case of CA. There are four possibilities: the *particular conversational interactions* under study; *audio- or video-recordings* of those interactions; *transcripts* of those recordings; or the analyst-as-member's *interpretations* of the transcripts and/or recordings.[15]

---

14  In practice, though, Potter and Wetherell do not write up their analyses in this way, for example by using 'new literary forms'. Instead, they adopt a mode of writing that has a fairly standard academic character, while yet seeking to distance themselves at various points from the implications that they take to be built into that mode of writing.

15  In a popular introduction to conversation analysis, Hutchby and Wooffitt claim that 'for CA, transcripts are *not* thought of as "the data". The data consist of tape recordings of naturally occurring interactions'. They state that '[transcripts] are not intended as "objective" representations of social reality [...]'. These are 'necessarily impressionistic: they represent the analyst/transcriber's hearing of what is on the tape'. At the same time, indeed on the same page, these authors argue that 'transcripts play a key role in the claim of CA to be a rigorous empirical discipline. An important aspect of this is that analyses produced by one researcher do not amount merely to idiosyncratic and untestable assertions about what is going on in a stretch of talk' (Hutchby and Wooffitt 1998:92). There is some ambiguity here; and this is not unrepresentative of discussions of the issue by conversation analysts.

If the first position is taken, a problem that arises – at least in terms of the parallel with phenomenology – is that the details of conversational interactions are not directly accessible to us in the way that it might be claimed experiential phenomena are. Furthermore, Sacks and other conversation analysts specifically reject any reliance on intuitive or remembered data, insisting on the use of recording and transcription; on the grounds that these provide for detailed, extended study, and the presentation of the data as evidence for readers of research reports.

If the second answer is given, we must note that recordings are not the same as the social interaction they record. They are selective. Much went on before they started and after they stopped. Furthermore, what is 'picked up' in audio-recordings, or is 'in shot' for a camera, is only part of a much wider realm of happenings. Sacks recognises this, but claims that 'other things, to be sure, happened, but at least what was on the tape had happened' (Sacks 1984:26). But this is to assume that what is included in the recording is analytically separable from what is not; an assumption that would be difficult to justify.

Next, if it is the transcripts that are treated as the data (and we should remember that the recordings are not usually available to readers of CA research reports), this neglects the fact that transcripts are themselves constructions (see Ochs 1979; Atkinson 1992; Edwards and Lampert 1993; Lapadat 2000). Decisions have to be made about what to include and how to represent the talk; and these can affect readers' interpretations. Specific issues are: how to identify speakers (are they given numbers or names; and, if given names, are these real names, pseudonyms or role names; are titles and surnames, or just first names, provided; is gender indicated; is any other information provided about speakers?); how the speech is to be represented (so as to match the sound or so as to capture as clearly as possible what is taken to be the message?); what non-verbal phenomena are to be included (laughter, coughing, etc.); and how the talk is to be laid out on the page (in the form of a playscript, in separate columns for each speaker, or in some other manner)? In specific respects, different decisions about these and other matters will produce different data; in other words, they may lead to or favour different inferences about what is going on.[16]

Finally, if the data are the analyst-as-member's interpretations of what was going on in the interaction, questions arise about the status of those interpretations. On what grounds can we take them to be *members'* interpretations? And this links to the deeper problem of what a 'member' is a member of.[17] The

---

16 There is also the issue of the implications of different forms of transcription for the ease of reading and analysis. It is questionable whether the very detailed forms of transcription used by conversation analysts present the original interaction in a manner that is analogous to how it was for the participants. Could this be evoked more effectively by less detailed transcripts?

17 This is a question raised, but not answered, by Watson (1994). Lynch (1993:253) provides an answer, though not one, it seems to me, that solves the problem.

very nature of ethnomethodology appears to prevent any analytic specification of the boundaries of membership (see Moerman 1968; Sharrock 1974), and thereby of what would (and would not) count as a member's interpretation of a recording or transcript. To try to specify this would be to rely on common-sense understandings as a resource, and to attribute substantive and distinctive psycho-social characteristics to members. After all, membershipping is itself an everyday practice (see, for example, Payne 1976). Furthermore, treating analysts-as-members' interpretations as the data involves a reliance on intuitions, not unlike that of some conventional linguists – even though these may be interpretations of careful and detailed transcriptions.

A related problem concerns the very possibility of an analytic approach that is without presuppositions; in ethnomethodological terms, an approach that does not trade on unexplicated commonsense assumptions and methods as resources. Husserl never managed to solve this problem. What he proposes in his later writings is that, while there can be no presuppositionless starting point, the outcome of phenomenological analysis will be a full explication of the pre-suppositions of the phenomenological project: a demonstration of their apodictic character (Elveton 1970:Introduction). A presuppositionless starting point looks no more possible in the case of ethnomethodology and CA than it was with phenomenology. Yet the claim that this is possible sometimes appears to underpin CA's restriction of evidence to what is 'observable' in the data. So, the question arises: if CA itself trades on members' resources, why is it superior to conventional sociology given that this is held to be the latter's main failing?

Garfinkel's argument is that people construct-and-display social order in the course of interaction. If they did not do this, then there would be no order to find. In other words, the fact that they do this not only makes society possible, it simultaneously makes a *science* of society possible. But the question that arises is: by whom are the constitutive practices that generate order observable? Or alternatively, though it probably amounts to the same thing, *how* are they observable? Is what is observable only observable to 'members'; in other words, does it rely on 'members' methods'? Or is it observable in some more direct sense, so that analysts (and readers) can see the evidence without relying on those methods? If the first answer is given, it is clear that there cannot be a presuppositionless starting point. If the second answer is given, some justification needs to be provided for what is an implausible claim in the light of twentieth-century philosophical criticism of direct perception, and of foundationalism more generally.

The argument that the process of conversation analysis can be self-explicating, in the way that the later Husserl claimed for phenomenology, is no more convincing. Here, in doing the analysis, the researcher is simultaneously engaged in constituting the social order that he or she is claiming to document. The threat of circularity looms. At best, CA could only be self-explicating if there were a finite and fixed set of members' methods. But it is not clear whether conversation analysts believe this, or what grounds they could have for doing so. Furthermore, CA is not directed towards explicating its own rationale in the way that phenomenological philosophy is: it is intended to be a science rather than a philosophy; though, as will become clear in the next paragraphs, there are questions about its status in this respect.

A third issue is the question of the nature of the methods which ethnomethodology and CA claim to document. There have been attempts to clarify this, but these raise more problems than they solve (see, for instance, Heap 1979; Coulter 1983). For example, Coulter claims that some of the sequential structures that conversation analysts have identified, such as adjacency pairs, are synthetic a priori in epistemological status. He notes that no amount of evidence of unanswered questions could reasonably persuade us that answers do not follow questions, or lead us to conclude that they usually follow some other kind of speech act. Rather than treating as counter-evidence cases that do not display this structure, we rightly judge them, or at least those that are clearly not intended as snubs, to be the product of incompetence on the part of participants, or the result of interactional accident or misunderstanding.

However, Coulter argues that while these structures are a priori – not susceptible to disproof by empirical evidence – this does not mean that they are immediately intuitable; and on this basis he claims that empirical data can play a role in their discovery. Coulter uses parallels with chess and mathematics to try to establish this point. He cites Vendler (1971:255–6), who points out that when, in a game of chess, we see two pawns of the same colour standing in the same column we can conclude that one of them must have taken an opposing piece in a previous move. And we know this not inductively, on the basis of observing what happens in many chess games, but because (given the rules of chess, along with the assumption that these have been followed) this is the only way in which that arrangement of pieces could have happened. However, while the empirical evidence cannot confirm this conclusion, since it is true a priori, the evidence may bring it to our attention. Without observing a game in which this arrangement of pieces occurred, we might never have recognised the possibility. Vendler also offers an example from mathematics. There is a theorem that, for any $n$, the sum of the first $n$ odd integers is equal to $n$ squared. However, recognition of this fact, and the logical proof of it, were stimulated by a great deal of study of integers and their properties, rather than being deduced from the premises of arithmetic.

Now, the existence of a priori synthetic truths has been a controversial matter ever since Kant formulated the distinctions between a priori and a posteriori, and between analytic and synthetic, knowledge.[18] Furthermore, Coulter's

18  For a useful discussion of these distinctions, see Bennett (1966).

position has some important implications for the practice of CA. As he makes clear, it runs against the notion of proof employed by Sacks, Schegloff and Jefferson (1978), which implicitly treats sequential structures in conversation as a posteriori in epistemological terms, appealing to the evidence of participants' understandings displayed in the data and/or to the capacity of an analysis to explain all of the data (Schegloff 1968). Indeed, in a much more recent article, Schegloff specifically contrasts CA with approaches that rely on a priori knowledge (Schegloff 1997). As already noted, Coulter's argument implies that close analysis of empirical materials may not be *essential* in order to discover sequential structures, suggests that those materials cannot establish the existence of such structures, and proposes that any contradictory data can be dismissed as the product of snub, incompetence, or accident. Furthermore, it follows from this that these sequential structures are normative in character. As a result, in so far as it is primarily concerned with these a priori sequential structures, CA is not an empirical science. It is perhaps closer in character to a form of philosophy.

This argument raises a question about the relationship of CA to Garfinkel's original project since, as we saw, this was designed to produce a rigorous empirical science of social life. Coulter's interpretation reintroduces a normative conception of social order, such that any failure of what actually happens to match the analysis can be treated as a case where the world failed to be orderly. In other words, it breaches the scientific presupposition that the world is already orderly in a factual way, and that the task is to discover the details of that orderliness.

A further issue concerns how use of the conversational rules which CA identifies to explain the form that any particular conversation takes can escape Garfinkel's original point: that the application of rules always involves interpretation or judgement.[19] And if the argument is that CA involves not explanation of social interaction but explication of its constitution, what exactly does that mean? After all, Husserl did not see his constitutive phenomenology of natural science as *replacing* the causal and functional explanations for physical phenomena generated by physicists and chemists. Nor did Schutz see his phenomenology of the social world as replacing social science. Yet, as noted earlier, ethnomethodology *does* seem to imply the impossibility of a science of social life concerned with causal analysis.[20]

---

19  For one attempt to respond to this criticism, see Clayman and Maynard (1995:17).

20  There is a dispute about whether Schutz's work implies a radical re-specification of conventional sociology or is simply an attempt to explicate its foundations (see Helling 1984). The attitude of ethnomethodologists and conversation analysts towards what they often refer to as 'constructive analysis' seems to oscillate between 'indifference', whereby conventional sociological work simply becomes more grist for the analytic mill, and radical methodological critique.

Finally, there is the question of what the *product* of CA is intended to be. There are at least two possible answers to this. First, the goal could be knowledge of the universal, though context-sensitive, methods or practices through which social life, or at least orderly conversation, is constituted (with examples used solely for evidence and illustration). Or, secondly, the intended product could be explications of particular stretches of talk. The first answer is justifiable in principle, but runs into the various problems I have outlined. The second, idiographic, interpretation of the goal of CA may escape some of those criticisms, but it raises a question about what the *point* of this form of analysis is. Why would such explications be of interest and value to readers? Schegloff draws a parallel with literary criticism (Schegloff 1997);[21] but the reason why readers are interested in literary criticism is because it deals with important works of art that are taken to have intrinsic meaning and value. The same is not obviously true of extracts from mundane conversations that have not been selected on value-relevant grounds.

### Constructionism and DA

Rather different problems face the constructionist rationale that underlies DA. In many respects, these result precisely from the fact that it does not re-specify the topic of analysis in the very radical way that ethnomethodology does. Where, for the latter, the focus is on the methods through which social phenomena are constituted, for constructionist discourse analysts it is the constructed character of particular social phenomena that is highlighted. More than this, as noted earlier, there is often a concern with the socio-historical purposes and interests underlying the ways in which accounts are constructed, and the social consequences of those constructions. In this respect, it is an updated version of ideology-critique. Thus, the discursive construction of realities is located, explicitly or implicitly, in a larger social theory or philosophy which supplies knowledge of the motivating forces that lead to the world being discursively constructed one way rather than another. As a result, the topics for analysis are the same as, and as diverse as, those of other kinds of social inquiry. In Potter and Wetherell's own work, for example, these include natural science as a form of practice, the nature of racism, and forms of masculinity.

What is distinctive about constructionist analyses of these and other topics, as compared with conventional accounts, is that the phenomena concerned are treated as discursive products, rather than as features of the social world that are caused by psychological or social forces; though, as already noted, such forces may be appealed to in order to explain the character of discursive productions. By contrast with ethnomethodology, interest is not confined to the identification of

---

21 Moerman (1988:ch 1) does the same. Of course, neither argues that literary criticism and CA are identical in character.

'members' methods'. This probably reflects the influence of post-Husserlian forms of phenomenology; as well as a residual commitment to the topics addressed by mainstream social science. At the same time, the intended product of DA does not seem to be simply explications of what is going on in particular texts. Rather, discourse analysts make claims on the basis of such explications about discursive practices that are available to various categories of actor in particular societies, and about the functions and effects of specific discursive strategies.

There are several problems with this rationale. One is that – to the extent that DA is presented as a new, superior paradigm – it involves treating a particular theoretical model of the actor as if it were exhaustive, or sufficient for all purposes. This model is what we might call *homo rhetoricus* – where the actor is primarily concerned with formulating accounts that are as persuasive as possible, in order to serve his or her interests. As Crossley and others have pointed out, this is a very thin and partial model, one which leaves out much of the person and of social life that we might reasonably think is important (see Crossley 2000:30–2). There is no problem with using such a model to learn what it can teach us about human behaviour. But there *is* a problem if discourse analysis based on such a model is treated as a self-sufficient way of understanding such behaviour. Furthermore, while the model of the actor is a thin one, the model of the social context in which he or she operates is, by comparison with CA, quite 'thick'. For example, in Wetherell and Potter's analysis of racist discourse in New Zealand, the discursive strategies that are the focus of inquiry, through which racism operates, are presented against the background of a society in which Maoris are an indigenous group that is exploited by the predominantly white settler community (Wetherell and Potter 1992). Here, questions arise not just about the adequacy of this background account, and about the justification for its evaluative slant, but also about the legitimacy within DA of such claims about social phenomena *as they are*, rather than as social constructions. If *these* social facts – for instance, the positions of different groups within New Zealand society – are not to be studied as discursive products, why should other phenomena be treated solely in this way? It is difficult to see what grounds there could be for differential treatment of this kind within DA. It parallels the kind of 'ontological gerrymandering' that Woolgar and Pawluch have identified in the constructionist literature on social problems (Woolgar and Pawluch 1985).

There is also a fundamental *methodological* problem involved in DA. It assumes the possibility of a process of generalisation that is by no means easy to validate. Much discourse analysis depends on the following argument: that, in the instance studied, one or more participants employed discursive practice X; that we can conclude from this that X was part of their repertoire; and, finally, that this can be taken as evidence that X is available to all participants who belong to some category or set of categories to which the people studied belong. Once again, Wetherell and Potter's account of the discursive strategies by which white New Zealanders construct a racist society is a case in point.[22] This argument raises various questions.

One is about the category of actor to which the discursive practice should be ascribed. Given that any participant is describable in terms of a large number of social categories, there are many alternative possibilities here. Yet, as already noted, discourse analysts are not concerned simply with documenting members' methods in the manner of CA. They seek to locate discursive acts in terms of the concerns of particular types of actor, for example those of white New Zealanders. There is an internal contradiction here.

A second question concerns why it can be concluded that the availability of this discursive practice to one or a few members of a category means that it is available to, or used by, most or all of them. This is the standard problem of generalisation from sample to population, but it is not addressed by discourse analysts. Indeed, Potter and Wetherell emphatically deny that sampling issues are relevant to the validity of discourse analysis accounts (Potter and Wetherell 1987:161–2). However, it is clear that they are not interested simply in what goes on in the data extracts they discuss, they want to make wider claims about the way particular discursive strategies function, for example in sustaining a sexist or a racist social order (Wetherell and Potter 1992; Edley and Wetherell 1995).[23]

A more general problem with DA and its constructionist rationale is that discursive practices are treated as having an ontological status that is different from that of the phenomena they are taken to construct. While most social phenomena are presented as occasioned constructions, the practices which generate them are treated as real and stable objects in the world. Yet, we must ask, are these practices themselves not also discursive constructions? Potter and Wetherell insist in a number of places that their own writing can itself be subjected to discourse analysis, but they do not address the major implications of this, one of which might be to threaten any claim to validity for their analyses.

---

22 For a very different approach to racism, inspired by ethnomethodology, though also locating itself within discursive psychology, see McKenzie (2003). Jonathan Potter (personal communication) has argued that the concept of interpretative repertoire has been dropped by many discourse analysts, especially those involved in discursive psychology. However, the same problems arise with the ascription of discursive strategies, and identification of the functions and consequences of these; which is central, for example, to his *Representing Reality* (Potter 1996a).

23 Elsewhere, Potter explicitly argues that DA provides a basis for generalisations about discursive strategies (see Potter 1996b). Similarly, in a later paper, Wetherell and Edley claim that the 'broad methods of self-accounting' they identify in interviews with male Open University students 'have a generality outside the interview context and in this sense are robust phenomena' (Wetherell and Edley 1999:339). In neither case is it explained how such generalisations are to be validated.

The central message of DA is that phenomena could always be constructed differently; and that how they are constructed has consequences, or fulfils certain social functions. But this raises questions about the appeal to data, and to consistency of argument, which discourse analysts make in supporting their own analyses. Why is their analysis itself not to be treated simply as a series of rhetorical moves designed to have particular effects on readers? If, as Potter and Wetherell insist, we should not be concerned with the correspondence between accounts and the world, does this mean that no correspondence is being claimed between *their* accounts and the discursive practices those accounts identify? As noted earlier, in pragmatic terms, what they write is suffused with a commitment to documenting the reality of discursive practices. If their own accounts can correspond to reality, on what grounds do they deny that this is possible for the discourse that they analyse?

While they note that some authors have employed 'new literary forms', they do not usually do so themselves.[24] But, even if they did employ these, thereby reminding readers that their own writing constructs the phenomena to which it refers, this would not escape the problem. Indeed, it leaves open the question of what possible justification there could be for discourse analytic research. It seems that it could only be justified in ethical or aesthetic terms, given that epistemic justification is taken to be no longer legitimate. But on what grounds can it be assumed that ethical and aesthetic criteria are any less 'constructed' than epistemic ones?

In short, constructionism seems logically to imply the reflexive application of DA to itself: having documented the discursive production of some phenomenon, it apparently then requires a reflexive analysis of how that documentation was itself discursively constructed; and so on, *ad infinitum*. And, given that this process of self-explication can never be completed, we might conclude that no progress towards self-explication is ever made. This suggests that the moral or political authenticity to which constructionists sometimes appeal is unattainable. Furthermore, this endless reflexivity undermines any claim for research as an activity distinct from fiction writing.[25]

## Conversation analysis and discourse analysis in practice

CA and DA are both going enterprises, in the sense that they produce interesting and convincing empirical findings. Should we conclude from this that

---

24  Though Potter has collaborated in an article of this kind, see Ashmore et al. (1995).

25  Some will embrace this last conclusion, but in my view those who do so ought to make their literary ambitions clear in claiming a livelihood as researchers and in bidding for research funds. I suspect that this would also be the view of many writers of novels and short stories who struggle to make a living without being able to draw on spurious institutional support.

the problems raised in the previous section have been solved or avoided? I think not. It seems to me that the viability of these two forms of analysis stems, to a considerable extent, from the ways in which they deviate from the two theoretical rationales I have outlined; and that this is associated with a partial abandonment of the two negative commitments I outlined at the beginning.

So, I want to look briefly at the actual practice of these two forms of analysis, in order to determine how far they live up to those commitments. To do this, I will use as a resource a debate between Schegloff, Wetherell and others in the pages of *Discourse and Society* (see, especially, Schegloff 1997; Wetherell 1998; and Schegloff 1998). Both the two main protagonists include some analysis of data within their papers, so I will focus on this.

While neither Schegloff nor Wetherell engages in the attribution of substantive distinctive psycho-social features to actors in the way that conventional research does, in practice they both do this in a more limited way. At the very least, they attribute occasioned orientations; and, as already indicated, DA often goes some way beyond this. Similarly, while neither relies on information from informants in the way that much social research would, they do both make some use of such information as background.

### Conversation Analysis in practice

In analysing the data extract in his paper, Schegloff makes explicit that he is focusing on 'the overtly displayed concerns of the participants themselves, the terms in which they relate to one another, the relevancies to which they show themselves to be oriented'. Indeed, he emphasises that what he is interested in is 'what was going on in [this exchange] for the participants, in its course' (Schegloff 1997:174). This formulation of his purposes plays a central role in the rationale he presents for CA, as against any kind of critical discourse analysis, which he treats as (at best) premature. He comments: 'if the parties are hearing that way and responding that way – that is, with an orientation to this level of turn design – we are virtually mandated to analyze it that way' (1997:175). Thus, he objects to critical discourse analysis because it begins by imposing the analyst's own concerns on what is happening, rather than attending (at least first of all) to what are the participants' concerns.

For my purposes here, the questions that arise about Schegloff's mode of analysis are: Why is the attribution of occasioned orientations legitimate, whereas that of stable and distinctive perspectives, attitudes, worldviews, etc. is not? On what basis is it assumed, as it seems to be, that the kind of orientation to what is going on in the talk on which Schegloff concentrates exhausts available participant orientations? In other words, why should we assume, even for the purposes of analysis, that people engage in interaction solely on the basis of resources available to 'anyone', and that they are primarily (even if unwittingly) concerned with displaying what they are doing to one another? One answer to this question would appeal to a theoretical model of human behaviour, one which assumes a very thin and standardised actor. And this is a model whose application in CA work produces illuminating insights. However, it is no more exhaustive of the character of human behaviour than is, say, *homo economicus*, or the model of human behaviour that I suggested was built into discourse analysis. The problem is not the adoption of this theoretical model, but the implied claim that it is the only scientific basis for understanding human social life, or that it provides the essential foundation for other kinds of analysis.

A rather different answer to the question of why the attribution of occasioned orientations is legitimate is that they are observable. I will put aside here the problem I noted earlier about what is observable to whom and how, since this answer does not necessarily rely on ethnomethodology. Instead, it can be formulated in methodological terms. In effect, the claim is that the ascriptions made in CA are much less open to reasonable doubt than are those of conventional sociologists. And this is very often true. But we must then ask: what is the appropriate threshold above which ascriptions are too speculative to be acceptable? After all, while Schegloff's ascriptions of occasioned orientation may be less open to question than conventional sociological attributions of perspectives and attitudes, some of the latter could also be beyond reasonable doubt. Why draw the line below these rather than above them? Schegloff does not address this issue; yet it raises questions about the sharp, and questionable, distinction he makes between what is observable and what is not.

My argument here is similar in some respects to Lynch and Bogen's (1994) criticism of CA's empiricism; even though it comes from a different direction. I am suggesting that what distinguishes CA from other kinds of analysis of social interaction, such as that of ethnographers, may be not so much a commitment to ethnomethodology as to what we might call methodological severity: a refusal to put forward claims about the orientations of participants that cannot meet a very strict threshold, and one that demands reliance on transcribed talk.[26] If this is correct, then what becomes crucial for any defence of CA as a self-sufficient approach to understanding the social world is a justification for the adoption of such a strict threshold. But this is not supplied.

Turning to the other issue – the rejection of what people say as a source of information about the world – we can note that here too, in practice, Schegloff does not abide by the principle completely. Thus, he begins by providing us with information about the two participants in the data extract that he analyses: that one is male and the other female, that they are in a strained relationship, that they

---

26 'Methodological severity' is a version of 'methodological purism', in one of its meanings. The latter term emerged in a rather different context (see Troyna 1995). For a discussion, see Hammersley (2000:ch 5).

are 'the parents – now separated or divorced – of the teenaged Joey, who lives with this father in northern California, but has just spent a period of vacation from school with his mother in southern California'; that the day of the telephone call was when he was 'scheduled to drive back up north'. This information is not available in the transcript which is provided. But, even if it were, Schegloff would still be using these data as a source of information about the world rather than as a topic for analysis.

The first point to be made about the use of such data, even to provide context, is that it surely undermines any argument that this sort of information is in principle illegitimate or of no value. So, the questions arise: Why not use it more extensively and systematically? Why is only *this* information provided? And, what would be the effect on our interpretation of the data extract if we were given *more* contextual information? Perhaps, if that had been done, we would have been able to move a little further up the methodological gradient, in terms of what aspects of the orientations of conversational participants we could produce convincing knowledge claims about. In a sense, it is by *not* providing more information about the people and the situations from which their data come that conversation analysts render those data largely immune to conventional sociological investigation.

### Discourse Analysis in practice

DA also attributes occasioned orientations; but it goes beyond this, for example in seeking to 'map' the discursive or interpretative repertoires drawn on by particular categories of actor, and also in identifying the functions of discursive strategies. Wetherell defines an interpretative repertoire as: 'a culturally familiar and habitual line of argument comprised of recognizable themes, commonplaces and tropes (doxa)' (Wetherell 1998:400). In her analysis of the range of discursive strategies employed by a group of male students involved in a discussion about relations with the opposite sex, she identifies a number of such repertoires: 'male sexuality as performance and achievement, a repertoire around alcohol and disinhibition, [and] an ethics of sexuality as legitimated by relationships and reciprocity [...]' (1998:400). Moreover, she indirectly links these to the concept of ideology by suggesting that the young men's discursive strategies can be seen as seeking to deal with 'ideological dilemmas' (see Billig et al. 1988).

This amounts to the ascription of relatively stable sets of resources that are held to be constantly available to the young men. And it arises, in part, from Wetherell's attempt to integrate CA with elements drawn from post-structuralism. She summarises the argument of Mouffe: that 'subject positions, and thus the identities of participants in social life, are determined by discourses and in this sense are prior, already constituted, and could be read off or predicted from knowledge of the relevant discourse'. She denies that discourses should be treated as the agent here, but she seems nevertheless to accept that interpretative repertoires exist prior to the interaction in which they are used, which implies that they must be relatively stable features of the orientations of the participants.

Furthermore, she argues that there should also be a focus on discursive resources that are *not* drawn on. She suggests that, in relation to her data:

> We should also be interested in the 'heteronormativity' (Kitzinger, personal communication) evident throughout this discussion which supplies a further taken for granted discursive back-cloth organizing these young men's participant orientations and their members' methods for making sense. A more adequate analysis of 'why this utterance here?' would also explore the silences and absences in this material – the argumentative threads which are hearably not part of these participants' orientations and everyday sense-making. Crucially, it would be concerned with the ideological dilemmas [...] evident in the struggle and collaboration over how to formulate Aaron [one of the young men interviewed] and his actions.

Thus, she notes that:

> It is important and interesting from a feminist perspective that these young men only appeal to some notion of autonomous female sexuality at this point in their conversation [that is, where they are trying to justify the promiscuity of one of their number]. (Wetherell 1998:404)

Wetherell presents her work as part of critical discursive social psychology, which 'is concerned with members' methods and the logic of accountability while describing also the collective and social patterning of background normative conceptions (their forms of articulation and the social and psychological consequences)'. She describes critical discursive social psychology as 'a discipline concerned with the practices which produce persons, notably discursive practices, but seeks to put these in a genealogical context' (1998:405).[27] Here there is the suggestion that which discursive strategies are used reflects, in part, stable features of the actors, and also that those features have been shaped by discursive practices in the past. Earlier on in the article, Wetherell quotes Antaki to the effect that the ascription of a tendency to drunkenness in the course of a conversation 'gives a person their (portfolio of) identities' (Antaki et al. 1996:488). The argument here seems to be that, as a result of the discursive practices employed by others, people gain particular, stable reputations and that these shape how they will be treated in the future; and perhaps even how they come to view themselves and therefore their mode of orientation. There is a hint here of some version of the labelling theory of deviance.[28]

---

27 This kind of psychology also seems to involve an evaluative stance. Thus at one point Wetherell judges the interpretative resources used by the young men she studied from a feminist perspective, describing them as of a 'crass and highly offensive nature' (Wetherell 1998:403).

28 The epistemological ambiguity of that theory is significant in this context (see Hammersley 2000:ch 3).

So, even more obviously than with CA, what is involved in DA is not a rejection of all attributions of psychological or social attributes to people, but rather an insistence that only *certain kinds* of attribute be applied. In effect, DA treats attribution of those orientations deriving from recent processes of discursive interaction as legitimate, while rejecting any produced by genetic constitution or by early upbringing. In other words, rather than no psychological theory being involved in DA, one kind of theory is being promoted against another. Yet this is done by methodological, epistemological, or even ethical fiat; rather than on the basis of empirical evidence.

Turning to the second negative commitment, we find that Wetherell also provides some contextual information about her data, though no more than Schegloff. She tells us that the interviewees were 17–18-year-old male students attending the sixth form of a single sex boys' independent school in the United Kingdom. And she describes her data as arising from a 'relatively large-scale project on the construction of masculine identities', and indicates that this involved 'an intensive reflexive ethnography' (Wetherell 1998:389).[29] The information about the young men and their context must have come from descriptions provided by the boys themselves, by some representative of the school, or from documents. And, whatever its origin, this information is being used as resource rather than as a topic for analysis.

In addition, in analysing the data Wetherell tells us that the data refer to 'Aaron's behaviour at a pub on the Friday night and at a party on the Saturday night and the nature of his involvement with four different young women' (Wetherell 1998:389). Here too it seems clear that these data are not being treated as a focus for analysis but rather as a source of, albeit minimal, information about the events to which the young men's discussion refers.

As with Schegloff, the fact that Wetherell breaches this second commitment not only indicates that this kind of data can be useful, but also that rejection of it is not part of a consistent stand on the part of those who engage in DA. Again, the question arises: why is there not more of this kind of information? Indeed, such data would be of even greater significance for Wetherell's analysis than for Schegloff's, precisely because the latter stays so close to the interactional ground in its focus. Wetherell's claims about discursive repertoires and their consequences might have been supported much more effectively by drawing on information about the social situations in which these students

---

29 It is clear from other publications relating to this research that observational data were collected, and also data from interviews with school staff. However, while more use is made of these data in those other publications than here, they are still employed almost entirely as a source of background information. The main focus remains detailed analysis of the discourse of the young men in interviews (see, for example, Edley and Wetherell 1995; and also Edley and Wetherell 1997;). In later work on a similar theme, reliance is placed entirely on the interview data (see Wetherell and Edley 1999).

participate. Data sources such as observation of their activities in a wide range of contexts, interviews with their peers, with parents, and with the women concerned, etc. could be of considerable value in seeking to understand why they behave as they do, including what they say in interviews.

Here my argument parallels Wetherell's own criticism of Schegloff and CA. She argues that 'it is the conversation analyst in selecting for analysis part of a conversation or continuing interaction who defines [...] relevance for the participant. In restricting the analyst's gaze to [a] fragment, previous conversations, even previous turns in the same continuing conversation, become irrelevant for the analyst but also, by dictat, for the participants. We do not seem to have escaped, therefore, from the imposition of theorists' categories and concerns' (1998:403). My argument is that by restricting the primary data to discursive acts in audio-recorded interviews, discourse analysts may also fail to provide adequate context for their analyses.

## Conclusion

In this chapter, I began from the question of whether CA and DA should be treated as self-sufficient paradigms, in the way that their proponents tend to treat them. I identified two negative methodological commitments which serve as defensive barriers around CA and DA, leading them to be treated in this way. I looked at the rationales for these commitments, which I suggested were different in each case. I argued that the ethnomethodological rationale that CA often seems to rely on, while distinctive and challenging, involves some fundamental problems. And, in my view, these are at least as serious as those which ethnomethodologists ascribe to conventional sociology.

This is not necessarily damaging for CA, because it is unclear how heavily it depends upon the ethnomethodological rationale. I hinted that it could rely on a different, *methodological*, one. In these terms, CA succeeds in documenting important features of human social interaction that had hitherto been overlooked. And it does this relatively uncontentiously, for the most part, because its claims are of a kind that, generally speaking, can be established by the sort of data it uses. Nevertheless, there are problems with this methodological rationale. In some ways, it amounts to a new form of behaviourism, and suffers from the same weaknesses as the older kind.[30] One of these is that it relies on a notion of observability that is indefensible. What we are faced with in our experience of the world, surely, is not a sharp contrast between the observable and the unobservable, but a gradient of credibility. And, once that is recognised, we need to ask about where on that gradient we should draw the line between what is sufficiently credible to be accepted as true, until further notice, and

---

30 On the methodological character of psychological behaviourism, see Mackenzie (1977).

what is not. That we should draw the line where conversation analysts draw it is by no means self-evident.

A second weakness shared with psychological behaviourism is a tendency to treat anything that is not observable in the defined sense as having a different ontological status from that which is. At the very least, it is treated as constituted rather than constituting; and, therefore, even if it is not presented as less real, it is treated as less fundamental and determinate in character. The effect of this is to operate on the basis of a very thin model of the human actor, one whose concerns are exhausted by what is 'observable' and is therefore preoccupied with achieving interactional coordination. This may be a useful theoretical model for understanding an important aspect of human social relations, but it is unlikely to be the only useful one in social science. Furthermore, while knowledge of what Goffman referred to as 'the interaction order' may force us to rethink various features of our accounts of other aspects of social life, it is yet to be established that those accounts must always start from the interaction order, any more than that they should always end with it.[31]

The constructionist rationale to which DA appeals is also problematic. Ironically, this is partly because it does not re-specify the focus of inquiry in the fundamental way that ethnomethodology does. Instead, it displays an ambiguity about the ontological status of social phenomena. It sometimes implies that those phenomena are constituted by, rather than independent of, the accounting practices we use to talk about them; but it exempts some phenomena from such treatment, such as racism and sexism, as well as the accounting practices that are its focus. Here it is open to the charge of ontological gerrymandering.

If, on the other hand, we interpret DA as not denying the independence of social phenomena from accounts of them, then it is open to methodological question about the sufficiency of the evidence it puts forward, and is able to present on the basis of the kind of analysis and data it uses. What can we infer from the fact that a particular participant or set of participants used one discursive repertoire on a particular occasion? What discourse analysts *want* to be able to conclude, it seems, is that this person or these people use this repertoire on other occasions, that there are reasons or causes for why just this repertoire and not others was used, and that this usage is widespread and has determinate and systematic effects. In other words, they are claiming to document a pattern or regularity. But they do not set out to validate this in the way that is necessary. This would require showing, first of all, that the use of this repertoire on this

---

31 The relation between CA and Goffman's analysis of 'forms of talk' is, of course, a contested one (see Schegloff 1988; and Watson 1992). And, in fact, it seems to me that Goffman alerts us to some of the explanatory resources, for example notions of civility and politeness, that are necessary even if we limit our focus to the character of conversation in Western societies. For a historical account of the development of conversation in this context, see Burke (1993).

occasion was indicative of a general tendency on the part of the participant(s) concerned; and/or on the part of other members of the designated category. The second task would be to try to show *why* this particular interpretative repertoire is employed by that category of person. This is a complicated issue since discourse analysts wish to take account of the local reasons for the way the repertoires are used, but at the same time to explain why particular repertoires are available for use within a setting and why they are likely to be used by the relevant categories of actor. In order to test such interpretations we would need data about those types of actor from across situations that involve variation in the candidate explanatory factors. This would be necessary to provide evidence that it is *these* factors rather than others which play the key role. That discourse analysts do not do this renders their accounts largely speculative.

Furthermore, like CA, DA also relies on a very partial model of the human actor. This is that of *homo rhetoricus*, an actor who is preoccupied with persuading others to accept his or her point of view in order to further particular goals or to protect particular interests.[32] Again, this theoretical model may give us considerable insight into an aspect of human social action in many spheres, but it is not exhaustive. It involves a very limited vocabulary of motives. So, when it is presented as if it gives a full account, or in a way that implies its sufficiency, it is systematically misleading.

There is no doubt about the value of conversation analysts' and discourse analysts' work, nor that their methodological and philosophical arguments point to significant problems with conventional social science. What I am questioning here is whether they offer a solution to those problems, in the sense of an approach that does not involve other difficulties that are at least as severe. Furthermore, the drift of my argument is towards suggesting that both these forms of analysis could be usefully combined with other qualitative and even quantitative approaches. My inclination is towards trying to draw together the diverse methodological approaches that currently make up social research, in the belief that this fragmentation – especially when 'paradigmised' – is a barrier against progress towards more effective scientific study of social life.[33]

In specific terms, I am suggesting that conversation analysis can and should be detached from ethnomethodology; and that discourse analysis can and should be detached from constructionism. This does not mean that I believe that nothing is to be learned from those two lines of theoretical argument. But it seems to me that in so far as they propose a radical re-specification of sociological topic, or a radical change in view about the ontological status of social

---

32  This model is especially obvious in Potter (1996a).

33  In that sense I am another example of what Watson and Sharrock, in replying to Atkinson's critique, referred to as the 'incorporationist tendency'. I make no apologies for this, but I hope that it does not lead to my arguments being dismissed as 'misguided to the point of prejudice' (Watson and Sharrock 1991).

phenomena, they lead us in the wrong directions: away from the search for general knowledge of the social forces and institutions that structure human social life. It may be that the only justification for the possibility of such general knowledge is that all of us in the course of our lives act as if we have it or could have it. That would be a sad reflection on the considerable work done by many generations of social scientists – and an unfair one too, in my judgement, given what has been achieved – but it would still be sufficient. One of the oddest features of both ethnomethodology and constructionism is that, while they insist that they respect the orientations of the people they study, rather than judging those orientations from some scientistic vantage point, both effectively deny what seems, in practice, to be universally taken for granted in human experience and action, and which has been the driving concern behind much conventional social science. This is that we are part of a causal nexus of physical and social events which shapes how we think and act, and what we are able to accomplish. CA and DA have shown that to focus instead on how the social world is 'constituted' or 'constructed' through discourse can be illuminating. However, this focus cannot tell us all there is to know about human social life. As a result, these approaches cannot be replacements for more conventional forms of social scientific research. They offer important supplements and correctives. Nothing less, but nothing more.

# 7

# The Dadaist Alternative: 'Postmodernist' Qualitative Research

Over the past fifty years, qualitative research has become increasingly influential in many social science fields, often replacing previously dominant quantitative approaches. At the same time, the 'centre of gravity' of much of this work has shifted along at least three dimensions: from an ideal of disinterested 'appreciation' to one of purported political, ethical, and/or practical engagement; from realism or naturalism towards various kinds of constructionism; and from the guidance of logic or method to that of rhetoric or poetics. As part of such changes, there has been an increasing tendency by some to treat research as properly directed towards political goals and/or as embodying substantive ethical and/or aesthetic ideals. Most obviously, these moves stem from a rejection of positivism and empiricism, but more fundamentally they often amount to abandoning any commitment to science, in favour of appeals to philosophy, politics, literature or art. This shift is frequently framed as a rejection of Enlightenment thinking; though the meaning and implications of this are far from straightforward.[1] It is a move that arises, in large part, from that body of French philosophical work that has come to be labelled, in the Anglo-American intellectual context, as 'postmodernist'; whose sources are often traced to Nietzsche, Freud, and Heidegger, and other nineteenth- and twentieth-century writers who (with varying degrees of cogency) are seen as challenging science

---

1 Schmidt (1998) points out that critiques of 'the Enlightenment project' run together strands of thought that are neither logically nor always historically related, ignore important parts of what is usually included under the heading of the 'Enlightenment', and have been used to draw discrepant conclusions. He notes that 'what is bravely called the Enlightenment project [...] turns out to be a pastiche of arguments, each of which – when viewed separately – would find critics within the Enlightenment itself' (Schmidt 1998:422).

or rationalism.[2] Another important, and sometimes neglected, influence here has been the sort of approach to art and literature pioneered by the Dadaists, and subsequently developed by the Surrealists and those associated with them.[3]

## From Dadaism and the Surrealists to post-structuralism

The Dadaists were primarily intent on 'shocking the bourgeoisie', with the aim of challenging the whole cultural and social order that had been pre-eminent in Europe before the First World War – and which they saw as responsible for that war.[4] Theirs was an attempt to subvert the notion of art, as this had become institutionalised; indeed, to subvert the very intelligibility of the social order. There was a rejection of Western rationality, and of the idea of art as a conscious process of creation aimed at realising an ideal. Instead, art works were to be generated through chance processes, or by letting the subconscious speak, and/or through drawing on the art and rituals of the primitive societies that mainstream Western thought tended to dismiss as irrational. Furthermore, the boundaries between different forms of art – indeed between art, drama, and the various genres of literature – were to be erased.

Dadaism fed into Surrealism, and this, along with some figures loosely associated with it, most notably Georges Bataille and Walter Benjamin, had a considerable influence in France on what came to be called *la nouvelle critique*; in particular, on those writers associated with or influenced by the magazine *Tel Quel*, not least Barthes, Derrida, and Foucault (see Ffrench 1995). This involved a direct challenge to realism in literature, with an emphasis on revealing the textual devices that are used in creating literary effects, and the tensions among these; and an attempt to subvert prevailing taken-for-granted notions of reality and rationality. These moves were also influenced by structuralism in linguistics, by Russian

---

2 Postmodernist readings of these and other authors are by no means beyond challenge. This is true even in the case of Nietzsche (see Clark 1990; and Sadler 1995). To some degree, usage of the word 'postmodernism' has now gone the same way as that of 'positivism' – towards always being used for the purposes of negative dismissal – though there are still those who self-declare as postmodernists (see, for example, MacLure 2006). While I will be critical of many of the ideas and practices that normally go under this heading, I am not using the term in a dismissive way, as a substitute for argument, and am keen to resist any tendency in this direction.

3 This influence is made explicit in Clifford (1988); Lather (1996, 1997 and 2007); and MacLure (2003 and 2006). However, it is quite widespread across what I am referring to here as 'postmodernist' work.

4 Of course, they also drew on pre-war trends. For example, while they reacted against the symbolists they also took over much from them. On symbolism, see Wilson (1961).

formalism in literary theory, and by the rational epistemology of Bachelard and Canguilhem. Later, they broadened out into post-structuralism.[5]

Structuralism and post-structuralism were a reaction against the previously dominant intellectual movement in France, existentialism. However, they did not amount to total rejection (Merquior 1986b; Fox 2003). For example, while Barthes challenged Sartre's views about the form literature ought to take, he shared the idea that it should have an intellectually and politically subversive role. What was distinctive was that he insisted that the very forms of expression normally employed in literature should be challenged. Thus, he praised Brecht's drama for its distancing effect, for preventing the audience from taking what is happening on the stage for reality, and he championed the writing of Robbe-Grillet and other exponents of the '*nouveau roman*' for the same reason. By contrast, he criticised traditional bourgeois literature for its realism, for lulling audiences into treating linguistic signs as naturalistic representations of the world.[6]

At the heart of this intellectual movement was a rejection of humanism (Merquior 1986b). This amounted not only to a denial that consciousness is the starting point for all knowledge, and that texts represent what is outside them, but also rejection of influential conceptions of meaning as teleological: texts were not to be seen as carrying a message intended by their author, nor was History to be regarded as having intrinsic meaning inscribed in a process of linear or dialectical development. Instead, meaning came to be viewed as a (necessarily arbitrary) projection, and often not so much a product of any individual will-to-power but rather of psycho-socio-cultural forces that *constitute* individual subjectivities in historically and geographically specific, and also relatively unstable and conflictual, forms; relationships among which are 'incommensurable' or 'undecidable'. Also implied here was a rejection of the Western tradition of humanist ethical ideas; a rejection inspired by Nietzsche's celebration of the ancient Greek ethics of nobility as against the 'slavish' morality perpetrated by Christianity.

## Ethnographic postmodernism

What has come to be called 'postmodernism' in the Anglo-American world drew on all this, and focused in particular on 'the crisis of representation' it

---

5 Also significant, of course, is the influence of psycho-analysis, and particularly the work of Lacan. The Surrealists were the main champions of psycho-analysis in France in the 1930s and 1940s, against a background of considerable resistance. The general attitude in France changed in the 1960s, and Lacan was a central figure in this, with most of those who would be listed as post-structuralists attending his seminar (see Turkle 1993:21). Lacan's reading of Freud was subversive in ways not far removed from the subversiveness of Surrealism, and was very much a structuralist or even post-structuralist reading – in fact, in a broad sense, a poetic one, in which the symbolic (or symbolist) language of the unconscious is privileged.

6 On Barthes, see Culler (2002).

generated. The idea of representation was challenged in both its epistemological and political senses. This initially had most impact within anthropology. Previous ethnography had usually sought to provide factual representations of cultures, institutions, or patterns of social interaction; and, as part of this, to document the perspectives of the people involved. However, questions now began to be raised about the very possibility of such representation. It came to be emphasised, more than before, that ethnographers *construct* their accounts of the world, and that in doing so they draw on the same techniques as writers producing fictional literature. Moreover, what they write cannot but reflect who they are, in socio-cultural terms. And it was noted that most ethnographers have come from quite a restricted socio-cultural background: they have tended to be Western, white, middle-class, and predominantly male. So, the charge was that – rather than producing universally valid, objective, scientific knowledge, as they claimed to do – anthropologists' accounts of other cultures are, in large part, simply a reflection of the interests, preoccupations, assumptions, rhetorical resources, etc. of a highly restricted social group. Particularly problematic was their claim to represent the perspectives of the people they studied; in other words, to understand those people's experiences and to portray them 'in their own terms' (rather than from some 'external' point of view). It was argued that not only is this impossible, but that the whole enterprise of speaking 'on behalf of others' in this way is ethically and politically indefensible, particularly in the form of men writing about women or Western scholars writing about non-Western societies. Challenging this became a major preoccupation of many who were influenced by 'postmodernism'.

The earliest and most sophisticated development of this 'ethnographic postmodernism' is to be found in the work of writers associated with Clifford and Marcus's edited collection *Writing Culture* (Clifford and Marcus 1986; see also Clifford 1988). While there had been some previous attention to how social scientists write research reports, including the rhetorical devices that they use, this volume had the effect of making this a central preoccupation for many qualitative researchers. Anthropological writing was no longer to be seen as a matter of representation, or at least of unmediated or literal representation; rather, it was now treated as constituting the realities it portrayed; and as doing this in a 'partial' way, in both senses of that word. As Clifford notes: 'Literary processes – metaphor, figuration, narrative – affect the ways cultural phenomena are registered, from the first jotted "observations", to the completed book, to the ways these configurations "make sense" in determined acts of reading' (Clifford 1986:4). In an important respect, this echoes Derrida's treatment of writing as an underlying force that creates the world, though Clifford is ambiguous about the 'fictional' character of all writing (1986:6-7). He declares that 'as commonly used in recent textual theory' this word 'has lost its connotation of falsehood'. However, he then adds that '[…] it is important to preserve the meaning not merely of making, but also of making up, of inventing things not actually real'. This is because '[…] all constructed truths are made possible by powerful "lies" of exclusion and rhetoric'. He concludes that: 'Even the best ethnographic texts – serious, true fictions – are systems, or economies, of truth. Power and history work through them, in ways their authors cannot fully control' (1986:7).

Central to this ethnographic postmodernism is a questioning of two central features of much nineteenth- and early twentieth-century writing, whether historiography, anthropology, novels, or contemporary commentary. These are the notions of *character* and *plot*. The idea that human beings have essential identities that are preserved as stable over time and across contexts is challenged. Also put in doubt are the usual plot lines that are employed to make sense of social events: not just conventional forms of progressivism, but also narratives of lost worlds, along with those more complex notions of dialectical development that were so influential in the twentieth century for some intellectuals. The emphasis, instead, is on complexity and fragmentation, and on the written – in other words, constructed and artificial – character of biography, history, and culture. Texts exclude as well as include, they formulate and reformulate, and they are therefore always fictional and contestable. Clifford reports that: 'New historical studies of hegemonic patterns of thought (Marxist, Annaliste, Foucaultian) have in common with recent styles of textual criticism (semiotic, reader-response, post-structural) the conviction that what appears as "real" in history, the social sciences, the arts, and even in common sense, is always analyzable as a restrictive and expressive set of social codes and conventions' (Clifford and Marcus 1986:10).

In part, the stance that Clifford and others take reflects a sense of the changed nature of reality, according to which we now live in a *postmodern* world, a world in flux, where boundaries have been eroded, where everything has started to get mixed together, and so on. In other words, a world where 'All that is solid melts into air', to use the famous quotation from Marx (see Berman 1983). However, this idea of a changed world is not easily separated – and for some writers cannot, in any principled way, be distinguished – from a recognition that all characterisations and histories are constructions produced in particular contexts, via particular cultural resources, by particular people, for particular purposes. In other words, accounts could never have been simply representations that corresponded to how the world was, even in the past.

What many qualitative researchers have taken to follow from this is the need to abandon, or at least to put into question, the traditional ethnographic concern with producing factual, descriptive accounts of the cultures and practices of particular groups of people operating in local situations, along with attempts to place these within some larger socio-historical context, or to explain them. Instead, what is required, some conclude, is a form of research that adopts political and ethical goals without trading on the idea that it is possible to supply objective representations of the world, or to 'speak on behalf of' others.

And what is involved here is not the pursuit of some revolutionary political future or the championing of a new human ethic, since these would inevitably entail reliance on cultural resources that are integral to existing society, and are therefore discredited. The sort of politics that has resulted is one in which the task is to 'trouble', or destabilise, the existing social order, and particularly its associated intellectual order – since, in parallel with influential forms of Western Marxism (Merquior 1986a), the latter is seen as structuring society. In other words, the purpose of writing becomes to show that the existing order is not natural and inevitable; and perhaps also to open the way for something Other – something different whose nature cannot be anticipated. In this spirit, Maggie MacLure writes: 'I want firstly to suggest that [...] research might try to generate some of the defamiliarising energy sought by Benjamin and the surrealists – not in order to be able to "look back" at the familiar and see it more clearly, but rather to split it open: to see what might burst out of the "dehiscent gap" (Buci-Glucksmann, 1994, p. 49)'.[7]

It is worth noting that, in their 'reception' in Anglo-American intellectual contexts, the radicalism of post-structuralist ideas has often been tempered or watered down in some respects, and mixed with other elements. For example, while there is now widespread rejection of the idea that research can produce objective accounts, the notion of the researcher being able to represent her or his own experience, and perhaps that of others, is often retained – despite the 'death of the subject' announced by post-structuralism. This is evident, for example, in Denzin and Lincoln's characterisation of qualitative research as 'bricolage', where diverse materials are pieced together to produce an emergent construction which they describe as: 'A complex, dense, reflexive collage-like creation that represents the researcher's images, understandings and interpretations of the world or phenomenon under analysis' (Denzin and Lincoln 2005:6). The idea that a research report should be 'collage-like' clearly reflects the influence of 'ethnographic postmodernism', and beyond that of Surrealism and Dadaism. As Kim Levin comments: 'From our vantage point at the end of the century we can now begin to see that collage has all along carried postmodern genes' (in Hoffman 1989:ix). In using this concept, Denzin and Lincoln are proposing a view of research in which materials (including both 'data' and the researcher's own interpretations or thoughts) are juxtaposed in a way that is open-ended and designed to provoke readers rather than to convey some closed message. Yet the assumption that the researcher can represent and convey her or his 'images, understandings and interpretations' would appear to assume some (unitary?) Subject capable of doing this. What seems to be recommended here is a form of auto-ethnography that will represent the

---

7 According to the dictionary, 'dehiscent' has two meanings, referring in Botany to the spontaneous opening at maturity of some part of a plant structure, such as a fruit, to release its contents; and, in medicine, to a rupture or splitting open, as of a surgical wound, to discharge its contents.

experience of the ethnographer, and necessarily that of others as well. As Silverman has argued, what we have here is a pastiche that combines post-modernist themes with Romantic ideas about empathy, lived experience, emotion, and deep personal truths (Silverman 2007:ch 5).

Furthermore, the form that most auto-ethnographies, and other products of this genre, have taken has been at odds with the implications of post-structuralism in another way. In practice, they have not, generally speaking, been collage-like in character but much more conventional in artistic terms. And this is also true of the poetry and dramatic performances developed by qualitative researchers: these have not usually been 'experimental', in the manner of literary modernism or of influential twentieth-century art; even though they represent a clear break with conventional modes of reporting research.[8]

There has also been some backsliding in political terms. As we saw, post-structuralism challenged humanistic forms of Marxism, as well as liberalism (see Introduction, pp. 8–9). There is a contrast here, I suggest, with the orientation behind much *avant-garde* qualitative inquiry. Take, for example, Denzin and Giardina's summary of the kind of work they recommend:

> What is required is a methodology of the heart, a prophetic, feminist post-pragmatism that embraces an ethics of truth grounded in love, care, hope and forgiveness. When the divisions disappear between reality and its appearances, critical inquiry necessarily becomes disruptive, explicitly pedagogical, and radically democratic. Its topics [are]: fascism, the violent politics of global capitalist culture, the loss of freedom in daily life. [...] [In investigating these] Sociologists, anthropologists, and educators continue to explore new ways of composing ethnography, writing fiction, drama, performance texts, and ethnographic poetry. (Denzin and Gardina 2006a:xvi-xvii)

There is no acknowledgement here of the serious debates about the implications of post-structuralism for the very possibility of feminist politics (see Thornham 1998). Furthermore, pragmatism is drawn into the mix despite the commitment of Peirce and Dewey to the scientific ideal. And the appeal to 'love, care and hope' clearly has humanist resonances that would be challenged by many post-structuralists. It is not surprising then, that the 'sacred epistemology' proposed by Denzin and Lincoln (Lincoln and Denzin 2000; Denzin and Lincoln 2005:36–7), drawing on the work of Reason (1993, see also Reason and Bradbury 2006:11–12) and Christian (2005: 36–7), is

---

8 See, for example, Ellis (1993 and 2004); Packwood and Sikes (1996). As these examples illustrate, the reason why fairly conventional literary forms have often been adopted is that post-structuralist themes are not the only ones shaping the Anglo-American qualitative work that is often listed under the heading of 'postmodernist'. The notion of personal voice, and the role of emotion in understanding, have also been powerful influences, and have tended to encourage more traditional forms of expression.

sharply at odds with 'sacred sociology' championed by Bataille and others, which promoted a Nietzsche- and Durkheim-inspired mythology of death as absorption into Life (see Hollier 1988; Falasca-Zamponi 2006). Indeed, the ethics and politics assumed by Denzin and his colleagues seem to be hemmed in by vague, and rather conventional, Leftist commitments to democracy and multiculturalism.[9]

To a large extent, then, what is involved in the *avant-garde* qualitative research championed by Denzin and Lincoln is a watered down, syncretic collection of ideas, some of which were originally very radical in epistemological, artistic and political terms.[10] However, contrary to much current usage, I am not implying here that 'radical' means 'good'. Indeed, I believe that post-structuralism is founded on some false premises, or at least half-truths that have been exaggerated for dramatic effect. Unfortunately, despite deviation from it, many qualitative researchers today seem to have inherited these misconceptions, in one form or another. This is partly because they resonate with what has been taken over from other sources, notably an emphasis on the constructed and situated nature of accounts, and a felt imperative to challenge all claims to authority.

## Problems with the post-structuralist legacy

There are several problems with post-structuralism as a rationale for qualitative inquiry. These relate to fundamental assumptions on which it relies.

A first one is the idea that because we cannot produce accounts of social phenomena that capture their *essential* character, or describe and explain these phenomena *exhaustively* or *completely*, this means that objective representation is impossible – that any account is always necessarily arbitrary or partial in character, so that claims to have produced true accounts of the world must always be misleading and deceptive (see Clifford 1986:6–7). This argument is false because we can answer questions about the world correctly without assuming that our answers somehow grasp its essential nature entirely, whatever that might mean. Much depends upon what is meant by 'essence' here, but we

---

9 It is important to remember that democracy has been questioned as an ideal political arrangement on the Left, among both Marxists and anarchists, as much as it has been on the Right. Often, of course, the target of criticism has been *representative* democracy, with some form of discursive or deliberative democracy being advocated, implicitly or explicitly. However, even the latter is undermined by post-structuralist and postmodernist ideas, since they emphasise the role of differences in view that are incommensurable or undecidable and often reject the value of consensus and unity. For a sharp, and not entirely fair, political critique of postmodernist ideas and some of their sources, see Wolin (2004).

10 This kind of dilution is not uncommon: see Turkle's (1992:4–5) discussion of the reception of Freud's work in the United States.

certainly do not need to assume that every phenomenon has a single true character that must be captured if any knowledge of it is to be achieved. And, once we abandon that assumption, achieving knowledge becomes feasible even if what is produced is always fallible (Hammersley 2004b).

A second false premise is that because discursive meaning can never be tied directly to some form of presence, and is therefore not literally anchored to the world, it inevitably continually escapes us. Yet, we do not need a language that is entirely fixed, explicit, and stable in structure in order to produce and communicate knowledge. We manage to do this routinely on a daily basis. All we need is a language that is intelligible enough for the practical purposes concerned; and, to one degree or another (depending on the purposes), we already have this. Another version of this second argument is that because all accounts involve rhetorical strategies and devices they cannot represent or convey the truth. This involves the false assumption that rhetoric necessarily implies misrepresentation, but this would only be true if we assumed that what is required is language that transparently 're-presents' the phenomena to which it refers. But there is no reason to assume this.[11]

A third premise of ethnographic postmodernism is the idea that because all accounts are from a particular perspective, and because threats to validity can never be known to have been entirely eliminated, we should abandon the goal of producing knowledge in favour of pursuing political goals or seeking to exemplify ethical or aesthetic ideals.[12] Yet such epistemological scepticism corrodes *all* value commitments, not just the concern with pursuing knowledge. Value judgements necessarily depend upon factual assumptions. Furthermore, acceptance of 'the death of the subject' in effect erases any notion of agency; and this is essential to any kind of evaluation. It is also important to recognise that everyday forms of action, not just research, all presuppose that we can know the social world. This is not an optional assumption, it is *constitutive*. No one could actually live as an epistemological sceptic.

A final false assumption is the idea that there is something intrinsically oppressive about claims to scientific knowledge, that these necessarily operate in such a way as to suppress equally legitimate alternative views. It is certainly true that there is a history of scientism in the West, in some quarters: in other words, an exaggeration of the certainty with which scientific conclusions can be known to be sound; an over-extension of methods that have proved effective in one field to others where they are ineffective; and a failure to recognise the limits to what science can tell us. It is also the case that the development

---

11 On this and the previous argument, as represented in the work of Clifford, see Hammersley (2007c).

12 There are, of course, other arguments for supplementing or replacing the goal of knowledge production with political and ethical ideals, and I have argued against these elsewhere (see Hammersley 2000).

of science was closely associated with the growing power of the state in some societies, notably France, and with the rise of capitalism in Western Europe generally. But science also provides us with improved knowledge about the nature of our world, and about ourselves, and it has been responsible for many changes in our lives that, while rarely unalloyed benefits, have nevertheless brought considerable improvement in the quality of human lives in material and other respects. It also provides resources for arguing against injustices of various kinds, such as those stemming from sexism and racism. In addition, we should note that any claim that scientific knowledge is oppressive relies on precisely the kind of essentialism that post-structuralism purportedly challenges.

If we refuse to accept these false premises, then there is no reason for qualitative researchers to abandon the goal of discovering and representing relevant socio-cultural facts about the world. Indeed, there are good reasons for their continuing to pursue this goal in an age when advertising, public relations, political spin, and (in some quarters) appeals to religious 'givens', play such a major role in the public sphere.[13]

## The damage done by Dadaism

There are at least two respects in which it seems to me that Dadaist-inspired postmodernism has been particularly damaging for qualitative research. These relate to the analysis of data and to the writing of research reports.

### *The importance of testing interpretations*
One effect of postmodernist and other questioning of the capacity of research to produce knowledge, in the usual sense of that word, has been to legitimise and reinforce a downgrading within qualitative inquiry of the idea that the researcher has a responsibility to try to ensure that the conclusions he or she reaches are sound. Indeed, the tendency is to license speculative, exaggerated conclusions; to discourage careful attention to how well evidence supports the knowledge claims made; and to stimulate a preoccupation with whether research accounts are in line with political, ethical, or aesthetic preconceptions. It is not difficult to see how these consequences could follow from postmodernism, or why they would be damaging to the pursuit of knowledge. Moreover, the growing influence of postmodernism occurred at a time when speculative social theorising was, in any case, on the rise within many fields of social science.

Symptomatic of the way in which postmodernism has had this effect is the considerable influence of the idea that research should be a form of bricolage

---

13  It is striking that, in seeking to challenge 'methodological conservatism', Denzin and Giardina (2006a) unselfconsciously fall back on traditional notions of science and truth.

(Denzin and Lincoln 1994, 2000, 2005; Kincheloe 2001; Lincoln 2001; Kincheloe and Berry 2004). In contemporary French usage, 'bricolage' refers to 'do it yourself', and 'bricoleur' is usually employed to refer to a 'handyman'. On this interpretation, bricolage is recognised as being second-best (albeit perhaps good enough in the circumstances), in contrast to doing the job with the appropriate tools and on the basis of substantial expertise. This does not necessarily imply criticism of the *bricoleur*. The nurse who carries out a tracheotomy on a fellow airplane passenger with a knitting needle may well be that person's only hope of survival. While a surgeon in an operating theatre would probably have done a better job, that option was not available. But it is still the case that the quality of the work is likely to be substandard, when compared to a professional model. It is also significant that, in its original senses, bricolage was a form of action in which there was a clear indicator of success: namely, whether the problem was solved, at least temporarily. With the transfer of this term to the context of research, both these elements of its original meaning have generally been lost.

This transfer occurred via Lévi-Strauss's use of the concept in attempting to understand myths (Lévi-Strauss 1966).[14] He was concerned with the contrast that is often drawn between 'primitive' and 'civilised' thought, but unlike some previous writers he did not regard this distinction as marking, unequivocally, inferior and superior ways of thinking. Rather, they are different modes of orientation towards the world, and Lévi-Strauss has a distinctive understanding of the value of the way of life of primitive societies (see Merquior 1986b:ch 3). At the same time, the contrast between these two forms of thought seems to be based on something like Bachelard's conception of science as involving a 'rupture' with commonsense (see Gutting 1989 and 2001). Thus, whereas bricolage focuses on surface features, on things as they appear, and seeks similarities and other relationships among them, science goes beyond surface appearances to find underlying generative structures. Also, a distinctive feature of myth as bricolage is that there is a drive to produce a complete picture from whatever intellectual resources are currently available; whereas the scientist or engineer will accept that some things are not currently knowable or do-able, and will insist on only using adequate intellectual resources.

Despite his distinction between the two, there are passages in Lévi-Strauss that come close to treating bricolage as a form of art:

> Once it materialises the project will therefore inevitably be at a remove from the initial aim (which was moreover a mere sketch), a phenomenon which the surrealists have felicitously called 'objective hazard'. Further, the 'bricoleur' also, and indeed principally, derives his poetry from the fact that he does not

---

14  It was subsequently elaborated on and developed by others (see Weinstein and Weinstein 1991; Nelson et al. 1992).

confine himself to accomplishment and execution: he 'speaks' not only with things [...] but also through the medium of things: giving an account of his personality and life by the choices he makes between the limited possibilities. The 'bricoleur' may not ever complete his purpose but he always puts something of himself into it. (Lévi-Strauss 1966:21)

This is clearly quite close to what Denzin and Lincoln recommend for qualitative research. Lévi-Strauss also implies that what the *bricoleur* produces is writerly rather than readerly, to use Barthes' terms. In other words, it is open-ended and uncertain in character, leaving scope for audiences to make their own sense of it, rather than directing them to a particular message:

[...] in the case of 'bricolage', and the example of 'styles' of painters shows that the same is true in art, there are several solutions to the same problem. The choice of one solution involves a modification of the result to which another solution would have led, and the observer is in effect presented with the general picture of these permutations at the same time as the particular solution offered. He is thereby transformed into an active participant without even being aware of it. Merely by contemplating it he is, as it were, put in possession of other possible forms of the same work; and in a confused way, he feels himself to be their creator with more right than the creator himself because the latter abandoned them in excluding them from his creation. And these forms are so many perspectives opening out on to the world that has been realized. (Lévi-Strauss 1966:24)

Officially at least, Lévi-Strauss does not see social science as a form of bricolage, or view his own analysis in this way: he is explicitly wedded to a scientific version of research modelled on structural linguistics.[15] In this respect, he is different from those who have used bricolage as a model for qualitative inquiry. They have sometimes insisted on the need for 'rigour', but generally speaking it is quite unclear what that term means in this context (Kincheloe 2001; Kincheloe and Berry 2004). Furthermore, as the quotations from Lévi-Strauss indicate, this model would legitimate speculative qualitative analysis, in which politically, ethically, aesthetically, or personally appealing 'patterns' are identified on the basis of highly selective use of data. Ironically, there is a link here to the common anthropological criticisms made of Lévi-Strauss's fieldwork, and of his use of sources. An example is provided by Leach, by no means an unsympathetic commentator:

[...] Lévi-Strauss, like Frazer, is insufficiently critical of his source material. He always seems to be able to find just what he is looking for. Any evidence however dubious is acceptable so long as it fits with logically calculated expectations; but wherever the data runs counter to the theory Lévi-Strauss will either by-pass the evidence or marshal the full resources of his powerful invective to

---

15 Lévi-Strauss refers to geology as his first love, and it seems to have had an important effect on his conception of science. At the same time, as several commentators have noted, his actual relation to science is ambiguous (see Boon 1972; Merquior 1986b:37).

have the heresy thrown out of court! So we need to remember that Lévi-Strauss's prime training was in philosophy and law; he consistently behaves as an advocate defending a cause rather than as a scientist searching for ulti-mate truth. (Leach 1970:19–20)

We could formulate this criticism as suggesting that Lévi-Strauss was himself a bricoleur after all. And, indeed, Geertz has portrayed him as a 'Barthesian author-writer' (Geertz 1988:27).

It is perhaps not surprising, then, that statements from recent commentators who portray qualitative research as bricolage also seem to underplay the role of checking interpretations against evidence, with a view to discovering their truth or falsity. Like Lévi-Strauss, they tend to exaggerate the power of theory. Here, for instance, is Kincheloe: 'Using the x-ray vision of contemporary social-theoretically informed strategies of discourse analysis, post-structural psychoanalysis, and ideology-critique, the ethnographer gains the ability to see beyond the literalness of the observed' (Kincheloe 2001:686). There is nothing wrong with speculation, with seeking to develop ideas whose relationship to the data may be remote. Indeed, this is an important part of the research task. However, it is equally important to test out the ideas that have been developed against evidence and existing knowledge, to determine which are and are not cogent descriptions, explanations and theories. The problem is that the models of bricolage, visual art and imaginative literature, as typically interpreted, do not encourage this, quite the reverse.[16]

### The need for clarity

An important part of what is involved in postmodernist ethnography is oppo-sition to scientific language, and more generally to clarity as an ideal in writ-ing. For example, MacLure (2003:114) dismisses this as indicating a 'puritan methodology' that lives in fear of 'the threat of writing'. This is probably not intended to be a historical claim, but a brief historical foray may be of value in addressing the issue.

The idea that scientific writing should be clear and plain seems to have first arisen most influentially in the seventeenth century. One key figure here was Francis Bacon, and he was motivated by at least two considerations. First, an awareness that the ways in which language was commonly used threatened the drawing of valid inferences. For example, he argued that everyday language includes names for things that do not exist and thereby encourages belief in

---

16 It is striking that despite appeals to philosophy, literature and art as models for a new kind of qualitative research, very little seems to have been learned from the huge critical literature that is available in these areas, or from histories of work in these fields. The main exception is the work of Clifford.

fictitious entities. Perhaps more importantly, words in conventional usage have multiple and sometimes vague meanings, which make it difficult to know what is and is not being claimed; and, in particular, whether the distinctions and arguments being made have any practical value. The second motive, less direct but more distinctive to Bacon, was the belief that what was needed to bring about a major improvement in scientific knowledge was a move against humanist reliance on individual insight and genius towards use of a method, in particular eliminative induction, that would protect against some of the main threats to valid conclusions.[17] A key aspect of this method is that it does not rely on private or esoteric expertise but rather is public and collective in character. The relevant point here is that the operation of this method requires that knowledge claims, and the distinctions they involve, be formulated in ways that are intelligible to a broader constituency, rather than only to the erudite humanist. While he was a Protestant, Bacon attacked the puritans precisely because they made claims to knowledge on the basis of personal communion with God, which he saw as the substitution of zealotry for learning (see Gaukroger 2001:69 and *passim*). In my view, Bacon's concerns are far from outdated, even if we can now be rather more sophisticated about how language works, and thereby about what 'clarity' can and should mean, its benefits and dangers.[18]

Just as Clifford claimed that ethnographic accounts are necessarily fictions that involve 'lies', so MacLure (writing about life histories) suggests that, as fabrications, they are 'always a matter of copies, imitations and forgeries' (MacLure 2003:131). She also claims that clear writing disguises 'the effects of power and exclusion' (2003:118), following Lather's reference to 'the violence of clarity' (Lather 1996:529). Along the same lines, clarity is sometimes portrayed as an attempt by dominant groups to make others conform to their ways of speaking and writing; in other words, there is a 'politics of clarity' (Giroux 1992). And it is claimed that plain writing appears plain precisely because it maps easily on to taken-for-granted, and probably ideological, assumptions.

As an alternative to clarity, Lather proposes a 'Dada practice', which she defines, following Welchman (1989:64), as 'to mix and collide incommensurable discourses as a way to situate research as a gesture, a performance, a staging of the problems of representation that disrupts the traditional signifying economy,

---

17 There is quite a close relationship between eliminative induction and analytic induction, as discussed in Chapter 4.

18 For a recent defence of clarity, in the context of a critique of the American feminist Judith Butler, see Nussbaum 1999. It is also important to mention that, as Gaukroger makes clear, the key model behind Bacon's attempt to promote a new approach to natural philosophy was the tradition of rhetoric developed by Renaissance scholarship, and especially the role of rhetoric in legal contexts.

opening up another space for worlding the world' (Lather 1996:543). Thus, in place of the scientific goal of clear representation, there is a preference for literary and artistic forms that are more engaging or challenging, and that do not present any single line of argument – they are open-ended, so as to leave audiences to draw their own conclusions (or better, perhaps, to *make up* their own interpretations).

Postmodernists are opposed to what is regarded as the drive within mainstream social and educational research towards 'closure', 'simplification', reduction of the strange to the familiar, rational understanding of the irrational, and so on. In this spirit, MacLure expresses the hope that the '"preposterous", anachronistic postmodern method' she is developing '[...] might encourage new ways of "reading" and "writing" the social, based on anti-taxonomic, analogical, juxtapositional strategies such as collage or montage. Its architecture might more closely resemble a cabinet of curiosities, or a labyrinth, than the hierarchies of a "table" or paradigm' (MacLure 2006:230). The implication is that the drive for closure and control is built deep into modes of discourse that privilege clarity, and that these need subverting.

In part, what seems to be involved here is a rejection of the theory of communication that is believed to underlie the idea of clear scientific language, and the forms of scientist governance to which it is often assumed to lead. This theory is taken to imply that thoughts can be translated into language via some sort of semantic code book, transmitted, and then translated back into ideas at the other end by means of the same code book. This theory proposes that it is possible for statements to be absolutely clear or transparent. Against this, it is argued that language is not a tool that we use, that we can have control over. Rather, to a large extent it speaks through us, and any meaning which we seek to convey is continually dissipated, with audiences making sense of what is said in a contingent fashion that is not under their control either. As we have seen, there are also political and ethical arguments against clarity, to the effect that purporting to speak or write in a clear way obscures the real nature of discourse, as just outlined, and amounts to inauthenticity; indeed, that it constitutes a totalitarian attempt to impose meaning on others and a reinforcement of the status quo as natural and right.

Now, it is certainly true that the semantic translation model I have just sketched does not capture the nature of human communication; either in general or specifically in the case of science (Sperber and Wilson 1986). However, we do not need to treat clarity as an impossible transparency, in the sense of full explicitness for any audience. In other words, in arguing for the importance of clarity it is not necessary to claim that it is possible to speak or write without rhetoric, in absolutely plain language that says exactly what it means and no more. It is possible to control the meaning of what one writes and says to some extent so as to convey an intended message, without assuming any guarantee of complete success; just as it is possible to try to understand what others are intending to say, albeit again without assuming that success is guaranteed. We take this for granted in our everyday communications, and if we were seriously to doubt it then we would have to doubt just about everything else we routinely believe; leaving us in an epistemological scepticism that is impossible to sustain, both theoretically and practically.

Moreover, there is no reason why attempts at controlling the meaning of our communications should be treated as inherently undesirable; quite the reverse. Regarding them in this way is rather similar to the widespread assumption that power is always bad; an assumption, incidentally, that cannot be squared with Foucault's position, despite his distinction between power and resistance. Whether or not power is bad depends upon how it is used and with what effects; and this applies, for example, in the context of arguments about whether or not research communities should be 'policed' (see, for example, Scheurich 1997:84). In much the same way, attempts at clear communication are not essentially bad; any more than they are *essentially* good.

MacLure and others see a direct parallel between the ideal of scientific clarity and the scientist notion that public policy requires procedural transparency to facilitate 'the administrative gaze'. But we can reject such modes of governance without abandoning the idea of seeking to convey our research findings clearly to relevant audiences.[19] Moreover, publicising findings clearly is one of the key commitments of any kind of social science, qualitative research included. For this reason, drama, collage, poetry, etc., are not, for the most part, appropriate for the purpose of research – which is to produce and publicise warranted knowledge claims and the evidence relevant to them. I would not want to rule out the use of these artistic and literary forms completely from qualitative inquiry, but I *am* arguing that their use should be subordinated to the distinctive purpose of research (see Hammersley 1993).

We ought to avoid living up to the jibe, frequently directed at ethnographers in the past, that we are failed novelists or poets. Even less should we confirm it by producing poor quality literature or drama instead of pursuing the more prosaic task of reporting our findings as clearly as we can. Where previously social scientists had tended to ape natural science, envying its success, now the aspirational model seems to be art and literature; but this is simply the same kind of mistake in a different context. There is nothing wrong with learning from other kinds of enterprise, but this can only be worthwhile when the distinctiveness and value of the task in which we are engaged is not forgotten.

---

19 In a critique of clarity as an ideal in the context of systematic reviews, MacLure (2005) effectively runs these together. In doing so she uses the phrase 'clarity bordering on stupidity' which comes from Breton's manifesto for Surrealism. It is striking, though, that in fact Maclure writes clearly and uses a fairly conventional mode of academic expression. For a critique of the notion of procedural transparency from a rather different direction, see Hammersley (2001 and 2006b).

## Conclusion

In this chapter, I have sketched the influence of Dadaism and Surrealism on a very influential strand of methodological thinking about qualitative research that is often labelled 'postmodernist'. This approach rejects the older concern with documenting and explaining cultural phenomena in order to further human understanding, on the model of science, in favour of a view of research as necessarily constructing the 'realities' it presents, and as properly judged in political, ethical, and/or aesthetic terms. I have argued that this postmodernist approach is founded on some false assumptions that undermine the distinctive nature of social research. In effect, it amounts to abandoning the primary task of inquiry, which (perhaps it needs saying) is to produce knowledge about the world. Instead, resort is made to models from modernist art and literature. I have argued that one consequence of this has been a legitimation of speculative theorising; another has been a celebration of obscurity, and associated denunciations of clarity. In these various respects, many of the ideas and practices usually listed under the heading of postmodernism pose a major threat. It is not that nothing is to be learned from them. They warn of the dangers of premature closure, of oversimplification, of assuming that the world is more systematic and coherent than it is, and so on. However, not only are they by no means the only sources from which those lessons can be learned, but many of the conclusions that have been drawn from postmodernism by qualitative researchers are false and misleading. Their influence leads towards an abdication of the responsibility for clear and careful argument aimed at discovering what truths qualitative inquiry is capable of providing.

# 8

# Is Qualitative Research Just Rhetoric?

In the last few decades of the twentieth century, considerable attention began to be paid to the writing that social scientists do. The numerous books and articles produced were not concerned simply with providing advice about writing (see, for example, Becker 1986; Woods 1999/2007; Wolcott 2001), but also with analysing the rhetorical devices employed by researchers (see, for instance, Bruyn 1966:ch 5; Brown 1977; Atkinson 1982, 1991 and 1992; Edmondson 1984; Clifford and Marcus 1986; Van Maanen 1988; Sanjek 1990; Denzin 1997).[1] The core of what is offered in much of this literature is descriptive accounts of various rhetorical strategies used by researchers, especially in doing qualitative work. However, in some of these publications, these accounts are laced with philosophical, ethical, and political claims about the functions or effects of the strategies employed. In particular, a great deal of this work involves a critique of the realism that has long been, and for the most part continues to be, integral to research writing. The grounds for this critique are several: that realism disguises the fictional character of all writing, including that of scientists; and that it is an ideological form that is central to the reproduction of modern forms of social organisation. On the basis of this critique, there has been advocacy of so-called 'experimental' modes of writing, for example modelled on twentieth-century art and literature, that do not project a single, persuasive narrative voice. It is argued that, by avoiding this, they renounce the authority of social science and open the way for the voicing of suppressed discourses, thereby furthering social justice.[2]

---

1 For a review of this literature, see Hammersley (1994). More recent examples and discussions include Behar and Gordon (1995); James et al. (1997); Atkinson and Coffey (1995); Hammersley and Atkinson (2007:ch 9).

2 See, for example, the concern with 'how the discourses of qualitative research can be used to help create a free democratic society', which motivates some of the discussion in the relevant section of the third edition of the *Handbook of Qualitative Research* (Denzin and Lincoln 2005:909).

In more detail, there are three central, and interrelated, arguments frequently involved here:

1.  The fact that many of the rhetorical devices social scientists use are shared in common with writers of imaginative literature, especially realist novelists, is held by some to underline the inappropriateness of natural science as a model for social research. Science is seen as founded on a binary between factual and fictional writing that (so the argument goes), like all binaries, is also a hierarchy that privileges one side. It is claimed that the boundary between these forms of writing is socially constructed, and should be erased, or transgressed. Another formulation insists that all kinds of language-use, including scientific writing, are rhetorical, in the specific sense that they are governed by a concern with creating some type of effect in an audience. Both these strands can be included under the heading of what I will call the 'all-texts-are-rhetorical' argument.[3]
2.  It is declared or assumed that the rhetorical devices employed in research texts play an active role in constituting the very phenomena to which those texts refer. In other words, research texts do not represent pre-existing phenomena, but instead are in a broad sense performative: they *construct* the phenomena they claim to document. And this too is often taken to reinforce the idea that literature is a better model for social research than science. More specifically, what is held up as an exemplar are modernist forms of literature that specifically challenge or subvert their own enactment of 'reality'. I will call this idea 'constructionist anti-realism'.
3.  Finally, it is often claimed that the realist rhetoric employed in most research texts not only misrepresents the nature of inquiry but by doing so enables these texts to serve undesirable political functions. Realism is portrayed here as a means of legitimating power, not just that of social scientists but also that of dominant groups within Western societies, thereby reinforcing the socio-political status quo. It is suggested that what are required, instead, are textual strategies that challenge realism, thereby unsettling dominant assumptions and disturbing existing social arrangements, opening the way for the voices of subordinated groups – or, more abstractly, the Other – to be heard (see Lather 1996). I will call this the 'realism as ideology' argument.

The first two of these arguments each contains a grain of truth, but they are frequently over-extended to the point of being seriously misleading. The third, it seems to me, is fundamentally misconceived. This evaluation will be developed by comparing the recent literature on research rhetoric with a much

---

3  For an example of this argument, see MacLure (2003: Introduction and *passim*).

older tradition of work on rhetoric in political and other contexts, dating from at least the time of the Sophists in ancient Greece.[4]

### Blurred genres and the ubiquity of rhetoric

In common parlance, today, the term 'rhetoric' is used to refer to forms of language that are concerned with illegitimately manipulating audiences.[5] This usage dates from at least the time of Plato's attack on the Sophists, above all for what he saw as their unscrupulous teaching of persuasive ways of speaking to *anyone* and *for any purpose*. Thus, the dominant current meaning of 'rhetoric' is very close to the much more recently invented sense given to the word 'spin', referring to politicians' and others' attempts to control public impressions of themselves and their activities in order to mobilise and sustain support, sell products, etc. In these terms, by implication at least, not all speech or writing involves rhetoric; and, furthermore, rhetoric is (usually) viewed as undesirable. However, the older discipline of Rhetoric and the much more recent work focusing on discursive strategies in research texts are at odds with this common understanding. Both insist that there is a rhetorical dimension to *all* language-use: that we always employ language with a view to having an effect on an audience, and so formulate what we say or write in such a way as to achieve that goal. Equally important, following on from this, they argue or imply that the use of rhetoric is neither good nor bad in itself: its value depends upon the purposes for which, or the way in which, it is used.

Recent writing on research rhetoric has stressed the common textual strategies used by those engaged in quite different intellectual activities; in particular, science and imaginative literature. A first move towards this conclusion, in line with what is sometimes described as the discursive turn in twentieth-century thought, was to formulate science as primarily a *genre of writing*; and the second move was to emphasise the commonalities between the forms of writing characteristic of science and literature *rather than their differences*. As already noted, particular emphasis came to be placed on the way in which social scientists employ rhetorical devices that are very similar to those used by novelists, especially realist novelists (Brown 1977; Atkinson 1982 and 1991). And this, for some, signified a more general move away from treating natural science as an appropriate model for social inquiry, and towards seeking inspiration from

---

4 On the Sophists, see Guthrie (1971). For a detailed account of the history of rhetoric, and advocacy of its importance, see Vickers (1988). There has also been quite a lot of work in the USA on rhetoric, often in the context of teaching students to write more effectively. Becker (1986) draws on this work. There was an influential attempt to revive the study of rhetoric in Europe in the 1950s and 1960s (see Perelman and Olbrechts-Tyteca 1969; and also Perelman 1982).

5 An exception to this meaning is the notion of a rhetorical question, or 'interrogatio', a question that is not intended to elicit an answer (see Dixon 1971:36).

the humanities. To a large extent, this stemmed from a reaction against a previous tendency for science to be presented as the model for all forms of engagement with the world; and as an enterprise that generates knowledge whose validity is guaranteed through following fixed methodological procedures. Of course, work in the philosophy of science had long challenged such views, but an emphasis on the rhetorical dimension of scientific work represented an important elaboration of what were taken by some to be the implications of this philosophical criticism.

Now, while this attention to the rhetorical dimension of research is certainly of value, there is a tendency to draw false conclusions from it. It is true that all language-use is recipient-designed.[6] This means that however plain a piece of writing is, however much there is an attempt at straightforward clarity, it is still structured for an audience; at the very least, in terms both of what is judged to be intelligible and of interest to that audience. It is also true that many textual strategies are shared across different forms of writing. However, in order to understand *any* form of language-use, it is essential to locate it within the context of the larger activity of which it forms part; in other words, to recognise its social function. Writers in the tradition of Rhetoric recognised this: early commentators differentiated between forensic (legal) and political rhetoric, and later work concentrated more on poetic rhetoric (see Dixon 1971). In other words, while rhetoricians have stressed the ubiquity of rhetoric, they have not assumed that this ubiquity undercuts the distinctions among genres and the different activities associated with them. The tendency of some recent writers on research rhetoric to erase those distinctions, and particularly that between science and literature, is of course a reaction to a previous tendency to neglect the rhetorical dimension of scientific writing, and to exaggerate the differences between these two enterprises. However, it is an *over*-reaction.

While scientific writing is designed to persuade readers of the truth of what is claimed, it occurs within an institution that is concerned with the production of knowledge; and pursuit of persuasion is properly constrained by that larger enterprise. Much language-use in the context of politics and the law is also concerned with persuading an audience to accept particular policies or proposals, and there are constraints there too. However, the constraints are different, arising from contrasting institutional contexts and functions.[7] By contrast, much modern literary writing is not aimed at persuasion in any straightforward sense: it is designed to evoke some 'world' in which the reader can participate imaginatively, or to celebrate, poke fun, intrigue, puzzle, and so on. The fact that there are some common textual strategies across these genres

---

6  Schegloff (1971) shows that this is true even in the most mundane forms of communication, such as giving directions.

7  For an account of the differences between the contexts of research and public politics, as regards the role of criticism, see Hammersley (2005a).

does not undermine the importance of distinguishing between the different activities with which they are associated, and recognising their distinct purposes. Yet the all-texts-are-rhetorical argument generally ignores, denies, or seeks to challenge these differences.

Of course, as already noted, one of the motivations behind attempts to blur, erase, or transgress the boundaries between research and other kinds of writing stems from recognising the falsity of claims sometimes made for science. Scientific research has on occasion been portrayed as able to supply knowledge whose validity is absolutely certain, which can serve as a superior foundation for organising society, or for living one's life, to those provided by common sense, religion, or art. One of the arguments forcing recognition that such claims are exaggerated pointed to the active role that researchers play in constructing the knowledge they produce, this often being used to draw relativist or sceptical conclusions about that 'knowledge'. And, indeed, from the beginning of the rhetorical tradition, some writers have relied on sceptical arguments that challenge any idea of philosophy or science as capable of producing knowledge, arguments that also undermine any role for truth and honesty in other genres of speech and writing. Recent work on research rhetoric has also been very strongly influenced by twentieth-century versions of such ideas.[8] Reacting against an Enlightenment view that treats both science and art as concerned with producing true understanding, it is argued that they are both engaged in fabrication, such that any distinction between fact and fiction is weakened if not eliminated. Given this, they must be evaluated in non-epistemic terms: according to political intent or consequences, ethical values, or aesthetic qualities. This is what I have labelled constructionist anti-realism.

### Constructionist anti-realism

Plato portrayed the Sophists as committed to a sceptical or relativist view of knowledge that gave spurious justification to their role as teachers of rhetoric. He contrasted rhetoric with the dialectic (or logic) that is employed by philosophers in seeking true knowledge. However, while some of the Sophists, notably Gorgias, seem to have fitted Plato's picture of them, many writers on rhetoric challenged Plato's critique, not only by pointing to the unavoidability of a concern with persuasion in talk and writing but also by insisting on the compatibility of this with a commitment to truth and honesty.[9]

By contrast, many recent writers dealing with the rhetoric employed by researchers have more or less accepted the idea that the unavoidability of rhetoric undermines conventional claims to knowledge or truth. Indeed, they

---

8 For an illuminating history of the waxing and waning of the influence of scepticism over the course of Western history, see Popkin (1979).

9 An example is Isocrates, on whom see Vickers (1988:149–59).

argue that 'clear' writing, what Barthes calls readerly text (Barthes 1975), is simply another strategy of persuasion; and one that is especially misleading since it pretends to be transparent – to do nothing more than reveal truth to the reader (see Chapter 7). They infer from the fact that research texts are human constructions, produced by particular people, in particular circumstances, for particular audiences, using rhetorical devices of various kinds, that they cannot be accurate representations of phenomena that are independent of them. Yet this does not follow at all.

What often underpins this false conclusion, despite the influence of post-structuralism, is what we might call a subjectivist, or expressivist (see Taylor 1975), epistemology. This portrays knowledge as reflecting the characteristics of the subject that produced it *rather than* those of any objects to which it refers. It is important to emphasise that the subject here may be individual or collective (for example, it could be a particular social class, or a particular cultural entity such as 'the West'). Such subjectivism, in various forms, was influential throughout much of the eighteenth, nineteenth and twentieth centuries. However, an important change took place in its character over the course of this period. In the work of Hegel and other absolute idealists, and in the writings of Marx and some later Marxists, this kind of subjectivism was linked to a teleological account of historical development that was directed towards the re-integration of Subject and Object; and, thereby, the achievement of true knowledge. However, the late nineteenth and early twentieth centuries witnessed the decomposition of this project, and in particular the abandonment of its teleological component. What remains is an influential subjectivist account of the nature of human thought – represented early on by some versions of the sociology of knowledge and later by some kinds of constructionism – that has no place for truth as the key criterion of knowledge; since the metaphysics of a teleological reconciliation of Subject and Object has been abandoned. A parallel decomposition, important for post-structuralism and postmodernism, took place within phenomenology: from Husserl's attempt to ground objectivity in the transcendental ego through to the tendency of some later philosophers influenced by phenomenology to see meaning as either an imposition on an irrational world (Sartre) or as the product of wordplay by some mystical Other (to 'caricature' Derrida).[10] What is wrong here, I suggest, is the assumption that

---

10 On structuralism and post-structuralism, see Merquior (1986b). One might trace similar decompositions within pragmatism from Peirce to James, and from Dewey to Rorty; and there is also a strong strain of subjectivism, in the sense that I am using the term here, within British empiricism. It may, of course, seem odd to label post-structuralism as subjectivist, but while that philosophical trend rejects the idea that knowledge derives from individual human subjects, it retains from structuralism a concern with tracing back appearances to some generative process and applies this idea in a way that challenges claims to knowledge, in the conventional sense of that term – including its own.

knowledge must be a reflection *either* of an object *or* of a subject; that it cannot be *both* objective and subjective in these senses.[11]

Now, it is worth noting that while scepticism and relativism have a long history, going back to the beginnings of the rhetorical tradition, so too do criticisms of those positions. Moreover, the criticisms are cogent. In broad terms, these take both a positive and a negative form. First, contrary to what sceptics and relativists suggest, dogmatism is not the only alternative to their position; and, even more importantly, the other possibilities do not simply occupy some middle ground. Perhaps the most important example is fallibilism, which rejects a key assumption that dogmatism and scepticism share in common: the definition of knowledge as that which is known beyond all possible doubt. Fallibilists argue that this definition is fruitless, since (as sceptics rightly point out) no knowledge claim can ever meet its requirements; yet routinely, in everyday life, we distinguish among potential beliefs in terms of their likely validity, judging some to be much more reliable than others. Therefore, fallibilists conclude, 'knowledge' should be defined as what is true, and we should treat claims that we currently have good reason to believe are true as knowledge; while recognising, of course, that we may have to revise our assessment of them later.[12]

In other words, my argument here is that constructionist scepticism takes over a fundamental and mistaken assumption from what it opposes. It assumes that in order for language to represent real phenomena it must be transparent and unmotivated. And it is concluded from this that since it cannot be transparent and unmotivated it cannot represent phenomena that exist independently of it. But why should we accept the initial premise here? There seems no good reason to do so. Indeed, ironically, it is a premise that is wedded to the metaphysics of presence, the target of Derridean deconstruction.

The second, this time negative, line of argument is that scepticism is simply not a sustainable position, for a reason that has long been recognised even by many sceptics themselves: it is self-refuting. Moreover, attempting to avoid this by making no knowledge claims whatsoever, as did the ancient Pyrrhonian sceptics, is futile. We cannot think at all without treating *something* as knowledge. Other sceptics have tried to go through the mirror: declaring that they recognise that scepticism cannot be consistently held, but insisting that different people mean different things by 'consistent'; or suggesting that we must just accept that it is in the nature of our finite lives as human beings that we cannot be consistent in our beliefs, it is something we have to live with (see Smith 2004; Smith and Hodkinson 2005; Hammersley 2008d). Yet, in practical terms scepticism *cannot* be lived with, and I doubt

---

11  Much of the trouble here stems from the multiple meanings of these terms, see Hammersley (2004c).

12  Foe a fallibilist defence of science, see Haack 2003

whether any modern relativist or sceptic ever attempts to do this in a significant way. After all, it leaves us with no basis for acting one way rather than another, other than by backstop appeals to such things as tradition or personal taste or the throw of a die. Even in the context of research, modern relativists and sceptics do not act in line with absolute scepticism. Instead of treating all claims about knowledge as equally true or untrue, they almost always treat *some* as false.[13]

There are, of course, difficult philosophical issues surrounding the question of in what sense knowledge *represents* phenomena in the world (Hammersley 2004b). It is true that all knowledge claims are constructed, and that even the conceptual resources they employ are themselves human constructs. Knowledge is never simply given by the world; it is never a matter, for example, of 'sense *impressions*' or of logical derivations from these.[14] It is also true that multiple knowledge claims can always be made about the same phenomenon. Furthermore, there may be contradictory beliefs among which no reasonable adjudication can be made at particular points in time. However, what there cannot be are contradictory *truths* about the world. Accepting that there could be such 'truths' not only undermines any possibility of knowledge, it breaches the grammar required for any talk about knowledge, even that involved in denying its possibility. This is where the performative contradiction built into scepticism bites deepest.

### Realism as ideological

The third argument I listed earlier – that realism is ideological – seems to be distinctive to writing about research rhetoric; as far as I can tell it is not to be found in the older rhetorical tradition. It is an argument to the effect that realism is not only mistaken but is also an ideological form that serves the political status quo. This is often portrayed as an inversion of dominant Enlightenment ideas, and an application of the Enlightenment concept of ideology to the Enlightenment itself. Where, before, it was superstition, religion, and the political ideas supporting the *ancien régime* that were diagnosed as ideological, now various writers treat rationalism, empiricism and science as

---

13  They do not usually question the reality of rape, childhood abuse, or the holocaust, in the way that they question, for example, claims about biological differences between the sexes. For the interesting case of postmodernism and holocaust denial, see Eaglestone (2001). I have run relativism together with scepticism here, and some will wish to insist that they are different. However, to the extent that relativists claim that there are multiple realities which are at odds with one another, in other words to the extent that they propose that different frameworks involve incompatible truths, they are using the terms 'reality', 'knowledge', and 'truth' in a way that implies epistemological scepticism.

14  Even the metaphor of sense impression implies that the nature of any impression will be determined as much by the medium that is 'impressed' as by that which presses on it.

themselves open to this diagnosis.[15] What this amounts to is treating these modes of thought in functionalist terms: as arising so as to serve a social purpose or function, whether to promote the interests of a particular social group, not necessarily just social scientists but perhaps others too, or to establish and sustain a particular type of society.

At the level of discourse, what this involves is not just emphasising that even scientific texts rely on rhetorical devices, but also arguing that these devices disguise themselves as transparent, thereby obscuring their constitutive character – the fact that they reflect the socio-historical characteristics and location of the researcher, and serve particular interests. Moreover, it is argued that any purported 'view from nowhere' invariably serves the interests of the powerful, because it invests how things are with an apparent inevitability. Given this, the task for the authentic researcher becomes to subvert all claims to knowledge, and particularly those made in the name of science, or of research more generally. Moreover, a fully reflexive version of this position requires recognition that even the best-intentioned researcher will necessarily make ideological claims to knowledge, so that it is necessary for him or her to adopt forms of writing that continually subvert themselves by revealing the rhetorical constructions they employ. This is analogous, in some respects, to what Salvador Dalí recommended as the 'paranoic-critical method'. He writes: 'I believe the moment is at hand when, by a paranoic and active advance of the mind, it will be possible (simultaneously with automatism [that is, with automatic writing] and other passive states [probably an allusion to spiritualism]), to systematize confusion and thus to help discredit completely the world of reality' (from Dalí's *The Rotten Donkey*, quoted in Brandon 1999:378). Interestingly, this position not only goes against the views of those within the older tradition of Rhetoric, like Isocrates, who upheld the need to speak truly, but is also at odds even with Sophists who embraced scepticism. The latter saw the task of the orator as to *persuade* others to believe something, even though he or she knows that there can be no knowledge.[16] In this context, scepticism was, if you like, the guilty occupational secret of the rhetorician, and one that had to be protected for business purposes. Now, it seems, the task is to convince people that what is being said is, like everything else, unconvincing.

The interest in research rhetoric began most influentially in anthropology, where it was closely linked to concerns about the relationship between Western anthropologists and the non-Western societies and communities they had typically studied. Of course, concerns about imperialism and ethnocentrism had

---

15 For an excellent brief account of recent critiques of the Enlightenment, and the problems with them, see Schmidt (1998).

16 This is captured in a quotation from Plato reprinted on the front cover of Vickers (1988): 'The orator is one who intends to mislead another without being misled himself'.

long been present among anthropologists, but what was novel about this latest version of them was the belief that there is a close connection between the realist orientation of much anthropology and what was seen as its neo-imperialist role. Whereas earlier anthropologists had viewed themselves as documenting the diversity of cultures, and thereby at the very least championing the value of toleration, these more recent anthropologists suggested that the very commitment to providing realistic descriptions of diverse cultures was itself imperialist, in that it inevitably reflected dominant Western philosophical and political commitments and interests (see, for example, Clifford and Marcus 1986).

Here, what arises from the decomposition of subjectivism, especially in its Hegelian Marxist and phenomenological forms, is a scepticism about Western claims to knowledge, a tendency to see those claims as telling us about the West rather than about the phenomena they purport to describe, and, in particular, a suspicion that the interests and preoccupations of the West are deeply embedded in our whole way of thinking and writing. Given this, the task becomes to expose these interests and their disguises, one of which is believed to be the commitment to scientific realism.

From this perspective, the mission of social research might be seen as to adopt a 'just rhetoric', employing forms of writing that continually resist the tendency to treat Western forms of thought as superior, that seek to preserve space for subordinated or marginalised discourses without pretending to speak on their behalf, and that thereby promote social justice.[17] Equally, subverting realism may be viewed as opening up space for the creative play of Discourse or of some broader process of 'worlding'. From this point of view, we are condemned to rhetoric, but rather than it being a form of original sin that we must lament, it is regarded as a saving grace. By drawing attention to it we can assert our equality with those about whom we write; though Westerners must be seen, and must treat themselves, as subject to the continual temptation of claiming knowledge and thereby superiority – so that *their* only hope of salvation is by the grace of the Other, variously interpreted.

There are some very serious problems with this third argument. One is a matter of internal consistency: the concept of ideology involves some assumptions that are impossible to sustain on the basis of constructionist anti-realism. In particular, 'ideology' is defined by contrast with science, or with sound knowledge or rationality of some sort; yet this distinction is untenable for anti-realism. As a way round this, reliance tends to be placed on the idea that a commitment to realism has determinate socio-political consequences. Yet this argument is also incompatible with anti-realism since it assumes a form of

---

17  The argument can, of course, also be formulated in gender terms, with Western thought portrayed as inherently patriarchal.

essentialism – whereby the consequences of holding a particular belief are built into the very character of that belief. Thus, it is assumed that realism necessarily serves injustice, whereas anti-realism promotes justice. But on what grounds could a constructionist justify this? And, in any case, where is the evidence that it is true?

A further problem is that it is quite unclear why it should be assumed that realism is distinctively Western in character. Much depends here on what is meant by that term, of course. For present purposes, the core meaning seems to be the belief that there is a single reality about which knowledge is possible. On this interpretation, there are grounds for treating this belief as constitutive of all human life: in doing the simplest things we assume that the world has certain characteristics and that these are available to those with whom we interact as well as to ourselves (see Schutz 1962). In fact, historically there might be a stronger argument for claiming that scepticism and relativism are distinctively Western, rather than realism (at least as defined in this minimalist way).

A further criticism relates to the recommendation of forms of writing that subvert themselves. What are subverted here are not just claims to knowledge but in fact the very possibility of persuasiveness itself. In other words, what is proposed is a kind of anti-rhetoric: researchers are required to write in ways that are specifically designed to be *un*persuasive. But what could be the point of this? And is it only *researchers* on whom this obligation is placed, or only Westerners, or is it everyone? Moreover, what could be the justification for requiring it of some and not of others? Is the implication that non-Westerners, or at least the marginalised and oppressed, already write in ways that are properly unpersuasive, or is it that they must be allowed to write persuasively to counter intellectual imperialism? If the latter, what are the grounds for this recommendation – some kind of standpoint theory that treats subordinated discourses as epistemologically privileged? But if this *is* the basis, once more we run into inconsistency, since such a theory both involves a commitment to realism and is very much a product of nineteenth-century Western thought.

Finally, there is the question of why we should assume that the Other in general, or even specific marginalised discourses, are inherently just, or that they deserve a hearing. Why is opening up spaces for other discourses always a good thing? Presumably, what lies behind this is not the liberal assumption that openness and liberty lead to truth, of the kind to be found, for example, in the writings of John Stuart Mill or Karl Popper. After all, this too, is incompatible with constructionist anti-realism. And is complete openness good? If so, why? In addition, we might ask whether the very notion of justice that underpins some of the arguments against realist rhetoric is not as Western an idea as the realist concept of truth. What we have here is simply an inversion of the close link assumed by many Enlightenment thinkers between truth and justice. Whereas many, though by no means all, eighteenth-century *philosophers* believed that pursuit and publication of knowledge would necessarily serve the cause of justice or progress, these constructionist and postmodernist critics argue that the claim to scientific knowledge necessarily serves injustice. Yet, neither of these mirror-image positions seems plausible. The relationship between inquiry and justice, like that between the true and the good more generally, is contingent; it is neither necessarily positive nor inevitably negative.

## Conclusion

The attention that has been given to the textual strategies employed by researchers, to the rhetorical character of their work, is of considerable benefit. As Atkinson has argued (Atkinson 1991; Atkinson and Delamont 2004), it is important that we are reflectively aware of the writing strategies we employ, and of the assumptions that they involve. However, quite a lot of the work in this field has been committed to theoretical ideas – about the impossibility of knowledge, and the ideological character of realist accounts – that are unconvincing. By contrast, notwithstanding Plato's critique, the ancient tradition of Rhetoric was not, generally speaking, wedded to scepticism or relativism, though it was certainly fallibilist: aware of the difficulties of gaining knowledge, and of both the relationship and the difference between truth and persuasiveness. Moreover, it was centrally concerned not just with effective ways of speaking and writing, but also with what are and are not legitimate rhetorical strategies for particular purposes. And it seems to me that this is a very important, and very neglected, issue in the context of social research. It emerges in some books about research writing concerned with helping novice researchers (for example, Becker 1986). However, it is generally dealt with only marginally, and in a largely atheoretical way without being linked to explicit arguments about how particular sorts of writing do and do not serve the purposes of research, and the central role that communal discussion and assessment must play in the research process.

One aspect of research rhetoric that might repay sustained attention is the various functions served by citation of secondary literature: we need to consider whether all of these are legitimate, and what it takes for these functions to be met effectively. Sometimes it is far from clear why a particular reference is being cited, or what aspect or part of the work referred to is relevant. There is also a tendency for certain publications to become standard references in ways that are systematically misleading.[18] Another area of useful rhetorical inquiry would be the ways in which data extracts are used in qualitative research. Many years ago, Glaser and

---

18 Two examples are Becker's article 'Whose side are we on?' (Becker 1967; Hammersley 2000:ch 3) and Rosenthal and Jacobson's *Pygmalion in the Classroom* (Rosenthal and Jacobson 1968; Hammersley 2004a).

Strauss (1967) dismissed what they referred to as 'exampling', but it is less than clear what is good practice as regards the inclusion of qualitative data in research reports. What do data extracts stand for, and for whom and to what do they speak?[19]

Of course, there are those who are likely to see any attempt to lay down guidelines for what rhetorical strategies should and should not be used by social researchers as yet another attempt at policing the research field, which they regard as unnecessary and as authoritarian. It is certainly true that guidelines can quickly become transformed into fixed rules that are rigidly enforced. However, what we should be opposed to are not guidelines themselves, in this or any other area, but rather the abuse of these through their mechanical application. Guidelines, like laws, can serve an important function. Moreover, blanket opposition to policing, even policing carried out by citizens on themselves (this being rejected as Foucaultian surveillance), typically relies on an anarchist political philosophy that is underpinned by the sorts of philosophical ideas that I have challenged in this chapter. It is time that these were abandoned in favour of a more realistic perspective.

So, qualitative research is not *just* rhetoric, even though it necessarily relies on rhetorical strategies, as does all other writing. Nor should the primary concern be to ensure that this rhetoric is just in the sense of serving social justice. It should, however, be honest about the likely validity of the findings being reported. The primary concern must be with truth not justice.

---

19 For an interesting discussion of the rhetorical roles of examples in literature, see Gelley (1995). There has also been some discussion of the rhetoric of quantitative data (see McCloskey 1985; and Porter 1995). Other issues that might repay attention include the use of bugbear words, like 'positivism' and 'postmodernism'; usage of quotation marks as 'scare quotes' and 'sneer quotes' (on the latter, see Haack 1998:117); the use of adjectives like 'relative' and 'neutral' without clarification of the particular comparative frame being used; and the employment of nouns like 'emancipation' and 'empowerment' (in effect, as political slogans) without specification of from what people are to be freed or of what it is they are to be given the power to do. For an excellent explication of the logical grammar of 'freedom', see MacCallum (1972).

# 9

# The Issue of Quality in Qualitative Research

In recent years, the quality of qualitative research has increasingly been questioned. There are those who argue that much of it is of a poor standard. More usually, the complaint is that there is no clearly defined set of criteria available for judging it, so that it is of *uncertain* quality. There are two assumptions underpinning this second criticism that need to be addressed. First, what is involved here is an at least implicitly *comparative* assessment: it is usually assumed that clearly defined criteria of quality already exist for quantitative research.[1] The other assumption is that explicit assessment criteria are *needed*. There seem to be two reasons why they are thought to be necessary. First, it is believed that unless researchers operate on the basis of such criteria their work will be of poor or very variable quality. Secondly, it is argued that *users* of research require some reliable means of judging its quality, and that a set of criteria would meet this need.

In this chapter, I will examine some of the arguments about whether criteria are necessary, and then go on to consider whether a single set is possible given the present state of methodological pluralism within qualitative inquiry.

## Are criteria necessary?

Whether there are criteria by which qualitative research can be judged, and if so what character these should have, are issues about which there has been much debate but little agreement. There have been many attempts to identify criteria.[2] Some writers have tried to apply what they see as traditional

---

1 I have suggested elsewhere that this is a misconception (Hammersley 2007b).

2 These are lucidly reviewed and consolidated by Spencer et al. (2003), (see also Altheide and Johnson 1994).

quantitative criteria, such as (internal and external) validity and reliability, to qualitative work. Others have reformulated these epistemic criteria and, sometimes, added non-epistemic ones, whether in terms of 'giving voice' to the marginalised or bringing about practical or political outcomes of some kind – such as improving public services, challenging injustice and oppression, or 'troubling' the status quo. At the same time, there are some writers who appear to reject the very possibility of criteria, at least as conventionally understood. For example, many years ago, John Smith argued that 'there can be no criteria to reconcile discourse (to sort out the trustworthy from the untrustworthy results)' (Smith 1984:384; see also Smith 1989; Schwandt 1996; Garratt and Hodkinson 1998; ). Smith claimed that attempts to apply criteria to qualitative research would inevitably result in confusion and inconsistency, because criteria are incompatible with the basic philosophical assumptions of this type of inquiry. More recently, in a co-written article, he has insisted that 'criteria should not be thought of in abstraction, but as a list of features that we think, or more or less agree at any given time, and place, characterize good versus bad inquiry'. Furthermore, the list is open to revision: 'This is a list that can be challenged, added to, subtracted from, modified, and so on, as it is applied in actual practice – in its actual application to actual inquiries' (Smith and Deemer 2000:894). I suspect that, despite appearances, Smith's views have not changed much over the period concerned; the difference between the two formulations hinges on what is meant by the term 'criteria'. And this is a crucial issue.

We can provide two contrasting definitions which illustrate the scope for disagreement about this. At one end of the spectrum, 'criteria' means a finite set of observable indicators that can tell us whether or not the findings of a study are valid, or are of value in broader terms. What is involved here is a checklist that is sufficiently explicit and concrete in its reference for it to be completed with little error; moreover, it is comprehensive enough to cover everything that needs to be taken into account in judging quality. Very often proposed criteria of this kind relate to the research design employed, on the implicit assumption that this determines the validity of the findings. Towards the other end of the spectrum are the kind of criteria outlined by Smith and Deemer: a list of considerations, never fully explicit, that it is agreed in local circumstances should be taken into account in judging particular kinds of work, a list that can serve as no more than a reminder and that is always open to revision in the process of being used – indeed, which at least to some degree only gains meaning in particular contexts.[3] It seems to me that the

---

3 There could be a position that is beyond that of Smith and Deemer, where the whole point of criteria is to transgress them. Lather (1993) seems close to this. Also near this end of the spectrum would be Feyerabend's rejection of method (Feyerabend 1975).

second definition comes much closer to what is possible and desirable than the first.

The best place to start in thinking about the nature and role of criteria is with how researchers actually go about, and should go about, assessing quality in doing their work. This is, after all, integral to any form of inquiry, throughout its course. And, generally speaking, researchers do not do this by simply *applying* a set of explicit and concrete rules of assessment. Instead, they make specific, and often largely implicit, judgements: about particular items and sources of evidence, about inferences from them, about the reliability of the conclusions drawn, and so on. However, to some extent they can, and often will, explicate these judgements in terms of methodological principles. This picture is as true of quantitative as of qualitative researchers, whatever other differences there are between them. Moreover, I suggest that reliance on *judgement* is inevitable in both kinds of research. The task of assessing quality in the context of any relatively complex activity cannot be sensibly reduced to the application of explicit, concrete and exhaustive indicators. Instead, formulations of criteria, in terms of relevant standards and considerations that might need to be taken into account, *come out of* the process of judgement and are modified by it; to one degree or another. At the same time, they also feed back into it: they are used subsequently by researchers in judging quality in other situations; though they always have to be interpreted and may be *re*-interpreted in this process. Furthermore, they will be employed selectively, depending upon the nature of the knowledge claims and research involved.

While rejecting the idea of a finite set of explicit and exhaustive criteria that can substitute for judgement, or render its role minimal, this discussion at the same time indicates that criteria, in the form of guiding principles and lists of relevant considerations, can play an important role in the work of researchers. Such 'criteria' or 'guidelines' may facilitate reflection on previous judgements that enables us to learn from our own experience, and from one another. And this learning may also involve exploring the implications of applying locally-used criteria in *new* contexts, and considering the extent to which there are commonalities across fields. This is important because such reflection can lead us to conclude that locally used criteria need to be changed or developed, even as regards their original context. In other words, it seems to me that changes in criteria arise not just, as Smith and Deemer suggest, from the practical work of particular researchers in particular situations but also from attempts to systematise current criteria. The aim here is not to produce a single, universal set of assessment rules that will eliminate judgement, it is rather that the process of thinking about how the criteria would apply in other contexts and how they relate to one another is a productive force in the development of research practice.

In a much more mundane way, but no less importantly, criteria of this kind can *remind* researchers about what they ought to take into account in assessing their own and others' research. This is no small matter. When engaged in any complex activity, it is easy to overlook what one would, in other circumstances, routinely take into consideration. Stated criteria may also facilitate students' learning how to assess research; though here, especially, care must be taken to avoid the implication that criteria can in some sense be a substitute for acquiring through participation the practical capacity to make sound judgements.

It is worth pointing out that a distinction needs to be drawn between the standards in terms of which research is judged, and those considerations that might need to be taken into account in order to reach a sound assessment regarding each standard. Equally important is to recognise that 'assessing research' does not refer to a single task with one focus. There are different forms of assessment that imply different standards of evaluation and therefore different relevant considerations; even though there are interconnections and overlaps among them. At least the following foci of assessment can be identified:

1. How well a study is presented in a research report. Relevant standards here would include clarity and sufficiency of information for the relevant audience.
2. How significant are the findings of a study, or of a body of research? Standards here would be validity (that is, likely truth) and relevance to some general human concern.
3. How well was a piece of research, or a set of studies, carried out? Here standards would include effectiveness of methods, given the purpose; how well they were used; care in the assessment of evidence; and so on.
4. Whether the methods employed in a study or group of studies seem likely to be fruitful in other contexts. This would presumably involve the same standards as 3, but adjusted to take account of the target context.
5. Assessing the expertise or competence of particular researchers on the basis of the work they have produced; for example, in order to decide whether they should be awarded a PhD. The standards relevant to 1, 2 and 3 would apply here, adjusted to what is thought appropriate for this context.

In relation to at least some of these forms of assessment, there will be a range of recognised considerations that need to be taken into account in making judgements according to the relevant standards. In the boxes below I have outlined what these could be for the first two types of assessment. I am not suggesting that these are complete or definitive statements of what is required, and they are based on assumptions about the nature of research that by no means everyone will share.[4] They are intended simply to indicate the difference, and relationship, between standards and relevant considerations for making judgements according to those standards.

---

4 For the approach on which they are based, see Hammersley (1997a).

**Box 1: Considerations in assessing the adequacy of
          research reports**

The following considerations cover both clarity and sufficiency as standards:

1.  The clarity of writing:

    a.  Consistency in use of terms
    b.  Are definitions provided where necessary?
    c.  Are sentences sufficiently well constructed to be intelligible and unambiguous?
    d.  Is there use of inappropriate rhetoric?

2.  The problem or question being addressed:

    a.  Is this clearly outlined?
    b.  Is sufficient rationale provided for its significance?

3.  The formulation of the main claims:

    a.  Are these made sufficiently clear and unambiguous?
    b.  Are the relations with subordinate claims (including evidence) made sufficiently
        explicit?
    c.  Is the character of each claim (as description, explanation, theory, evaluation,
        or prescription) indicated?

4.  The formulation of the conclusions:

    a.  Is there a distinction between main claims about the cases studied and gen-
        eral conclusions?
    b.  Is the basis for the conclusions signalled?

5.  The account of the research process and of the researcher:

    a.  Is there sufficient, and not too much, information about the research process?
    b.  Is there sufficient, and not too much, information about the researcher? (In
        other words, is what is necessary and no more provided for assessing the
        validity of the findings, the value of the methods, the competence of the
        researcher, according to what is appropriate?)

---

**Box 2: Considerations in assessing the significance of
          research findings**

As regards validity, the following considerations might be involved:

1.  The main claims and evidence:

    a.  Are the main claims plausible or credible enough to be accepted at face value?
    b.  If not, is evidence provided?
    c.  If so, is the evidence sufficient, both in terms of strongly implying the validity of the
        main knowledge claim and in being sufficiently plausible or credible to be accepted?

d. If not, is a further layer of evidence provided?

e. If so, is this evidence sufficient? And so on.

2. The relationship between the findings about the cases studied and the conclusions drawn:

a. Where these are empirical generalisations about some finite population, on the basis of whatever evidence is provided, are they sufficiently plausible or credible to be accepted?

b. Where they are theoretical statements of a conditional causal kind, on the basis of the evidence provided are they sufficiently plausible or credible to be accepted?

In relation to relevance, the considerations might be:

1. *The importance of the topic*: the research must relate (directly or indirectly) to an issue of importance to the intended audience, or to some potential audience.

2. *The contribution of the conclusions to existing knowledge*: the research findings must add something to our knowledge of the issue to which they relate. Research that merely confirms what is already beyond reasonable doubt makes no contribution (though research which corroborates what was previously suspected but not known with confidence *is* of value.)

In these terms, research findings may connect with an important topic but still not be relevant since they do not tell us anything new about it. Conversely, research may add new knowledge, but this may relate to no topic of any importance and so still lack relevance. Importance and contribution are necessary and jointly sufficient conditions for relevance.

I am arguing, then, that specifying standards, and considerations in terms of which they can be assessed, is likely to be of value even though it can be no substitute for practical judgement. However, as noted earlier, much of the pressure for qualitative criteria comes not so much from the context of *researchers* judging research, or even students learning to do this, but rather from that of lay 'users' of research (notably policymakers and practitioners) assessing its quality. It might seem, on the basis of the above discussion, that there is an insurmountable problem here: that, by contrast with researchers, lay people will not have the background knowledge, skill and experience necessary to judge quality; and if guidelines are provided they may be overly reliant upon these. This is true in one sense, and false in another. Moreover this ambiguity points to the crucial problem of the interface between research and other sorts of specialised activity; whether policymaking, pressure-group politics, or occupational work of various kinds (Hammersley 2002). It is true that lay users will not have equivalent knowledge of the research literature, or the experience of and capacity for making judgements about research that comes from practising it. And, as I have emphasised, no set of criteria can substitute for this. On the other hand, lay users of research are not simply ignorant or lacking in all skill, for example as regards assessing knowledge claims for relevance and validity. Indeed, this capacity is an essential element of many forms of activity, in fact of everyday life generally. The problem that faces lay users, then, is twofold: how to assess research findings in the terms in which these present themselves; and how to relate these findings to what they already know and take for granted, and the practical context in which they are operating. There seems to be a built-in tendency here for extreme reactions: for lay users either to adopt too reverent an attitude towards the products of research or simply to dismiss these where they conflict with what is taken to be existing knowledge. An oscilla- tion between these extremes can be difficult to avoid: it probably stems from the tensions between the relevant capacities that lay users do and do not have.

Any set of criteria offered by researchers could only deal with the first of these tasks: how to assess findings in research terms. It could not help with the problem of relating them to practical, experiential knowledge; not least because the latter will be highly variegated. Furthermore, to repeat the point, no set of criteria can remedy lay users' lack of practical experience of research. The implication of this is that, to a considerable extent, they must trust researchers: they must assume, unless there is strong evidence to the contrary, that the latter have carried out their work effectively, that they have presented their findings honestly, that the normal processes of criticism within the research community have reduced the danger of error, and so on. Whether researchers *deserve* such trust depends upon how they operate, but there is no mechanism that can check independently that the knowl- edge they produce is sound in research terms, or even that they have pursued this knowledge in the most effective way that is legitimate.

The need for trust cannot be eradicated in this context, any more than it can be in other forms of contact between specialised practitioners and lay people. As already hinted, trust does not have to be blind trust, it may be possible for lay users to make some judgement about the coherence and reasonableness of what researchers say, but they must take care not to dismiss what does not fit their current frame of reference *for that reason alone.* There is clearly a dilemma here. On the one hand, the whole point of research is that it may produce un- commonsensical conclusions, and therefore its findings must not be rejected because they are counter-intuitive. On the other hand, people's experience and background knowledge will often give them important resources with which to interrogate, modify, or reject research findings, especially in terms of how these relate to particular contexts of action with which they are familiar, and as regards their implications for practical action. But good judgement is required here by lay users, just as much as it is on the part of researchers.[5]

---

5 It is also important to note that it is quite legitimate, for certain purposes, for lay users of research to be less interested in the validity of particular research findings than in how these can be employed in promoting or defending some cause.

In short, I am arguing that it is not possible for researchers to make their judgements fully explicit, in the sense of being intelligible for and open to sound assessment by *anyone*, irrespective of background knowledge and experience. Indeed, there are limits to the extent to which these judgements can be made intelligible even to fellow researchers, because of the situated nature of judgement and differences even across the same field of research. Certainly, it is the case that such intelligibility is an *achievement*, it is not automatic: speakers need to be able to formulate the situation, the reasons for making the judgements that they did, and so on, in ways that facilitate understanding; and, equally importantly, the audience must be willing and able to draw the right inferences from what is said, on the basis of the background resources they have. The greater the experiential distance between speaker and hearer, the larger this problem of communication will be. And because the use of criteria always depends upon background knowledge and judgement, they cannot solve this problem even if they can serve as a useful resource in dealing with it.[6]

Indeed, guidelines can exacerbate the problem where lay audiences interpret them in ways that are at odds with the practical expertise of researchers, or treat them as if they *could* substitute for that expertise. And there are current circumstances that encourage this. The demand for qualitative research criteria that lay users can employ has arisen, to a large extent, in the context of the evidence-based practice movement (Trinder with Reynolds 2000; Thomas and Pring 2004) and against the background of what has been termed 'the new public management' (Pollitt 1990; Ferlie et al. 1996; Ridley 1996; Clarke and Newman 1997). A central theme here is 'transparency', for example it is demanded that the basis on which professionals work should be made explicit, so that the lay people who use their services can judge the quality of what is provided.

There are two ways in which social research is caught up in this. First, it is seen as capable of supplying the evidence on which more effective policy and practice can be based: it is regarded as offering the impersonal evidence that is essential in order to hold professional practice to account (Oakley 2000). But, and this is the crucial point in this context, in order for it to do this it must itself be 'transparent', so that lay users can determine which research findings can and cannot be relied upon. Fortunately or unfortunately, depending upon one's point of view, the idea that research can achieve this ideal is a mirage. For reasons already explained, and they parallel those that apply to other forms of professional practice, there is no possibility of full transparency; in the sense of lay people being in a position *consistently* to make judgements about the

---

6  Here I am, of course, abstracting away from the very real possibility that the judgements of both researchers and 'users' will be biased by their values, preferences and interests.

research quality of particular studies that are equally as good as those of researchers who work in the relevant field.

To a large extent, then, I think that qualitative researchers are right to resist demands for a fully explicit set of evaluation criteria: the nature of research (in general, not just of qualitative work) is such that these cannot operate in the way that is frequently assumed by those who demand them. And the same is true as regards lay use of research findings. Here too, good judgement is required and this cannot be reduced to explicit rules.

Even so, I believe that qualitative researchers need to give much more attention than they do currently to thinking about how they should assess their own work and that of others. This is not so much a matter of producing lists of criteria, in the sense of considerations that might need to be taken into account, useful though that undoubtedly is, but rather of collectively deliberating about what is involved in the various kinds of assessment relevant to research, and developing more of a consensus about relevant standards and considerations. However, currently there is a major obstacle to this process: the plurality of approaches to qualitative research that now exists, and the way that these are often regarded as incommensurable paradigms. These generate not just abstract methodological debates but also practical disagreement about the quality of particular studies; even if this is not always quite as great as might be expected on the basis of paradigmatic declarations.

## Is agreement about qualitative criteria possible?

It is an obvious fact about qualitative research today that it is divided not just in terms of substantive focus, or even according to the use of particular methods, but by some divergent theoretical, methodological, and value assumptions. These concern the nature of the phenomena being investigated, how they can and should be researched, and what research is for.[7] In other words, there are different, and to some extent competing, 'paradigms'. The key questions that this raises are whether it is possible and desirable to overcome these differences, and if so how this can be done.

The term 'paradigm', in the sense being used here, derives, of course, from the work of the historian and philosopher of science Thomas Kuhn. There has been much discussion of what Kuhn meant by 'paradigm', and it is clear that he used the word in somewhat different ways.[8] However, his core argument

---

7 I am not suggesting that by contrast quantitative research is entirely homogeneous, it is not. Experimental and survey research have conflicting orientations in some key respects. However, the differences do not lie at so deep a level as in the case of qualitative research.

8 For excellent recent discussions of Kuhn's work, see Hoyningen-Huene (1993), Bird (2000) and Sharrock and Read (2002).

was that natural scientists working within a mature field operate with a set of assumptions, about the relevant region of the world and how to understand it, that are embodied in their use of certain studies as exemplars; in other words, they take these for granted as the basis for further work. Of course, there are always things that do not seem to fit into their current understanding, and the task of what Kuhn called 'normal science' is to treat these as puzzles that can be solved *without modification to paradigmatic assumptions*. However, he famously argued that, over time, some puzzles turn out to be anomalies that cannot be resolved within these limits; and that, at some point, an alternative paradigm will arise that takes over the field, because it is able to explain all of what the previous paradigm covered and also resolves the anomalies that had arisen within it. He labels this the process of scientific revolution.

Now there have been many disputes about the accuracy of Kuhn's account of natural science, but the task of applying it to social science is even more complex and uncertain. Kuhn regarded the social sciences as pre-paradigmatic, at best, and therefore as not characterised by competing paradigms, in his sense of the word. And, even were we to ignore this, there is very little social research that approximates to his notion of normal science. Instead, much of it, over the past three decades, seems to have been in a state of continual 'revolution', albeit of a kind that is not recognisably scientific in Kuhnian terms.

At the same time, it probably *is* the case that social scientists operate on the basis of exemplar studies and models, and that this is part of the reason why they often adopt rather different approaches to the same topic, and why they sometimes disagree so sharply about methodology. Interpreted correctly, Kuhn's work is an important counter to any tendency to adopt too cognitivist a conception of conflicting approaches among researchers. It is not that people first acquire epistemological and ontological assumptions and then decide how they are going to investigate the social world. Rather, they acquire particular research practices and various methodological and philosophical assumptions, consciously and unconsciously, more or less simultaneously; and each subsequently shapes the other. This means that the differences among qualitative researchers are embedded in diverse forms of situated practice that incorporate characteristic ways of thinking and feeling about the research process. Furthermore, we are not so much faced with a set of clearly differentiated qualitative approaches as with a complex landscape of variable practice in which the inhabitants use a range of labels ('ethnography', 'discourse analysis', 'life history work', 'narrative study', 'activity theory', 'interpretivism', 'feminist standpoint epistemology', 'postmodernism', and so on) in diverse and open-ended ways in order to characterise their orientation; and probably do this somewhat differently across audiences and occasions.

So what is involved in paradigm conflict is not simply a clash of ideas about what form social research ought to take; but, rather, a divergence in *practices*. I can develop one aspect of this by drawing on the methodological arguments of the sociologist Max Weber. He inherited the view, from neo-Kantianism and the German historical sciences, that social inquiry, by contrast with natural science, must be idiographic rather than nomothetic in orientation. What this means is that social scientists are primarily interested in understanding particular social phenomena in their socio-historical contexts, rather than in discovering universal scientific laws. Moreover, by contrast with other neo-Kantians, Weber believed that in identifying and conceptualising particular phenomena for study, social scientists could not draw on objective or eternal values to define what is worth investigation. Rather, value-relevance is perspectival: there are discrepant value perspectives, which give different aspects of the social world more or less importance, and among which there is no ultimate rational basis that can determine choice. So, social scientists can adopt a range of different value perspectives in order to identify relevant phenomena for investigation; though they need not believe, and certainly should not claim to have established through research or on any other basis, that the one they have adopted is the only legitimate or true one.

The point of this is that if, in order to identify phenomena that are worth investigating, we necessarily draw on some set of values, to which there are always alternatives – and if, as seems likely, what are involved here are not only values but also factual assumptions about the nature of the phenomena concerned – then there will inevitably be significant lines of division within social research. What I mean by this is that there will be forms of research within this field that operate within discrepant frameworks of assumption.

Now, the reason why I employed the work of Weber to make this point is because he did *not* believe that social science research is necessarily, even less that it should be, political; in the sense of being geared towards political goals. There are quite a lot of qualitative researchers today who insist that research ought to be political in this sense: that it should aim at the eradication of social inequality of various kinds, that it should improve the lives of some groups of people (ethnic minorities, the disabled, women, and children, for example), that it should serve the goals of public policy, and so on.[9] It is not hard to see that this is likely to lead to diverse paradigms sometimes reflecting incompatible orientations; unless one holds to the idea, characteristic of some Enlightenment thinkers, that there is a single, all-embracing conception of 'the good' that will be recognised (at least in the medium term) by everyone. Weber did not believe this, and this was why he thought social research should aim to be value-neutral: in other words, that practical values (values other than truth) should not constitute the goal of social science inquiry, *even though they are needed to provide the value-relevant framework in terms of which the phenomena to be studied are identified*. My point, then, is that if – even from *Weber's* point of view, rather than from a position which assumes that all social science is inevitably political (in

---

9  For discussion of these orientations, see Hammersley (2000 and 2004a).

the broadest sense of that word) and therefore necessarily divided by allegiances to discrepant worldviews, interests, etc. – we can see how social research could be characterised by competing paradigms (in a non–Kuhnian sense), then we perhaps should resist any inclination to dismiss paradigm differentiation in social science as entirely the product of bias, theoretical or methodological fashion, career-building, etc., as is sometimes done.

Weber did not believe that value relevance is a matter of partisan definition; he assumed that those who fundamentally disagree about an issue could nevertheless concur regarding its importance and what is relevant to it. Indeed, he argued that research could play a role in facilitating the resolution of disagreements through both providing relevant factual evidence and clarifying the implications of different value positions; though he recognised that there was no guarantee that it could completely resolve any disagreement, since there are ineradicable conflicts among fundamental values. However, it seems to me that it is also crucial to recognise that these conflicts can generate differences in view about what are and are not important issues, or about the relative priority of different issues. As a consequence, there may be research topics that are believed to be important by some researchers but which are regarded as pointless or as positively harmful, or at least as of little importance, by others. Let me try to illustrate this with an example from the field of education:

There has been a body of research on gender inequalities in children's participation in school classrooms, both in terms of level and kind of participation.[10] In order to accept that this is a worthwhile topic of inquiry, one must, first of all, believe that there should be equality between the sexes in some sense of that term. And this may not be accepted either by those on the religious Right or perhaps even by some radical feminists, both of whom identify fundamental differences in orientation between males and females, though of course they view these in sharply discrepant ways. In order to see this topic as important, one probably *also* has to assume that particular kinds of inequality in patterns of classroom interaction are consequential for educational achievement; and, in addition, one must value highly educational achievement, defined, for example, in terms of examination success. Yet, there are those who question whether gender inequalities, or those of other kinds, in classroom participation have determinate and consequential effects on outcomes; and there are others who deny that examinations measure education and/or who insist that examinations are at odds with true education. What I am trying to show, then, is that research in this field is framed by a range of both value and factual assumptions that are open to actual, and perhaps also reasonable, disagreement.[11] What is involved here is not an instance of absolute 'incommensurability' (a problematic term even in the context of Kuhn's work) between points of view; it is rather that the fewer of the assumptions underpinning a field of research

---

10  For a more detailed discussion of work in this area, see Hammersley (1990).

11  For a broader attempt to outline assumptions involved in research on educational inequalities, and to show that some of them are debatable, see Foster et al. (1996).

people share the more difficult it will be for them to understand the point of the research, and the less inclined they will be to see it as of value, or to accept its conclusions as valid. Moreover, while there is scope for persuasion, so that one might come to recognise the significance of a particular form of research one did not previously value, this may often require arguments about values not just about facts. And, as a result, there is little guarantee that even lengthy discussion will produce a consensus.[12]

So I am arguing that some of the variation to be found within social research derives from the fact that it operates in diverse value-relevance niches. And I believe that these niches have consequences not just for judgements about what sorts of work are and are not worthwhile in terms of relevance, but even for judgements of validity. This is because the threshold that knowledge claims must reach if they are to be accepted, in terms of likely validity, is determined by relevant research communities – it is not something that can be laid down by the philosophy of science or by any central authority. And this implies that judgements about the quality of particular studies may differ sharply because of differences in background assumptions.[13]

Besides this variation in orientation arising from researchers operating within different value-relevance niches, there are also some more abstract sources of paradigm differentiation. And these two aspects of methodological pluralism are not, of course, completely independent: those working within particular niches draw on, modify, develop, and perhaps even misuse, more general ideas for their own purposes. They also sometimes portray their own work in general terms, as if it were social research writ large, thereby contributing to the intellectual resources that others may draw on in facilitating, justifying, and challenging work in other fields.

What I want to do in the rest of this chapter is to discuss three general issues about which there are sharp disagreements within the literature of qualitative research methodology that have important implications for judgements about quality. These relate to:

- different conceptions of scientific method and rigour;
- the conflict between constructionism and realism;
- the relationship between research and various other kinds of practical activity, including politics.

---

12 Much the same scope for variation in value-relevant focus can be found in other areas. For example, there is likely to be a fundamental difference in orientation between those studying the work of the police within a framework which assumes that policing is essential in a large, modern society and those who approach this topic from within, say, an anarchist perspective. This example was prompted by unpublished work on the nature of policing by Simon Blackburn, a PhD student at the Open University.

13 Of course, where researchers see the goal of their work as going beyond the production of knowledge, the disagreement will be even sharper (see Hammersley 1995:ch 4; 2000:ch 5).

## Scientific method and rigour

Natural science was the methodological model for most social research during much of the twentieth century. Conceptions of scientific method determined what counted as rigorous investigation. However, this did not prevent considerable disagreement about how social research ought to be pursued. There are several, interrelated, reasons for this.

First, different natural sciences were sometimes taken as exemplifying scientific method: for example, some researchers treated physics as the premier science, others took nineteenth-century biology as a more appropriate guide. Furthermore, there were also disciplines broadly within the social sciences that were treated by those working in other fields as exemplifying scientific method. Key examples here are behaviourist psychology, neo-classical economics, and structuralist linguistics. The point is, of course, that different exemplars of science or rigour can lead to very different prescriptions and forms of assessment.

Secondly, there were divergent philosophical interpretations of the 'method' employed by natural scientists. For instance, broadly speaking, moving from the nineteenth into the twentieth century there was a shift from an inductivist conception of inquiry, in which scientific laws were logically derived from observation of repeated patterns of occurrence, towards one which stressed the testing of hypotheses deduced from theories that were necessarily a product of speculative thought and that perhaps could never be proven to be true, only falsified at best – through being tested against evidence. Quite a lot of the conflict between social scientists promoting quantitative and those adopting qualitative methods in the first seventy years of the twentieth century stemmed from commitment to different notions of scientific method along these lines, with qualitative researchers tending to adopt a more inductivist approach, very loosely defined. This, of course, is only one of the dimensions along which there has been variation in interpretation of scientific method. Others include realism versus instrumentalism or conventionalism (see Keat and Urry 1975), and the nature of and need for measurement (Cicourel 1964).

Finally, there was variation in views about the degree and character of the differences between physical and social phenomena, and what the implications of these were for how far the methods of natural science needed to be modified if they were to be applied in the social field. At one extreme, there were those who took physics as exemplifying scientific method, and who believed that there were no distinctive features of social phenomena, or that if there were these did not stand in the way of rigorous measurement and control of variables. By contrast, others insisted that social phenomena had to be approached quite differently from physical phenomena. Indeed, it was sometimes argued that whereas the latter could only be studied from outside, social phenomena could and should be understood from within, so that a deeper form of knowledge was available. And it was claimed that this inner understanding required the researcher to draw upon his or her psychological and/or cultural resources to grasp the meanings that informed the actions of the people being studied, since these meanings are crucial for what it is that people set out to do, and why. In particular, it was insisted that these meanings cannot be inferred from external behaviour. To use Clifford Geertz's example, taken from Gilbert Ryle: there are significant differences between a facial tic that forces the closure of one eye, a wink, someone pretending to wink, and someone practising winking (Geertz 1973a:6). The key point in this context is that it is not possible to infer from physical behaviour alone which of these is taking place. Given this, some other, or additional, means of access must be secured to the cultural meanings that inform people's behaviour if we are to be able even to describe it accurately, let alone to explain it. All this did not necessarily lead to a rejection of science, but rather to the construction of distinctive conceptions of it, ones judged as suited to studying the social world.

Now qualitative researchers today vary in whether they see their work as scientific and, if they do, in what they take this to imply. And, aside from this, there are significant differences concerning what is regarded as possible or legitimate in epistemic terms. A recent illustration is what has been called the 'radical critique of interviews' (Murphy et al. 1998:120–3; see Chapter 5). This does not just raise questions about over-reliance on interview data – a common complaint, for example, on the part of ethnographers who, in the past at least, tended to stress the centrality of participant observation. What makes recent criticisms of interview research radical is that they challenge the main ways that many qualitative researchers have used, and continue to use, interviews today.

It is worth pointing out that the radical critique of interviews challenges a conception of rigour that is central to some forms of ethnography – for example that exemplified by interpretative anthropology – and replaces it with a view of rigour that is characteristic of many forms of discourse analysis. Discourse analysts often insist that the data must be presented to readers so that the latter can assess directly the validity of the inferences made, and perhaps also that inference must not range beyond what is 'observable' in the data. By contrast, ethnographers often argue that it is not possible for them to make all their data available to readers, that the validity of their inferences depends upon the success with which they have learned the culture of the people they are studying, and thereby have become able to interpret accurately what meanings various phenomena have for them. Moreover, some would question whether discourse analysts are actually presenting, or can present, 'the data' to readers; given that transcriptions involve theoretical assumptions about language-use, that how they are read will depend upon cultural background, and so on (see Chapter 6).

So, without even touching on post-structuralism and postmodernism, the usual bogeymen in this context, I have tried to show that there are divergent conceptions of the requirements of inquiry to be found among qualitative researchers. And it is not difficult to see how these can lead to disagreement in judgements about what is good quality work.

## Realism versus constructionism

Constructionism is one of the sources from which the radical critique of interview analysis arose.[14] The generic move of constructionism against realism is to insist that social phenomena do not exist independently of people's understandings of them, in other words that those understandings play a crucial generative role. Of course, many realists would accept, indeed insist, that social phenomena are the product of 'people acting together' rather than entirely a result of social forces operating beyond their knowledge and control. What is distinctive about constructionism, in the broad sense of that term, is that it takes the fact that social phenomena are culturally constituted and draws from it the conclusion that these phenomena can only be understood by describing *the processes by which* they are culturally constituted as the things they are. In other words, a re-definition of the goal of inquiry is required. The focus becomes, not the phenomena themselves, and certainly not what might have caused them or what effects they produce, but rather the discursive processes by which they are constituted and identified by culture members. For example, rather than studying families as groups interacting within and beyond the context of their homes, thereby relying on some analytic definition of what a family is, the focus becomes how people talk about what families are, both explicitly and perhaps even more importantly implicitly, how they use notions of family life, ideas about kin obligations, etc. in the course of their interactions with one another. So people's accounts of these phenomena are not treated as descriptions of patterns of social relations that exist independently of them but rather as forms of language-in-action whose social significance lies in their practical functions rather than any representational capacity.

It is not just the realist/constructionist divide that generates divergences here in how research is assessed. There are important differences in orientation *within* this broadly defined constructionism. One version is modelled on ethnomethodology (see Zimmerman and Pollner 1971; Lynch 1993). It suggests that the constitutive processes by which social phenomena are ongoingly produced can be uncovered or displayed in a manner that does not involve any cultural interpretation or inference on the part of the researcher. All that is involved, it is claimed, is description, in the sense of explication. The terms of this explication are entirely those of the activity being explicated. This position does not imply any form of epistemological scepticism; in other words, it need not be denied that the actions and institutions people produce through their

---

14 I am using the term 'constructionism' in a broad way here to incorporate ethnomethodology and conversation analysis; though I will also address their distinctiveness.

actions have a real existence as particulars. What *is* denied, though, is that these can be grouped into natural kinds in any other way than in terms of the processes that constituted them; and perhaps not even in that way either. Furthermore, we must remember that there is no one-to-one correspondence between some constitutive cultural notion, like family form, and the actions it is used to produce and how these interrelate with other actions. This is because such notions may be 'honoured in the breach', 'stretched' in various ways, joked about, and so on.

A quite different way of operating, characteristic of epistemologically radical forms of constructionism, is to treat researchers as themselves necessarily engaged in constituting the social world, or particular social phenomena, through the writing process; rather than simply describing or displaying how others discursively construct the world through their actions.[15] This often leads to a blurring of the boundary between social research and imaginative literature. In fact, from this point of view, the whole of conventional social research cannot but be, in effect, simply a form of fiction which is falsely conscious of its own character and therefore operates in 'bad faith'.

These two approaches, which by no means exhaust the kinds of work constructionism has generated, imply very different modes of assessing research from one another, as well as from realism. For the first, the concern, presumably, is with whether particular descriptions of the constitutive processes of social life are accurate, in other words whether what is displayed is indeed these processes. By contrast, the second position rejects any idea of validity in this sense, and the accounts produced by researchers must be judged in non-epistemic terms, for instance according to aesthetic, ethical, and/or political criteria. One way of thinking about the shift from realism to this latter kind of constructionism is in terms of the replacement of Kuhn by Rorty as the patron philosopher of qualitative research. Whereas Kuhn still sees natural science as engaged in a process of inquiry, in which knowledge is accumulated, albeit in a discontinuous and diversifying rather than a continuous and cumulative way, Rorty abandons the residual realism to be found in Kuhn's account. In effect, he erases the distinction between inquiry, which is concerned with gaining knowledge, and conversation, conceived as guided by an interest in 'edification'. Indeed, he treats social inquiry, understood in its conventional way, as labouring under a mistaken conception of itself, one that assumes that it is possible (and desirable) to claim superior knowledge of reality.[16]

---

15 To a large extent, this approach arose from structuralism and the various moves beyond or behind it that have come to be labelled 'post-structuralism' (see Chapter 7). There are significant parallels, as well as important differences, between ethnomethodology, inspired by phenomenology, and structuralism.

16 The issues involved here are complex ones, and Rorty is open to different interpretations. However, see Putnam's criticisms of his position (Putnam 2002:99–100).

There are many varieties of both constructionism and realism, but I hope this discussion gives some sense of the major implications that such a contrast in orientation can have for judgements about the quality of particular pieces of research. The point is that these amount to fundamental differences that it may be impossible to bridge.

## Activism: the relationship of research to politics, policymaking and practice

What comes under the heading of 'activism', like that of 'constructionism', is quite diverse in character. But my point is that there are various qualitative approaches that explicitly reject the idea that the production of knowledge should be the only immediate goal of inquiry: in place of what they see as mere contemplation they insist on 'action'.[17] Advocates of some of these approaches believe that research should form an integral part of other kinds of practice, and argue that it is rendered useless, or at least debased in value, when separated out from these.[18] Indeed, there are those who claim that any process of institution-alisation, whereby inquiry is concentrated in special institutions, such as universities, is now being reversed through the rise of a new mode of knowledge production which occurs in the context of, and directly addresses, practical problems of various kinds (Gibbons et al. 1994; Gibbons 2000). Other approaches insist on the inevitably *political* character of research, requiring that it must be explicitly directed towards bringing about change of one sort or another: challenging capitalism, patriarchy, racism, the social conditions that generate disability, homophobia, and so on.[19]

Now, what is relevant here is that all these approaches introduce extra or alternative considerations in judging the quality of research findings, additional to or instead of the traditional epistemic ones concerned with the production of knowledge. The nature of these criteria varies, of course, depending upon the form of practice to which research is to be tied, or with which it is to be integrated. The criteria may be political, ethical, aesthetic, or even economic – for example, concerned with whether there is demand for what is being produced, whether it offers value for money, and so on.

---

17 The term 'activism' is not entirely satisfactory, not least because it might seem to imply that conventional kinds of social research are inactive, being the pastime of those closed off from the world in their ivory towers. Needless to say, I do not accept this implication.

18 Some advocates of action research seem to come close to this position (see Elliott 1988). For a critique of this, see Hammersley (2003a and 2004b).

19 In both cases, it is arguable that there is an unwarranted move from 'is' to 'ought' (see Hammersley 1995:ch 6 and 2008c).

In their early versions, these activist conceptions of research treated the goal of producing knowledge as compatible with, or even conducive to, the pursuit of practical goals. For example, in its original form, Marxism conflated epistemic with other considerations, on the basis of the Hegelian assumption that the development of knowledge and the realisation of other ideals are strongly interrelated in a historical dialectic. More recently, that assumption has been abandoned by 'critical' researchers, and as a result practical or political goals have often been raised above, or have replaced, epistemic ones. This has usually been done on the argument, associated with some kinds of constructionism or relativism, that the pursuit of knowledge, in the conventional sense of that term, is futile. Alternatively, there are arguments for interventionism that dismiss traditional kinds of qualitative research on ethical grounds as a form of voyeurism (see Denzin 1992:151). There are also interventionist approaches that are aesthetic rather than either scientific or ethical in character. Here research is to be a form of performance art, indeed it may be argued that it cannot but be this, and the requirement is that it be consciously shaped aesthetically, at most only hiding behind the masks of science or ethics in an ironic, knowing way.[20] It is not difficult to see that the criteria relevant here would be significantly different again.

## Conclusion

In this chapter, I have explored some of the issues surrounding the idea that agreement about assessment criteria for qualitative research is possible and desirable. I raised questions about what the term 'criteria' refers to, but suggested that outlining assessment standards and indicating considerations relevant to them can be desirable, so long as they are not seen as a substitute for the practical capacity to evaluate research. In the second half of the chapter, I argued that some fundamental differences in assumptions generate the methodological pluralism that is characteristic of qualitative research today, and that this has profound consequences for the prospect of agreement about criteria.

There have been various responses to this methodological pluralism, including the following:

1.  The apparent differences are spurious, amounting simply to rhetoric: when it comes to actually doing research there is much less variation than the methodological debates suggest. (From this pragmatist position, even the wilder flights of methodological fancy may be regarded as useful antidotes

---

20 I have not been able to find any clear presentation of this argument for intervention, but an example of the approach is Miller and Whalley (2005). I am not suggesting that these authors would accept my description as an accurate account of their motivation.

to traditional prejudices, but it will usually be insisted that one should not take any form of methodology straight or in large doses.)[21]

2.  There are deep-seated incompatibilities in approach, and we must simply recognise that diverse forms of social research will develop, each having its own distinctive conception of what is good quality work, and its own ways of applying this. And these differences must be respected.[22]

3.  There are serious differences in perspective, but some means needs to be found to at least reduce them, so as to increase the level of agreement across social researchers' judgements about what is and is not good quality work. Clarifying standards of assessment and considerations relevant to them may serve a useful function in this.

My position is, broadly speaking, the third. However, the sources of division I have identified in this chapter vary in character and in their implications for assessing quality. The first – diversity in value relevancies – is probably not a serious barrier to generating a common set of criteria, so long as it is recognised that these cannot be used as a fully explicit and exhaustive checklist, and that somewhat different considerations may apply in different substantive fields. As regards conflicting views of what counts as rigour, I suspect that (at least in the longer run) if this can be separated out from other issues it is open to resolution through reflection on and discussion about the research process: different conceptions of rigour must be judged in practical terms according to their productivity.

A selective strategy may be required as regards the realism–constructionism divide. In the case of those constructionists who focus on understanding discursive practices of various kinds, the conflict with older forms of realist social science may be resolvable by treating it as reflecting a difference in disciplinary orientation; in other words, as resulting from a fundamental difference in focus. In these terms, there is no need for competition or conflict, so long as neither side formulates its position in such a way as to render the other discipline illegitimate; and assuming that each side is suitably modest in the claims it makes for itself. Furthermore, while one might reasonably expect the same assessment *standards* to hold across disciplines, the considerations that need to be taken into account are likely to vary, depending upon the sorts of research question addressed and the kinds of data, methods, and forms of inference that these imply.

---

21  Seale (1999) provides an example of this sort of position.

22  Hodkinson (2004) illustrates this position, on which see Hammersley (2005b). It is worth noting that this does not have to be taken as implying that there are incommensurable paradigms, the exponents of which simply cannot understand one another. An alternative metaphor is of different language communities; where, though true translation is not possible, learning the other language is. This is an analogy that Kuhn uses in his later work, as against the perceptual analogy on which he relies in *The Structure of Scientific Revolutions* (Kuhn 1970 and 2003).

By contrast, in the case of more radical kinds of constructionism, the only response can be to try to insist that its advocates face the inconsistencies that their position implies. One way of doing this is illustrated by Harry Gensler in his book *Formal Ethics*. He offers an imaginary conversation with a Hegelian who denies the law of non-contradiction:

A:  Are you still a follower of Hegel?

B:  Of course! I believe everything he wrote. Since he denied the law of noncontradiction, I deny this too. On my view, P is entirely compatible with not-P.

A:  I'm a fan of Hegel myself. But he didn't deny the law of noncontradiction! You read the wrong commentators!

B:  You're wrong, he did deny this! Let me get my copy of *The Science of Logic*.

A:  Don't get so upset! You said that he did deny the law, and I said that he didn't. Aren't these compatible on your view? After all, you think that P is compatible with not-P.

B:  Yes, I guess they're compatible.

A:  No they aren't!

B:  Yes they are!

A:  Don't get so upset! You said that they are compatible, and I said that they aren't. Aren't these two compatible on your view? Recall that you think that P is compatible with not-P.

B:  Yes, I guess they're compatible. I'm getting confused.

A:  And you're also not getting confused, right?

(Gensler 1996:36–7)

Perhaps even more difficult to deal with the radical constructionism are the differences generated by what I have referred to as activism. As we saw, this either requires research to supplement its goal of producing knowledge with other goals, or proposes the adoption of these other goals in place of the pursuit of knowledge. The former position is likely to render research incoherent, unable to achieve any goal effectively – least of all the production of knowledge; while the latter amounts to the disguised abandonment of research in favour of some other activity (Hammersley 2000). Furthermore, aside from the problem of reconciling activist and non-activist conceptions of research, we should note that there is likely to be little agreement as regards assessment criteria even *among* activist researchers, given that they can be motivated by very different political or practical enterprises. In the case of activism, it seems to me that we need collectively to define exactly what can and cannot count as research. However, I am not optimistic that agreement can be reached about this. On Kuhn's account, reaching agreement is by no means straightforward even where there is consensus about the purpose and intended product of the enterprise; where this is not present it seems likely to be virtually impossible.

My conclusion is that criteria for qualitative research are desirable, for the reasons I outlined at the beginning of the chapter. However, the barriers to our being able to agree on these are formidable. At the same time, we should not simply accept methodological pluralism at face value, since doing so simply reinforces it by treating each qualitative approach as having its own unique set of quality criteria. Dialogue on this issue, across different approaches – and, indeed, across the qualitative–quantitative divide – is essential for the future of social research.

# Epilogue

'At least knowing where the difficulty lies, we should be prevented from engaging in the practice of the ostrich or in expecting some form of magic to make the problem vanish.' (Herbert Blumer)

I am confident that this book has lived up to its title: it has raised many questions about qualitative research. I began, in the Introduction, by sketching some of the very different approaches that are now available, and various dangers and problems associated with them. In Chapter 1, I argued that qualitative inquiry has developed over the past half-century in ways that do not match the claims that were originally made for it. In some respects, this indicates that parts of the original rationale need rethinking. Therefore, in subsequent chapters I explored the notion of complexity, which has been and continues to be a central theme in the justifications offered for many forms of qualitative research; and I examined two longstanding, and contrasting, approaches designed to deal with it. I argued that Geertz's notion of 'thick description', while of value in telling us something about the nature of human social life and how to understand it, involves unresolved tensions that reflect fundamental problems with interpretivism that have been recognised since the nineteenth century. By contrast, those who have promoted the notion of analytic induction have struggled with the conceptual and methodological problems it faces, and in doing so have advanced thinking about important matters that anyone committed to a science of social life must address, as well as pointing to strategies for dealing with them. While they have not been entirely successful in this, they have provided a basis on which others can build.

Unfortunately, at present, few qualitative researchers are inclined to attempt this. One reason is that commitment to a social *science* has been abandoned by many, or it has been re-specified in terms of an exclusive focus on discourse. In the second part of the book I examined the arguments for these moves. I looked at the 'radical critique of interviewing', the ethnomethodological and constructionist approaches that underpin this, and then at 'postmodernism' and the idea that qualitative research must be viewed as a form of rhetoric, literary and/or political.

The final chapter addressed an aspect of research methodology where the conflict between competing conceptions of qualitative research comes to a head: the question of how studies and their findings ought to be evaluated. I considered the problems surrounding the notion that there should be explicit criteria of assessment; and the reasons why, at present, there can be little hope of reaching agreement, even at a relatively abstract level, about how qualitative research should be judged. These relate to the methodological pluralism that I highlighted in the Introduction.

It should be clear from this book that I believe qualitative research, and social science more generally, faces some very difficult problems that require much more focused and sustained attention than they currently receive. One reason why they do not get this attention derives from what I have already identified as being a key part of the problem: the sharp methodological and theoretical divisions that now exist among researchers. This encourages the treatment of some ideas and practices as *defining features* of particular approaches, and therefore as beyond question for those committed to them. On the basis of this, criticisms are simply dismissed, for example as relying on a discredited positivism or as reflecting the assumptions of a different paradigm; in this way, many qualitative researchers protect themselves from awkward questions.[1]

The continual emergence of new paradigms reflects forms of epistemological and political radicalisation that arise, in part, from the pressure, deriving from both outside and within, for social science to produce grand and novel solutions to both private troubles and public issues. Yet, it cannot provide solutions to these on its own; and in most cases the problems are intractable and the potential alleviations already well known, along with their drawbacks. I am not suggesting that social science can have no value beyond itself, but rather that its value is more limited and more piecemeal than many of us might wish. Furthermore, the pursuit of new paradigms that will make social science a transformative enterprise in personal and social terms discourages and detracts from the careful, painstaking thought and investigation required, including the methodological reflection that is necessary, if the progress that can be made is to be achieved.

A central thesis of this book is that we must work to overcome, or at least to reduce, methodological pluralism. It is not that all research can or should be done in the same standardised way. Rather, my point is that any approach to methodological thinking needs to engage with the same general issues. I am under no illusions that bringing about such constructive engagement will be easy, or result (in the short, or even the medium, term) in a broad consensus. But I do believe that we must move in this direction. While toleration of alternative approaches is a virtue up to a point, like all virtues it can turn into a vice; even more so the celebration of difference and diversity. There needs to be more clarity about the purpose and intended product of particular forms of research, about the methodological issues that are implicated in these, and about

---

1 This 'paradigm mentality' has been in operation for a long time (see Hammersley 1984).

the relative value of different ways of dealing with them. I do not believe that any approach is free of all problems. But, as Herbert Blumer points out, we must not bury our heads in the sand or try to magic them away.

Another reason why methodological problems are not given the attention they deserve is because of the influence of a certain kind of pragmatism: an impatience with what are seen as 'philosophical' difficulties. This can be found in many quarters. For example, in his book *The Quality of Qualitative Research* Clive Seale has argued that 'intense methodological awareness, if engaged too seriously, can create anxieties that hinder practice'. His view of the role of methodology is that 'if taken in small doses it can help to guard against more obvious errors' (Seale 1999:475). I have some sympathy for this position. I do not believe that the problems facing social research can be resolved by 'philosophy' or methodology alone, and some of them do not need to be resolved in order to produce worthwhile findings. However, this sort of pragmatism can easily turn into simply accepting and following traditional or standard strategies because they are widely accepted and seem to work. Given that these strategies and rationales vary across different kinds of qualitative inquiry, it is also a recipe for researchers simply going on as normal, working within existing, discrepant 'paradigms' and ignoring the problems. Some balance is required between methodological angst and blinkered pragmatism, although just where that balance ought to be struck is, of course, difficult to determine.

I am more sceptical about current ideas and practices within qualitative research, and social science more generally, than many others would be; and I have explained the reasons for this. The tone of this book may be judged overly pessimistic by some readers, but it is designed to counter what seems to me to be excessive optimism about the current capacity of social science, of all kinds, to produce sound knowledge. I am not suggesting that our work is incapable of doing this; even less that it has little value (since it can make other sorts of contribution besides supplying reliable knowledge, including encouraging necessary scepticism and reflection). But the spirit in which we put forward the results of our research needs to be tempered by recognition of the serious methodological problems we face in our work, and the inadequacy, in many respects, of the means we have available for dealing with them.

So, I hope that this book will encourage deeper engagement with these problems and lead to their being resolved, or at least handled more effectively, in the future. While it raises many questions, this book provides few answers. However, I hope that it does show what are likely to be more (and less) fruitful directions in which to go.

# References

Allen, W. (1983) *Without Feathers*. New York: Random House.

Almeder, R. (1980) *The Philosophy of Charles S. Peirce: a critical introduction*. Oxford: Blackwell.

Altheide, D. and Johnson, J. (1994) 'Criteria for assessing interpretive validity in qualitative research', in N. Denzin and Y. Lincoln (eds), *Handbook of Qualitative Research*. Thousand Oaks, CA: Sage.

Anderson, L. (2006) 'Analytic autoethnography', *Journal of Contemporary Ethnography*, 35(4): 373–95.

Antaki, C., Condor, S. and Levine, M. (1996) 'Social identities in talk: speakers' own orientations', *British Journal of Social Psychology* 35: 473–92.

Ashmore, M., Myers, G. and Potter, J. (1995) 'Discourse, rhetoric, reflexivity: seven days in the library', in S. Jasanoff, G.E. Markle, J.C. Petersen and T. Pinch (eds), *Handbook of Science and Technology Studies*. Thousand Oaks, CA: Sage.

Atkinson, E. (2004) 'Thinking outside the box: an exercise in heresy', *Qualitative Inquiry* 10(1): 111–29.

Atkinson, P. (1982) 'Writing and ethnography', in H.J. Helle (ed.), *Kultur und Institution*. Berlin: Dunker and Humblot.

Atkinson, P. (1988) 'Ethnomethodology: a critical review', *Annual Review of Sociology* 14: 441–65.

Atkinson, P. (1991) *The Ethnographic Imagination: textual construction of reality*. London: Routledge.

Atkinson, P. (1992) *Understanding Ethnographic Texts*. Newbury Park, CA: Sage.

Atkinson, P. (2006) 'Rescuing autoethnography', *Journal of Contemporary Ethnography* 35(4): 400–4.

Atkinson, P. and Coffey, A. (1995) 'Realism and its discontents: the crisis of cultural representation in ethnographic texts', in B. Adam and S. Allen (eds), *Theorising Culture*. London: UCL Press.

Atkinson, P. and Coffey, A. (2002) 'Revisiting the relationship between participant observation and interviewing', in J.F. Gubrium and J.A. Holstein (eds), *Handbook of Interview Research*. Thousand Oaks, CA: Sage.

Atkinson, P., Coffey, A. and Delamont, S. (2003) *Key Themes in Qualitative Research*. Walnut Creek, CA: Alta Mira.

Atkinson, P. and Delamont, S. (2004) 'Qualitative research and the post-modern turn', in M. Hardy and A. Bryman (eds), *Handbook of Data Analysis*. London: Sage.

Atkinson, P. and Delamont, S. (2006) 'In the roiling smoke: qualitative inquiry and contested fields', *International Journal of Qualitative Studies in Education* 19(6): 747–55.

Atkinson, P., Delamont, S. and Hammersley, M. (1993) 'Qualitative research traditions', in M. Hammersley (ed.), *Educational Research: contemporary issues*. London: Paul Chapman. (Earlier version published in *Review of Educational Research* 58(2): 231–50.)

Atkinson, P.A. and Silverman, D. (1997) 'Kundera's *Immortality*: the interview society and the invention of the self', *Qualitative Inquiry* 3: 304–25.

Austin, J.L. (1962) *How To Do Things with Words*. Oxford: Oxford University Press.

Baker, C. (1984) 'The search for adultness: membership work in adolescent–adult talk', *Human Studies* 7: 301–23.

Baker, C. (1997) 'Membership categorisation and interview accounts', in D. Silverman (ed.), *Qualitative Research: theory, method and practice*. London: Sage.

Baker, C. and Johnson, G. (1998) 'Interview talk as professional practice', *Language and Education* 12(4): 229–42.

Ball, S.J. (1990) *Politics and Policy Making in Education: explorations in policy sociology*. London: Routledge.

Barnes, B. (1974) *Scientific Knowledge and Sociological Theory*. London: Routledge and Kegan Paul.

Barthes, R. (1975) *S/Z*. London: Jonathan Cape. (First published in French in 1970.)

Baruch, G. (1981) 'Moral tales: parents' stories of encounters with the health profession', *Sociology of Health and Illness* 3: 275–96.

Becker, H.S. (1963) *Outsiders*. New York: Free Press.

Becker, H.S. (1967) 'Whose side are we on?', *Social Problems* 14: 239–47.

Becker, H.S. (1986) *Writing for Social Scientists*. Chicago: University of Chicago Press.

Becker, H.S. (1992) 'Cases, causes, conjunctures, stories and imagery', in C. Ragin and H.S. Becker (eds), *What is a Case? Exploring the foundations of social inquiry*. Cambridge: Cambridge University Press.

Becker H.S. (1994) '"Foi por acaso": conceptualising coincidence', *Sociological Quarterly* 35(2): 183–94.

Becker, H.S. (1998) *Tricks of the Trade*. Chicago: University of Chicago Press.

Becker, H.S. and Geer, B. (1957) 'Participant observation and interviewing: a comparison', *Human Organization* 16(3): 28–32.

Behar, R. and Gordon, D. (eds) (1995) *Women Writing Culture*. Berkeley, CA: University of California Press.

Bennett, J. (1966) *Kant's Analytic*. Cambridge: Cambridge University Press.

Berger, P. and Luckmann, T. (1969) *The Social Construction of Reality*. Harmondsworth: Penguin.

Berman, M. (1982) *All that is Solid Melts into Air: the experience of modernity*. New York: Simon and Schuster.

Bhaskar, R. (1975) *A Realist Theory of Science*. Leeds: Leeds Books.

Bhaskar, R. (1989) *The Possibility of Naturalism* (2nd edn). Hassocks: Harvester.

Biesta, G. (2007) 'Why "what works" won't work: evidence-based practice and the democratic deficit in educational research', *Educational Theory* 57(1): 1–22.

Billig, M., Condor, S., Edwards, D., Gane, M., Middleton, D. and Radley, A.R. (1988) *Ideological Dilemmas*. London: Sage.

Bird, A. (2000) *Thomas Kuhn*. Princeton, NJ: Princeton University Press.

Bloch, M. (2004) 'A discourse that disciplines, governs, and regulates: the National Research Council's Report on Scientific Research in Education', *Qualitative Inquiry* 10(1): 96–110.

Blumer, H. (1956) 'Sociological analysis and the "variable"', *American Sociological Review* 21: 683–90.

Blumer, H. (1962) 'Society as symbolic interaction', in A.M. Rose (ed.) *Human Behavior and Social Processes*. Boston: Houghton Mifflin.

Blunkett, D. (2000) 'Influence or irrelevance: can social science improve government?', ESRC speech reprinted in *Research Intelligence*, 71:12–21.

Boon, J.A. (1972) *From Symbolism to Structuralism: Lévi-Strauss in a literary tradition*. New York: Harper & Row.

Brady, H.E. and Collier, D. (eds) (2004) *Rethinking Social Inquiry: diverse tools, shared standards*. Lanham, MD: Rowman & Littlefield.

Brandon, R. (1999) *Surreal Lives*. London: Macmillan.

Briggs, C. (1986) *Learning How to Ask: a sociolinguistic appraisal of the role of the interviewer in social science research*. Cambridge: Cambridge University Press.

Brown, R.H. (1977) *A Poetic for Sociology*. New York: Cambridge University Press. (Second edition, Chicago: University of Chicago Press, 1989).

Bruun, H.H. (2007) *Science, Values and Politics in Max Weber's Methodology* (2nd edn). Aldershot: Ashgate.

Bruyn, S.T. (1966) *The Human Perspective in Sociology: the methodology of participant observation*. Englewood Cliffs, NJ: Prentice-Hall.

Buci-Glucksmann, C. (1994) *Baroque Reason: the aesthetics of modernity*. London: Sage.

Bulmer, M. (1982) *The Uses of Social Research*. London: Allen and Unwin.

Burawoy, M. (2000) *Global Ethnography*. Berkeley, CA: University of California Press.

Burke, P. (1993) *The Art of Conversation*. Ithaca, NY: Cornell University Press.

Button, G. (1978) 'Comments on conversation analysis', *Analytic Sociology* 1(2).

Button, G. (ed.) (1991) *Ethnomethodology and the Human Sciences*. Cambridge: Cambridge University Press.

Button, G. and Sharrock, W. (1993) 'A disagreement over agreement and consensus in constructionist sociology', *Journal for the Theory of Social Behaviour* 23: 1–25.

Caputo, J.D. (1987) *Radical Hermeneutics: repetition, deconstruction and the hermeneutic project*. Bloomington, IN: Indiana University Press.

Carroll, L., 'Sylvie and Bruno Concluded', in L. Carroll (2001) *The complete stories and poems of Lewis Carroll*. New Lanark: Midpoint Press. p. 204.

Chouliaraki, L. and Fairclough, N. (1999) *Discourse in Late Modernity: rethinking critical discourse analysis*. Edinburgh: Edinburgh University Press.

Christians, C.G. (2005) 'Ethics and Politics in Qualitative Research', in Denzin and Lincoln (eds).

Christofferson, M. (2005) *French Intellectuals Against the Left: the antitotalitarian moment of the 1970s*. New York: Berghahn Books.

Cicourel, A.V. (1964) *Method and Measurement in Sociology*. New York: Free Press.

Clarke, J. and Newman, J. (1997) *The Managerial State*. London: Sage.

Clark, M. (1990) *Nietzsche on Truth and Philosophy*. Cambridge: Cambridge University Press.

Clayman, S.E. and Maynard, D.W. (1995). 'Ethnomethodology and conversation analysis', in P. ten Have and G. Psathas (eds), *Situated Order: studies in the social organization of talk and embodied activities*. Lanham, MD: University Press of America.

Clifford, J. (1986) 'Introduction', in J. Clifford and G.E. Marcus (eds), *Writing Culture: the poetics and politics of ethnography*. Berkeley, CA: University of California Press.

Clifford, J. (1988) *The Predicament of Culture*. Cambridge, MA: Harvard University Press.

Clifford, J. (1990) 'Notes on (field)notes', in R. Sanjek (ed.), *Fieldnotes: the makings of anthropology*. Ithaca, NY: Cornell University Press.

Clifford, J. and Marcus, G.E. (eds) (1986) *Writing Culture: the poetics and politics of ethnography*. Berkeley, CA: University of California Press.

Cohen, S. (1987) *Folk Devils and Moral Panics: the creation of the Mods and Rockers* (2nd edn). Oxford: Blackwell.

Connolly, P. (1992) 'Playing it by the rules: the politics of research in "race" and education', *British Educational Research Journal* 18(2): 133–48.

Coulter, J. (1983) 'Contingent and *a priori* structures in sequential analysis', *Human Studies* 6: 361–76.

Coulter, J. (1999) 'Discourse and mind', *Human Studies* 22: 163–81.

Coulter, J. (2003) 'Ryle's "Le Penseur"', *Revue Internationale de Philosophie* 57: 223.

Coulter, J. (2004) 'What is "discursive psychology"?', *Human Studies* 27: 335–40.

Crapanzano, V. (1986) 'Hermes' dilemma: the masking of subversion in ethnographic description', in J. Clifford and G.E. Marcus (eds), *Writing Culture: the poetics and politics of ethnography*. Berkeley, CA: University of California Press.

Crossley, M. (2000) *Introducing Narrative Psychology*. Buckingham: Open University Press.

Culler, J. (2002) *Barthes* (revised edn). Oxford: Oxford University Press.

Davies, P. (2000) 'Contributions from qualitative research', in H.T.O. Davies, S.M. Nutley and P.C. Smith (eds), *What Works? Evidence-based policy and practice in the public services*. Bristol: Policy Press.

Dean, J.P. and Whyte, W.F. (1958) 'How do you know if the informant is telling the truth?', *Human Organization* 17(2): 34–8.

Denzin, N.K. (1970) *The Research Act*. Chicago: Aldine de Gruytes.

Denzin, N.K. (1992) 'Whose Cornerville is it anyway?', *Journal of Contemporary Ethnography* 21: 120–32.

Denzin, N.K. (1997) *Interpretive Ethnography: ethnographic practices for the 21st century*. Thousand Oaks, CA: Sage.

Denzin, N.K. (2003) *Performance Ethnography: critical pedagogy and the politics of culture*. Thousand Oaks, CA: Sage.

Denzin, N.K. and Giardina, M.D. (2006a) 'Introduction', in N.K. Denzin and M.D. Giardina (eds), *Qualitative Inquiry and the Conservative Challenge*. Walnut Creek, CA: Left Coast Press.

Denzin, N.K. and Giardina, M.D. (eds) (2006b) *Qualitative Inquiry and the Conservative Challenge*. Walnut Creek, CA: Left Coast Press.

Denzin, N.K. and Lincoln, Y.S. (eds) (1994) *Handbook of Qualitative Research*. Thousand Oaks, CA: Sage.

Denzin, N.K. and Lincoln, Y.S. (eds) (2000) *Handbook of Qualitative Research* (2nd edn). Thousand Oaks, CA: Sage.

Denzin, N.K. and Lincoln, Y.S. (eds) (2005) *Handbook of Qualitative Research* (3rd edn). Thousand Oaks, CA: Sage.

Denzin, N.K., Lincoln, Y.S. and Giardina, M.D. (2006) 'Disciplining qualitative research', *International Journal of Qualitative Studies in Education* 19(6): 769–82.

Deutscher, I. (1973) *What We Say/What We Do: sentiments and acts*. Glenview, IL: Scott, Foresman and Co.

Dewey, J. (1922) *Human Nature and Conduct*. New York: Henry Holt.

Dewey, J. (1938) *Logic: the theory of inquiry*. New York: Henry Holt.

Dey, I. (1993) *Qualitative Data Analysis: a user-friendly guide for social scientists*. London: Routledge.

Dey, I. (1999) *Grounding Grounded Theory: guidelines for qualitative inquiry*. San Diego, CA: Academic Press.

Dingwall, R. (1997) 'Accounts, interviews and observations', in G. Miller and R. Dingwall (eds), *Context and Method in Qualitative Research*. London: Sage.

Dixon, P. (1971) *Rhetoric*. London: Methuen.

Dostal, R.J. (ed.) (2002) *The Cambridge Companion to Gadamer*. Cambridge: Cambridge University Press.

Downes, D. and Rock, P. (eds) (1979) *Deviant Interpretations*. London: Martin Robertson.

Eaglestone, R. (2001) *Postmodernism and Holocaust Denial*. Cambridge: Icon Books.

Edley, N. and Wetherell, M. (1995) *Men in Perspective: practice, power and identity*. London: Harvester-Wheatsheaf.

Edley, N. and Wetherell, M. (1997) 'Jockeying for position: the construction of masculine identities', *Discourse and Society* 8: 203–17.

Edmondson, R. (1984) *Rhetoric in Sociology*. London: Macmillan.

Edwards, D. (1997) *Discourse and Cognition*. London: Sage.

Edwards, J.A. and Lampert, M.D. 1993. *Talking Data: transcription and coding in discourse research*. Hillsdale, NJ: Lawrence Erlbaum.

Eisenhart, M. (2005) 'Science plus: a response to the responses to *Scientific Research in Education*', *Teachers College Record* 107(1): 52–8.

Eisenhart, M. (2006) 'Qualitative science in experimental time', *International Journal of Qualitative Studies in Education* 19(6): 697–707.

Elliott, J. (1988) 'Response to Patricia Broadfoot's presidential address', *British Educational Research Journal* 14(2): 191–4.

Ellis, C. (1993) '"There are survivors": telling a story of sudden death', *Sociological Quarterly* 34(4): 711–30.

Ellis, C. (2004) *The Ethnographic I*. Walnut Creek, CA: AltaMira Press.

Ellis, C. and Bochner, A.P. (2000) 'Autoethnography, personal narrative, reflexivity: researcher as subject', in N.K. Denzin and Y.S. Lincoln (eds), *Handbook of Qualitative Research* (2nd edn). Thousand Oaks, CA: Sage.

Elveton, R.O. (1970) *The Phenomenology of Husserl: selected critical readings*. Chicago: Quadrangle Books.

Erickson, F. (2005) 'Arts, humanities, and sciences in educational research and social engineering in Federal Education Policy', *Teachers College Record* 107(1): 4–9.

Erickson, F. and Gutierrez, K. (2002) 'Comment: culture, rigor, and science in educational research', *Educational Researcher* 31(8): 21–4.

Falasca-Zamponi, S. (2006) 'A Left sacred or a sacred Left?' The Collège de Sociologie, Fascism and political culture in interwar France', *South Central Review*, 23(1): 40–54.

Ferlie, E., Pettigrew, A., Ashburner, L. and Fitzgerald, L. (1996) *The New Public Management in Action*. Oxford: Oxford University Press.

Feuer, M.J., Towne, L. and Shavelson, R.J. (2002) 'Scientific culture and educational research', *Educational Researcher* 31(8): 4–14.

Feyerabend, P. (1975) *Against Method*. London: Verso.

Ffrench, P. (1995) *The Time of Theory: a history of Tel Quel 1960–83*. Oxford: Oxford University Press.

Flick, U. (1998) *An Introduction to Qualitative Research*. London: Sage.

Foster, P., Gomm, R. and Hammersley, M. (1996) *Constructing Educational Inequality*. London: Falmer.

Fox, N.F. (2003) *The New Sartre*. London: Continuum.

Garratt, D. and Hodkinson, P. (1998) 'Can there be criteria for selecting research criteria? A hermeneutic analysis of an inescapable dilemma', *Qualitative Inquiry* 4(4): 515–39.

Gaukroger, S. (2001) *Francis Bacon and the Transformation of Early-Modern Philosophy.* Cambridge: Cambridge University Press.

Gee, J.P. (2005) 'It's theories all the way down: a response to *Scientific Research in Education*', *Teachers College Record* 107(1): 10-18.

Geertz, C. (1965) *The Social History of an Indonesian Town.* Cambridge, MA: MIT Press.

Geertz, C. (1973a) 'On thick description: toward an interpretive theory of culture', in C. Geertz, *The Interpretation of Cultures.* New York: Basic Books.

Geertz, C. (1973b) *The Interpretation of Cultures.* New York: Basic Books.

Geertz, C. (1983) *Local Knowledge.* London: Fontana.

Geertz, C. (1988) *Works and Lives: the anthropologist as author.* Stanford, CA: Stanford University Press.

Geertz, C. (2000) *Available Light: anthropological reflections on philosophical topics.* Princeton, NJ: Princeton University Press.

Gelley, A. (ed.) (1995) *Unruly Examples: on the rhetoric of exemplarity.* Stanford, CA: University of California Press.

Gensler, H. (1996) *Formal Ethics.* New York: Routledge.

George, A.L. and Bennett, A. (2005) *Case Studies and Theory Development in the Social Sciences.* Cambridge, MA: MIT Press.

Gewirtz, S., Ball, S.J. and Bowe, R. (1995) *Markets, Choice and Equity in Education.* Buckingham: Open University Press.

Gibbons, M. (2000) 'Mode 2 society and the emergence of context-sensitive science', *Science and Public Policy* 26(5): 159–63.

Gibbons, M., Limoges, C., Nowotny, H., Schwartzman, S., Scott, P. and Trow, M. (1994) *The New Production of Knowledge: the dynamics of science and research in contemporary societies.* London: Sage.

Gilbert, G.N. and Mulkay, M. (1980) *Opening Pandora's Box: a sociological account of scientists' discourse.* Cambridge: Cambridge University Press.

Gillborn, D. (1995) *Racism and Antiracism in Real Schools.* Buckingham: Open University Press.

Giroux, H.A. (1988) 'Postmodernism and the discourse of educational criticism', *Journal of Education*, 170: 5–30.

Giroux, H.A. (1992) 'Language, difference and curriculum theory: beyond the politics of clarity', *Theory into Practice* 31: 219–27.

Glaser, B.G. and Strauss, A. (1967) *The Discovery of Grounded Theory.* Chicago: Aldine Press.

Gomm, R., Hammersley, M. and Foster, P. (eds) (2000) *Case Study Method: key texts, key issues.* London: Sage.

Gould, S.J. (1991) *Wonderful Life: the Burgess Shale and the nature of history.* Harmondsworth: Penguin.

Gubrium, J.F. and Holstein, J.A. (2002) 'Introduction', in J.F. Gubrium and J.A. Holstein (eds), *Handbook of Interview Research.* Thousand Oaks, CA: Sage.

Guthrie, W.K.C. (1971) *The Sophists.* Cambridge: Cambridge University Press. (First published as volume III of *A History of Greek Philosophy*. Cambridge: Cambridge University Press, 1969.)

Gutting, G. (1989) *Michel Foucault's Archaeology of Scientific Reason.* Cambridge: Cambridge University Press.

Gutting, G. (2001) *French Philosophy in the Twentieth Century*. Cambridge: Cambridge University Press.

Haack, S. (1998) *Manifesto of a Passionate Moderate: unfashionable essays*. Chicago: University of Chicago.

Haack, S. (2003) *Defending Science within Reason: Between Scientism and Cynicism*. Amherst, NY: Prometheus Books.

Hacker, P.M.S. (1996) *Wittgenstein's Place in Twentieth-century Analytic Philosophy*. Oxford: Blackwell.

Hammersley, M. (1984) 'The Paradigmatic Mentality: a diagnosis', in L. Barton and S. Walker (eds), *Social Crisis and Educational Research*. London: Croom Helm.

Hammersley, M. (1985) 'From ethnography to theory: a programme and paradigm for case study research in the sociology of education', *Sociology* 19(2): 244–59.

Hammersley, M. (1986) 'Measurement in ethnography: the case of Pollard on teaching style', in M. Hammersley (ed.), *Case Studies in Classroom Research*. Milton Keynes: Open University Press.

Hammersley, M. (1989) *The Dilemma of Qualitative Method*. London: Routledge.

Hammersley, M. (1990) 'An evaluation of two studies of gender imbalance in classroom interaction', *British Educational Research Journal* 16(2).

Hammersley, M. (1993) 'The rhetorical turn in ethnography', *Social Science Information* 32(1): 23–37. (Reprinted in C. Pole (ed.), *Fieldwork* (vol. 4). London: Sage, 2005.)

Hammersley, M. (1994) 'Ethnographic writing', *Social Research Update* 5.

Hammersley, M. (1995) *The Politics of Social Research*. London: Sage.

Hammersley, M. (1997a) *Reading Ethnographic Research* (2nd edn). London: Longman.

Hammersley, M. (1997b) 'On the foundations of critical discourse analysis', *Language and Communication* 17(3): 237–48.

Hammersley, M. (1998a) 'Get real! A defence of realism', in P. Hodkinson (ed.), *The Nature of Educational Research: realism, relativism, or post-modernism?* Crewe: Crewe School of Education, Manchester Metropolitan University. (Reprinted in H. Piper and I. Stronach (eds), *Educational Research: difference and diversity*, Aldershot: Ashgate, 2004).

Hammersley, M. (1998b) 'Partisanship and credibility: the case of antiracist educational research', in P. Connolly and B. Troyna (eds), *Researching Racism in Education: politics, theory and practice*. Buckingham: Open University Press.

Hammersley, M. (1999) 'Not bricolage but boatbuilding: exploring two metaphors for thinking about ethnography', *Journal of Contemporary Ethnography* 28(6): 574–85.

Hammersley, M. (2000) *Taking Sides in Research: essays on bias and partisanship*. London: Routledge.

Hammersley, M. (2001) 'On "Systematic" reviews of research literatures: a "narrative" reply to Evans and Benefield', *British Educational Research Journal* 27(5): 543–54.

Hammersley, M. (2002) *Educational Research, Policymaking and Practice*. London: Paul Chapman/Sage.

Hammersley, M. (2003a) 'Can and should educational research be educative?', *Oxford Review of Education* 29(1): 3–25.

Hammersley, M. (2003b) 'Discourse analysis: an introductory bibliographical guide', unpublished paper. Available at: www.tlrp.org/rcbn/capacity/Activities/Themes/in-depth/guide.pdf (accessed 22.01.2008).

Hammersley, M. (2004a) 'Should ethnographers be against inequality? On Becker, value neutrality and researcher partisanship', in B. Jeffrey and G. Walford (eds), *Ethnographies of Educational and Cultural Conflicts: strategies and resolutions*. Oxford: Elsevier.

Hammersley, M. (2004b) 'Action research: a contradiction in terms?', *Oxford Review of Education* 30(2): 165–81.

Hammersley, M. (2004c) 'Too good to be false? The ethics of belief and its implications for the evidence-based character of educational research, policymaking and practice', unpublished paper.

Hammersley, M. (2004d) 'Get real! A defence of realism', in H. Piper and I. Stronach (eds), *Educational Research: difference and diversity*. Aldershot: Ashgate.

Hammersley, M. (2004e) 'Some questions about research and evidence-based practice in education', in G. Thomas and R. Pring (eds), *Evidence-based Practice in Education*. Buckingham: Open University Press.

Hammersley, M. (2004f) 'Objectivity', in M. Lewis-Beck, A. Bryman and T.F. Liao (eds), *Encyclopedia of Social Science Research Methods*. Thousand Oaks, CA: Sage.

Hammersley, M. (2005a) 'Should social science be critical?', *Philosophy of the Social Sciences* 35(2): 175–95.

Hammersley, M. (2005b) 'Countering the "new orthodoxy" in educational research: a response to Phil Hodkinson', *British Educational Research Journal* 31(2): 139–55.

Hammersley, M. (2005c) 'Is the evidence-based practice movement doing more good than harm? Reflections on Iain Chalmers' case for research-based policymaking and practice', *Evidence and Policy* 1(1): 1–16.

Hammersley, M. (2006a) 'Philosophy's contribution to social science research on education', *Journal of Philosophy of Education* 40(2): 273–86.

Hammersley, M. (2006b) 'Systematic or unsystematic, is that the question? Reflections on the science, art, and politics of reviewing research evidence', in A. Killoran, C. Swann and M. Kelly (eds), *Public Health Evidence: changing the health of the public*. Oxford: Oxford University Press.

Hammersley, M. (2007a) 'What's wrong with quantitative research?', unpublished paper.

Hammersley, M. (2007b) 'Assessing validity in social research', in P. Alasuutari (ed.), *Handbook of Social Research*. London: Sage.

Hammersley, M. (2007c) 'A powerful "lie": the fictional character of all ethnographic accounts', unpublished paper.

Hammersley, M. (2008a) 'Troubles with triangulation', in M. Bergman (ed.), *Advances in Mixed Methods Research*. London: Sage.

Hammersley, M. (2008b) 'Educational research', in G. McCulloch (ed.), *Encyclopaedia of Education*. London: Routledge.

Hammersley, M. (2008c) 'Troubling criteria: a critical commentary on Furlong and Oancea's Framework for Assessing Educational Research', *British Educational Research Journal*, forthcoming.

Hammersley, M. (2008d) 'Challenging relativism: the problem of assessment criteria', *Qualitative Inquiry*, forthcoming.

Hammersley, M. (2009) 'Is social measurement possible?', in E. Tucker, M. Viswanathan and G. Walford (eds) *The Handbook of Measurement*. London: Sage. Forthcoming.

Hammersley, M. and Atkinson, P. (2007) *Ethnography: principles in practice, third edition*. London: Routledge.

Hammersley, M. and Woods, P. (eds) (1984) *Life in School*. Milton Keynes: Open University Press.

Hammond, M., Howarth, J. and Keat, R. (1991) *Understanding Phenomenology*. Oxford: Blackwell.

Hargreaves, A. (1982) 'Resistance and relative autonomy theories: problems of distortion and incoherence in recent Marxist theories of education', *British Journal of the Sociology of Education* 3(2): 107–26.

Hargreaves, D.H. (1978) 'Whatever happened to symbolic interactionism?', in L. Barton and R. Meighan (eds), *Sociological Interpretations of Schooling and Classrooms*. Driffield, England: Nafferton.

Harrington, A. (2000) 'Objectivism in hermeneutics? Gadamer, Habermas, and Dilthey', *Philosophy of the Social Sciences* 30(4): 491–507.

Harrington, A. (2001) *Hermeneutical Dialogue and Social Science*. London: Routledge.

ten Have, P. (1999) *Doing Conversation Analysis: a practical guide*. London: Sage.

Hayek, F. (1955) *The Counter-Revolution of Science: studies in the abuse of reason*. New York: Free Press.

Heap, J. (1979) 'What are sense-making practices?', *Sociological Inquiry* 46: 107–15.

Helling, I.K. (1984) 'A. Schutz and F. Kaufmann: sociology between science and interpretation', *Human Studies* 7: 141–61.

Heritage, J. (1984) *Garfinkel and Ethnomethodology*. Cambridge: Polity Press.

Hester, S.K. and Francis, D. (1994) 'Doing data: the local organization of a sociological interview', *British Journal of Sociology* 45(4): 675–95.

Hodkinson, P. (2004) 'Research as a form of work: expertise, community and methodological objectivity', *British Educational Research Journal* 30(1): 9–26.

Hoffman, K. (ed.) (1989) *Collage: critical views*. Ann Arbor, MI: UMI Research Press.

Hollier, D. (ed.) (1988) *The College of Sociology (1937–39)*. Minneapolis: University of Minneapolis Press.

Holstein, J.A. and Miller, G. (eds) (1993) *Reconsidering Social Constructionism: debates in social problems theory*. New York: Aldine de Gruyter.

Howe, K.R. (2004) 'A critique of experimentalism', *Qualitative Inquiry* 10(4): 42–61.

Howe, K.R. (2005) 'The question of education science: *experimentism* versus *experimentalism*', *Educational Theory* 55(3): 307–21.

Hoyningen-Huene, P. (1993) *Reconstructing Scientific Revolutions: Thomas S. Kuhn's philosophy of science*. Chicago: University of Chicago Press. (First published in German in 1989.)

Hughes, R. (2007) 'L'amour Fou', The *Guardian*, March 24.

Hutchby, I. and Wooffitt, R. (1998) *Conversation Analysis: principles, practices and applications*. Cambridge: Polity Press.

James, A., Hockey, J. and Dawson, A. (eds) (1997) *After Writing Culture*. London: Routledge.

Keat, R. and Urry, J. (1975) *Social Theory as Science*. London: Routledge and Kegan Paul.

Keddie, N. (1975) *Tinker, Tailor: the myth of cultural deprivation*. Harmondsworth: Penguin.

Kendall, P.L. and Wolf, K.M. (1949) 'The analysis of deviant cases in communications research', in P.F. Lazarsfeld and F. Stanton (eds), *Communications Research 1948–9*. New York: Harper and Bros. (Reprinted in P.F. Lazarsfeld and M. Rosenberg (eds), *The Language of Social Research*. Glencoe, IL: Free Press.)

Khilnani, S. (1993) *Arguing Revolution: the intellectual Left in postwar France*. New Haven, CT: Yale University Press.

Kincheloe, J. (2001) 'Describing the bricolage: conceptualizing a new rigor in qualitative research', *Qualitative Inquiry* 7(6): 679–92.

Kincheloe, J. and Berry, K.S. (2004) *Rigour and Complexity in Educational Research: conceptualizing the bricolage*. Maidenhead: Open University Press.

Kolenda, K. (ed.) (1979) *Gilbert Ryle: on thinking*. Totowa, NJ: Rowman & Littlefield.

Kuhn, T.S. (1970) *The Structure of Scientific Revolutions* (2nd edn). Chicago: University of Chicago Press.

Kuhn, T.S. (2003) *The Road Since Structure*. Chicago: University of Chicago Press.

Kuper, A. (1999) *Culture: the anthropologists' account*. Cambridge, MA: Harvard University Press.

Lapadat, J.C. (2000). 'Problematising transcription: purpose, paradigm, and quality', *International Journal of Social Research Methodology*, 3(3): 203–19.

Larson, M.S. (1977) *The Rise of Professionalism: a sociological analysis*. Berkeley, CA: University of California Press.

Lather, P. (1993) 'Fertile obsession: validity after post-structuralism', *Sociological Quarterly* 34(4): 673–93.

Lather, P. (1996) 'Troubling clarity: the politics of accessible language', *Harvard Educational Review* 66(3): 525–54.

Lather, P. (2000) 'Responsible practices of academic writing: troubling clarity II', in P. Trifonas (ed.) *Revolutionary Pedagogies*. New York: Routledge.

Lather, P. (2004) 'This is your father's paradigm: government intrusion and the case of qualitative research in education', *Qualitative Inquiry* 10(1): 15–34.

Lather, P. (2006) 'Foucauldian scientificity: rethinking the nexus of qualitative research and educational policy analysis', *International Journal of Qualitative Studies in Education*. 19(6): 783–91.

Lather, P. (2007) *Getting Lost: feminist efforts toward a double(ed) science*. Albany NY: State University of New York Press.

Lather, P. and Smithies, C. (1997) *Troubling the Angels: women living with HIV/AIDS*. Boulder, CO: Westview Press.

Latour, B. and Woolgar, S. (1979) *Laboratory Life: the social construction of scientific facts*. London: Sage.

Laub, J.H. and Sampson, R.J. (1991) 'The Sutherland–Glueck debate: on the sociology of criminological knowledge', *American Journal of Sociology* 96(6): 1402–40.

Leach, E. (1970) *Lévi-Strauss*. London: Fontana.

Lévi-Strauss, C. (1966) *The Savage Mind*. London: Weidenfeld and Nicolson. (First published in French as *La Pensée Sauvage* in 1962.)

Lewin, K. (1936) 'Some social and psychological differences between the United States and Germany', *Character and Personality* 4: 265–93.

Lieberson, S. (1992) 'Small n's and big conclusions: an examination of the reasoning in comparative studies based on a small number of cases', in C. Ragin and H.S. Becker (eds), *What is a Case? Exploring the foundations of social inquiry*. Cambridge: Cambridge University Press.

Lincoln, Y.S. (2001) 'An emerging new *bricoleur*: promises and possibilities – a reaction to Joe Kincheloe's "Describing the bricoleur"', *Qualitative Inquiry* 7(6): 693–6.

Lincoln, Y.S. and Cannella, G.S. (2004) 'Dangerous discourses: methodological conservatism and governmental regimes of truth', *Qualitative Inquiry* 10: 5–14.

Lincoln, Y.S. and Denzin, N.K. (2000) 'The seventh moment: out of the past', in N.K. Denzin and Y.S. Lincoln (eds), *Handbook of Qualitative Research* (2nd edn). Thousand Oaks, CA: Sage.

Lindesmith, A. (1937) *The Nature of Opiate Addiction*. Chicago: University of Chicago Libraries.

Lindesmith, A. (1952) 'Two comments on W.S. Robinson's "The logical structure of analytic induction"', *American Sociological Review* 17: 492–3.

Lindesmith, A. (1968) *Addiction and Opiates*. Chicago: Aldine de Gruytes.

Lindesmith, A. (1981) 'Symbolic interactionism and causality', *Symbolic Interaction* 4(1): 87–96.

Lock, M. and Gordon, D. (eds) (1988) *Biomedicine Examined*. Dordrecht: Kluwer.

Lyas, C. (1999) *Peter Winch*. Teddington, UK: Acumen.

Lynch, M. (1988) 'Alfred Schutz and the sociology of science', in L. Embree (ed.), *Worldly Phenomenology: the continuing influence of Alfred Schutz on North American Human Science*. Washington, DC: Center for Advanced Research in Phenomenology and University Press of America.

Lynch, M. (1993) *Scientific Practice and Ordinary Action*. Cambridge: Cambridge University Press.

Lynch, M. and Bogen, D. (1994) 'Harvey Sacks's primitive natural science', *Theory, Culture and Society* 11: 65–104.

Lyons, W. (1980) *Gilbert Ryle: an introduction to his philosophy*. Brighton: Harvester Press.

Mac an Ghaill, M. (1988) *Young, Gifted and Black*. Milton Keynes: Open University Press.

MacCallum, G. (1972) 'Negative and positive freedom', in P. Laslett, W.G. Runciman and Q. Skinner (eds), *Philosophy, Politics and Society* (Fourth Series). Oxford: Blackwell.

McCloskey, D. (1985) *The Rhetoric of Economics*. Madison, WI: University of Wisconsin Press.

Macdonald, K.M. (1995) *The Sociology of the Professions*. London: Sage.

MacIntyre, A. (1990) *Three Rival Versions of Moral Enquiry*. London: Duckworth.

Mackenzie, B.D. (1977) *Behaviourism and the Limits of Scientific Method*. London: Routledge and Kegan Paul.

McKenzie, K. (2003) 'Discursive psychology and the "new racism"', *Human Studies* 26: 461–91.

MacLure, M. (2003) *Discourse in Educational and Social Research*. Buckingham: Open University Press.

MacLure, M. (2005) '"Clarity bordering on stupidity": where's the quality in systematic review', *Journal of Education Policy* 20(4): 393–416.

MacLure, M. (2006) '"A demented form of the familiar": postmodernism and educational research', *Journal of Philosophy of Education* 40(2): 223–39. (Reprinted in D. Bridges and R. Smith (eds), *Philosophy, Methodology, and Educational Research*. Oxford: Blackwell, 2007.)

Manning, P. (1982) 'Analytic induction', in R.B. Smith and P.K. Manning (eds), *Qualitative Methods. Volume II: Handbook of Social Science Methods*. Cambridge, MA: Ballinger.

Marsh, P., Rosser, E. and Harré, R. (1978) *The Rules of Disorder*. London: Routledge and Kegan Paul.

Matza, D. (1969) *Becoming Deviant*. Englewood Cliffs, NJ: Prentice-Hall.

Maxwell, J.A. (2004) 'Re-emergent scientism, postmodernism, and dialogue across differences', *Qualitative Inquiry* 10(1): 35–41.

Merquior, J.G. (1986a) *Western Marxism*. London: Paladin.

Merquior, J.G. (1986b) *From Prague to Paris: a critique of structuralist and post-structuralist thought*. London: Verso.

Merton, R.K. (1948) 'The self-fulfilling prophecy', *Antioch Review* VIII: 193–210.

Merton, R.K. (1995) 'The Thomas Theorem and the Matthew Effect', *Social Forces* 74(2): 379–424.

Miller, J. and Glassner, B. (1997) 'The "inside" and the "outside": finding realities in interviews', in D. Silverman (ed.), *Qualitative Research: theory, method and practice*. London: Sage.

Miller, L. and Whalley, J.B. (2005) 'Stories from the field – "taking the piss": notes on collaborative practice as research', in B. Somekh and C. Lewin (eds), *Research Methods in the Social Sciences*. London: Sage.

Mishler, E.G. (1986) *Research Interviewing: context and narrative*. Cambridge, MA: Harvard University Press.

Moerman, M. (1968) 'Being Lue: uses and abuses of ethnic identification', in J. Helm. (ed.), *Essays on the Problem of the Tribe*. Seattle, WA: University of Washington Press.

Moerman, M. (1988) *Talking Culture: ethnography and conversation analysis*. Philadelphia: University of Pennsylvania Press.

Montaigne, M. (1958) *Essays*. Translated by J.M. Cohen. Harmondsworth: Penguin.

Moran, D. (2005) *Edmund Husserl: founder of phenomenology*. Cambridge: Polity Press.

Moss, P.A. (2005a) 'Toward "epistemic reflexivity" in educational research: a response to *Scientific Research in Education*', *Teachers College Record* 107(1): 19–29.

Moss, P.A. (2005b) 'Understanding the other/understanding ourselves: toward a constructive dialogue about "principles" in educational research', *Educational Theory* 55(3): 263–83.

Mosteller, F. and Boruch, R.F. (eds) (2002) *Evidence Matters: randomized trials in education research*. Washington, DC: Brookings Institution Press.

Murphy, E., Dingwall, R., Greatbatch, D., Parker, S. and Watson, P. (1998) 'Qualitative research methods in health technology assessment: a review of the literature', *Health Technology Assessment* 2(16): 1–260. Also available at: <http://www.hta.nhsweb.nhs.uk/execsumm/summ216.htm> (accessed 14.08.2002).

Nelson, C.K. (1994) 'Ethnomethodological positions on the use of ethnographic data in conversation analytic research', *Journal of Contemporary Ethnography* 23: 307–29.

Nelson, C., Treichler, P.A. and Grossberg, L. (1992) 'Introduction', in L. Grossberg, C. Nelson and P.A. Treichler (eds), *Cultural Studies*. New York: Routledge.

Nussbaum, M. (1999) 'The professor of parody', New Republic, February 22, 220(8): 37–45. Also available at: http://www.akad.se/Nussbaum.pdf (accessed 17.01.2008).

Oakeshott, M. (1986) *Experience and Its Modes*. Cambridge: Cambridge University Press.

Oakeshott, M. (1989) 'Education: the engagement and the frustration', in T. Fuller (ed.) *The Voice of Liberal Learning: Michael Oakeshott on education*. London: Yale University Press.

Oakley, A. (2000) *Experiments in Knowing: gender and method in the social sciences*. Cambridge: Polity Press.

Oakley, A. (2001) 'Evidence-informed policy and practice: challenges for social science', published by the Manchester Statistical Society, Manchester, UK, 13 February. (Reprinted in M. Hammersley (ed.), *Educational Research for Evidence-based Practice*. London: Sage.)

Ochs, E. (1979) 'Transcription as theory', in E. Ochs (ed.), *Developmental Pragmatics*. New York: Academic Press.

Orne, M.T. (1962) 'On the social psychology of the psychological experiment: with particular reference to demand characteristics and their implications', *American Psychologist*, 17: 776–83.

Packwood, A. and Sikes, P. (1996) 'Adopting a postmodern approach to research', *International Journal of Qualitative Studies in Education* 9(3): 335–45.

Palmer, R.E. (1969) *Hermeneutics*. Evanston, IL: Northwestern University Press.

Payne, G.C.F. (1976) 'Making a lesson happen: an ethnomethodological analysis', in M. Hammersley and P. Woods (eds), *The Process of Schooling: a sociological reader*. London: Routledge and Kegan Paul.

Pearson, G. (1975) *The Deviant Imagination: psychiatry, social work and social change*. London: Macmillan.

Perelman, C. (1982) *The Realm of Rhetoric*. Notre Dame, IN: University of Notre Dame Press.

Perelman, C. and Olbrechts-Tyteca, L. (1969) *The New Rhetoric: a treatise on argumentation*. Notre Dame, IN: University of Notre Dame Press. (First published in French in 1958.)

Phillips, D.C. (1990) 'Subjectivity and objectivity: an objective inquiry', in E.W. Eisner and A. Peshkin (eds), *Qualitative Inquiry in Education: the continuing debate*. New York: Teachers College Press.

Pollitt, C. (1990) *Managerialism and the Public Services*. Oxford: Blackwell.

Pollner, M. and Emerson, R.M. (2001) 'Ethnomethodology and ethnography', in P. Atkinson, A. Coffey, S. Delamont, J. Lofland and L. Lofland (eds), *Handbook of Ethnography*. London: Sage.

Popkewitz, T.S. (2004) 'Is the National Research Council Committee's Report on Scientific Research in Education scientific? On trusting the manifesto', *Qualitative Inquiry* 10(1): 62–78.

Popkin, R.H. (1979) *The History of Scepticism: from Erasmus to Spinoza*. Berkeley, CA: University of California Press.

Popper, K.R. (1990) *A World of Propensities*. Bristol: Thoemmes Antiquarian Books.

Porter, T.M. (1995) *Trust in Numbers: the pursuit of objectivity in science and public life*. Princeton, NJ: Princeton University Press.

Potter, J. (1996a) *Representing Reality: discourse, rhetoric and social construction*. London: Sage.

Potter, J. (1996b) 'Discourse analysis: theoretical background', in J.E.T. Richardson (ed.), *Handbook of Qualitative Research Methods*. Leicester: British Psychological Association.

Potter, J. and Edwards, D. (2001). 'Discursive social psychology', in W.P. Robinson and H. Giles (eds), *The New Handbook of Language and Social Psychology*. London: Wiley.

Potter, J. and Edwards, D. (2003) 'Rethinking cognition: on Coulter on discourse and mind', *Human Studies* 26(2): 165–81.

Potter, J. and Hepburn, A. (2005) 'Qualitative interviews in psychology: problems and possibilities', *Qualitative Research in Psychology* 2: 281–307.

Potter, J. and Wetherell, M. (1987) *Discourse and Social Psychology*. London: Sage.

Price, H.H. (1969) *Belief*. London: Allen and Unwin.

Priest, G., Beall, J.C. and Armour-Garb, B. (eds) (2004) *The Law of Noncontradiction: new philosophical essays*. Oxford: Oxford University Press.

Putnam, H. (2002) *The Collapse of the Fact–Value Dichotomy and Other Essays*. Cambridge, MA: Harvard University Press.

Ragin, C. (1987) *The Comparative Method: moving beyond qualitative and quantitative strategies*. Berkeley, CA: University of California Press.

Randall, J.H. (1944) 'The nature of naturalism', in Y.H. Krikorian (ed.) *Naturalism and the Human Spirit*. New York: Columbia University Press.

Reason, P. (1993) 'Sacred experience and sacred science', *Journal of Management Inquiry*. 2: 10-27.

Reason, P. and Bradbury, H. (eds) (2006) *Handbook of Action Research* (concise paperback edn). London: Sage.

Reay, D. (1995) '"They employ cleaners to do that": habitus in the primary classroom', *British Journal of Sociology of Education* 16(3): 353–71.

Reay, D., Davies, J., David, M. and Ball, S.J. (2001) 'Choices of degree or degrees of choice? Class, "race" and the higher education choice process', *Sociology* 35(4): 855–74.

Rescher, N. (1998) *Complexity: a philosophical overview*. New Brunswick, NJ: Transaction Publishers.

Ridley, F. (1996) 'The new public management in Europe: comparative perspectives', *Public Policy and Administration* 11(1): 10–29.

Riessman, C. (1990) 'Strategic uses of narrative in the presentation of self and illness: a research note', *Social Science and Medicine* 30(11): 1195–200.

Rist, R. (2000) 'Influencing the policy process with qualitative research', in N.K. Denzin and Y.S. Lincoln (eds), *Handbook of Qualitative Research* (2nd edn). Thousand Oaks, CA: Sage.

Ritchie, J. (2003) 'The applications of qualitative research methods', in J. Ritchie and J. Lewis (eds), *Qualitative Research Practice: a guide for social science students and researchers*. London: Sage.

Robinson, R. (1954) *Definition*. Oxford: University Press.

Robinson, W.S. (1951) 'The logical structure of analytic induction', *American Sociological Review* 16(6): 812–18.

Rock, P. (1973) 'Phenomenalism and essentialism in the sociology of deviance', *Sociology* 7(1): 17–29.

Rosenthal, R. and Jacobson, L. (1968) *Pygmalion in the Classroom*. New York: Holt, Rinehart and Winston.

Rothman, K.J. (1986) *Modern Epidemiology*. Boston: Little Brown.

Ryle, G. (1949) *The Concept of Mind*. London: Hutchinson.

Ryle, G. (1971a) 'Thinking and language', in G. Ryle, *Collected Papers* (vol. 2). London: Hutchinson.

Ryle, G. (1971b) 'Thinking and reflecting', in G. Ryle, *Collected Papers* (vol. 2). London: Hutchinson.

Ryle, G. (1971c) 'The thinking of thoughts', in G. Ryle, *Collected Papers* (vol. 2). London: Hutchinson.

Ryle, G. (1979) 'Adverbial verbs and verbs of thinking', in K. Kolenda (ed.), *Gilbert Ryle: on thinking*. Totowa, NJ: Rowman and Littlefield.

Sacks, H. (1984) 'Notes on methodology', in J.M. Atkinson and J. Heritage (eds), *Structures of Social Action: studies in conversation analysis*. Cambridge: Cambridge University Press.

Sacks, H., Schegloff, E.A. and Jefferson, G. (1974) 'A simplest systematics for the organization of turn-taking in conversation', *Language*, 50(4): 696–735.

Sadler, T. (1995) *Nietzsche: truth and redemption*. London: Athlone Press.

Sanjek, P. (ed.) (1990) *Fieldnotes: the making of anthropology*. Ithaca, NY: Cornell University Press.

Schegloff, E.A. (1968). 'Sequencing in conversational openings', *American Anthropologist* 70: 1075–95.

Schegloff, E.A. (1971) 'Note on a conversational practice: formulating place', in D. Sudnow (ed.), *Studies in Social Interaction*. New York: Free Press.

Schegloff, E.A. (1988) 'Goffman and the analysis of conversation', in P. Drew and A. Wootton (eds), *Erving Goffman: exploring the interaction order*. Cambridge: Polity Press.

Schegloff, E.A. (1997) 'Whose text? Whose context?', *Discourse and Society* 8: 165–87.

Schegloff, E.A. (1998) 'Reply to Wetherell', *Discourse and Society* 9: 413-16.

Scheurich, J.J. (1997) *Research Methods in the Postmodern*. London: Falmer.

Schmidt, J. (1998) 'Civility, Enlightenment, and society: conceptual confusions and Kantian remedies', *American Political Science Review* 92(2): 419–27.

Schofield, J.W. (1989) 'Increasing the generalizability of qualitative research', in E.W. Eisner and A. Peshkin (eds), *Qualitative Inquiry in Education: the continuing debate*. New York: Teachers College Press.

Schutz, A. (1962) *Collected Papers. Volume 1: The Problem of Social Reality*. The Hague: Martinus Nijhoff.

Schwandt, T. (2005) 'A diagnostic reading of scientifically based research in education', *Educational Theory* 55(3): 285–305.

Seale, C. (1998) 'Qualitative interviewing', in C. Seale (ed.), *Researching Society and Culture*. London: Sage.

Seale, C. (1999) *The Quality of Qualitative Research*. London: Sage.

Shankman, P. (1984) 'The thick and the thin: on the interpretive theoretical program of Clifford Geertz', *Current Anthropology*, 25(3): 261–80.

Sharrock, W.W. (1974) 'On owning knowledge', in R. Turner (ed.), *Ethnomethodology*. Harmondsworth: Penguin.

Sharrock, W.W. (1977) 'The problem of order', in P. Worsley (ed.), *Introducing Sociology* (2nd edn). Harmondsworth: Penguin.

Sharrock, W. and Read, R. (2002) *Kuhn: philosopher of scientific revolution*. Cambridge: Polity Press.

Shavelson, R.J. and Towne, L. (eds) (2002) *Scientific Research in Education*. Washington, DC: National Research Council, National Academy Press.

Sibley, F.N. (1970) 'Ryle and thinking', in O.P. Wood and G. Pitcher (eds), *Ryle*. London: Macmillan.

Silverman, D. (1973) 'Interview talk: bringing off a research instrument', *Sociology* 7(1): 31–48.

Silverman, D. (1997) 'Towards an aesthetics of research', in D. Silverman (ed.), *Qualitative Research: theory, method and practice*. London: Sage.

Silverman, D. (2007) *A Very Short, Fairly Interesting, and Reasonably Cheap Book about Qualitative Research*. London: Sage.

Slavin, R. (2002) 'Evidence-based education policies: transforming educational practice and research', *Educational Researcher* 31(7): 15–21.

Smith, J.K. (1984) 'The problem of criteria for judging interpretive inquiry', *Educational Evaluation and Policy Analysis* 6(4): 379–91.

Smith, J.K. (1989) *The Nature of Social and Educational Inquiry*. Norwood, NJ: Ablex.

Smith, J.K. (2004) 'Learning to live with relativism', in H. Piper and I. Stronach (eds), *Educational Research: difference and diversity*. Aldershot: Ashgate.

Smith, J.K. and Deemer, D.K. (2000) 'The problem of criteria in the age of relativism', in N.K. Denzin and Y.S. Lincoln (eds), *Handbook of Qualitative Research* (2nd edn). Thousand Oaks, CA: Sage.

Smith, J.K. and Hodkinson, P. (2005) 'Relativism, criteria and politics', in N.K. Denzin and Y.S. Lincoln (eds) *Handbook of Qualitative Research* (3rd edn). Thousand Oaks, CA: Sage.

Speer, S.A. (2002) ' "Natural" and "contrived" data: a sustainable distinction?', *Discourse Studies*, 4(4): 511–25.

Speer, S.A. and Hutchby, I. (2002) 'From ethics to analytics: aspects of participants' orientations to the presence and relevance of recording devices', *Sociology* 37(2): 315–37.

Spencer, L., Richie, J., Lewis, J. and Dillon, L. (2003) *Quality in Qualitative Evaluation: a framework for assessing research evidence*. London: Government Chief Social Researcher's Office, Strategy Unit, Cabinet Office. Prepared by the National Centre for Social Research on behalf of the Cabinet Office. Also available at: http://www.pm.gov.uk/files/pdf/quality-framework.pdf

Sperber, D. and Wilson, D. (1986) *Relevance: communication and cognition*. Oxford: Blackwell.

St. Pierre, E.A. (2002) '"Science" rejects postmodernism', *Educational Researcher* 31(8): 25–7.

St. Pierre, E.A. (2006) 'Scientifically based research in education: epistemology and ethics', *Adult Education Quarterly* 56(4): 239–66.

Stebbing, L.S. (1958) *Philosophy and the Physicists*. London: Methuen.

Stimson, G. and Webb, B. (1975) *Going To See the Doctor*. London: Routledge.

Stokes, D.E. (1997) *Pasteur's Quadrant: basic science and technological innovation*. Washington, DC: The Brookings Institute.

Stouffer, S.A. (1930) 'An experimental comparison of statistical and case-history methods of attitude research', unpublished PhD thesis, University of Chicago. (Reprinted Arno Press, 1980.)

Tashakkori, A. and Teddlie, C.B. (eds) (2002) *Handbook of Mixed Methods in Social and Behavioral Research*. Thousand Oaks, CA: Sage.

Taylor, C. (1975) *Hegel*. Cambridge: Cambridge University Press.

Thomas, G. (1998) 'The myth of rational research', *British Educational Research Journal* 24(2): 141–61.

Thomas, G. and Pring, R. (eds) (2004) *Evidence-based Practice in Education*. Buckingham: Open University Press.

Thomas, W.I. and Znaniecki, F. (1918) *The Polish Peasant in Europe and America* (vol. 1). Chicago: University of Chicago Press.

Thomason, B. (1982) *Making Sense of Reification: Alfred Schutz and constructionist theory*. London: Macmillan.

Thornham, S. (1998) 'Postmodernism and feminism', in S. Sim (ed.), *The Icon Critical Dictionary of Postmodern Thought*. Cambridge: Icon Books.

Trinder, L. with Reynolds, S. (eds) (2000) *Evidence-based Practice: a critical appraisal*. Oxford: Blackwell Science.

Troyna, B. (1995) 'Beyond reasonable doubt? Researching "race" in educational settings', *Oxford Review of Education* 21: 395–408.

Turkle, S. (1992) *Psychoanalytic Politics: Jacques Lacan and Freud's French revolution* (2nd edn). London: Free Association Books.

Turner, R.H. (1948) 'Statistical logic in social research', *Sociology and Social Research* 32: 697–704.

Turner, R.H. (1953) 'The quest for universals in sociological research', *American Sociological Review* 18: 604–11.

van den Berg, H., Wetherell, M. and Houtkoop-Steenstra, H. (eds) (2003) *Analyzing Race Talk: multidisciplinary approaches to the interview*. Cambridge: Cambridge University Press.

Van Maanen, J. (1988) *Tales of the Field*. Chicago: University of Chicago Press.

Vickers, B. (1988) *In Defence of Rhetoric*. Oxford: Oxford University Press.

Vendler, Z. (1971) 'Summary: linguistics and the *a priori*', in C. Lyas (ed.), *Philosophy and Linguistics*. London: Macmillan.

Voysey, M. (1975) *A Constant Burden: the reconstruction of family life*. London: Routledge and Kegan Paul.

Walker, R. (ed.) (1986) *Applied Qualitative Research*. Aldershot: Gower.

Watson, D.R. (1992) 'The understanding of language use in everyday life: is there a common ground?', in G. Watson and M. Seiler (eds), *Text in Context*. Newbury Park, CA: Sage.

Watson, D. R. and Sharrock, W.W. (1991) 'On the provision of "ethnographic context" in ethnomethodological and conversation-analytic research'. Paper presented at the International Conference on Current Work in Ethnomethodology and Conversation Analysis, University of Amsterdam, 15–19 July.

Watson, G. (1994) 'A comparison of social constructionist and ethnomethodological descriptions of how a judge distinguished between the erotic and the obscene', *Philosophy of the Social Sciences* 24: 405–25.

Watson, G. and Seiler, R.M. (eds) (1992) *Text in Context: contributions to ethnomethodology*. Newbury Park, CA: Sage.

Weinstein, D. and Weinstein, M.A. (1991) 'Georg Simmel: sociological *flâneur bricoleur*', *Theory, Culture and Society* 8: 151–68.

Welchman, J.C. (1989) 'After the Wagnerian bouillabaisse: critical theory and the Dada and Surrealist word-image', in J.C. Freeman (ed.) *The Dada and Surrealist Word-Image*. Los Angeles: Los Angeles County Museum of Art/Cambridge, MA: MIT Press.

Werthman, C. (1963) 'Delinquents in schools: a test for the legitimacy of authority', *Berkeley Journal of Sociology*, 8(1): 39–60.

West, P. (1990) 'The status and validity of accounts obtained at interview: a contrast between two studies of families with a disabled child', *Social Science and Medicine* 30(11): 1229–39.

Wetherell, M. (1998) 'Positioning and interpretative repertoires: conversation analysis and post-structuralism in dialogue', *Discourse and Society* 9: 387–412.

Wetherell, M. and Edley, N. (1999) 'Negotiating hegemonic masculinity: imaginary positions and psycho-discursive practices', *Feminism and Psychology* 9(3): 335–56.

Wetherell, M. and Potter, J. (1992) *Mapping the Language of Racism*. New York: Harvester Wheatsheaf.

Wetherell, M., Taylor, S. and Yates, S.J. (eds) (2001) *Discourse Theory and Practice: a reader*. London: Sage.

Williams, M. (1999) 'Single case probabilities and the social world: the application of Popper's propensity interpretation', *Journal for the Theory of Social Behaviour* 29(2): 187–201.

Willis, P. (1977) *Learning to Labour*. Aldershot: Gower.

Wilson, E. (1961) *Axel's Castle*. London: Fontana. (First published in 1931.)

Wilson, T.P. (1971) 'Normative and interpretive paradigms in sociology', in J.D. Douglas (ed.), *Understanding Everyday Life*. London: Routledge.

Winch, P. (1958) *The Idea of a Social Science*. London: Routledge and Kegan Paul.

Wolcott, H.F. (2001) *Writing Up Qualitative Research* (2nd edn). Thousand Oaks, CA: Sage.

Wolin, R. (2004) *The Seduction of Unreason: the intellectual romance with fascism from Nietzsche to postmodernism*. Princeton, NJ: Princeton University Press.

Woolgar, S. and Pawluch, D. (1985) 'Ontological gerrymandering: the anatomy of social problems explanations', *Social Problems* 32: 314–27.

Woods, P. (ed.) (1980) *Pupil Strategies*. London: Croom Helm.

Woods, P. (1999) *Successful Writing for Qualitative Researchers*. London: Routledge. (Second edition, 2007).

Yoshida, K. (2007) 'Defending scientific study of the social: against Clifford Geertz (and his critics)', *Philosophy of the Social Sciences* 37(3): 289–314.

Zimmerman, D.H. and Pollner, M. (1971) 'The everyday world as a phenomenon', in J.D. Douglas (ed.), *Understanding Everyday Life*. London: Routledge.

Znaniecki, F. (1934) *The Method of Sociology*. New York: Farrer and Rinehart.

# Author Index

# Subject Index